T0356959

The New Nuclear Age

For Lindsay, my partner in all things.

The New Nuclear Age

At the Precipice of Armageddon

ANKIT PANDA

polity

Copyright © Ankit Panda 2025
The right of Ankit Panda to be identified as Author of this Work has been
asserted in accordance with the UK Copyright, Designs and Patents Act 1988.

First published in 2025 by Polity Press

Polity Press
65 Bridge Street
Cambridge CB2 1UR, UK

Polity Press
111 River Street
Hoboken, NJ 07030, USA

ISBN-13: 978-1-5095-5746-2

A catalogue record for this book is available from the British Library.

Library of Congress Control Number: 2024943101

Typeset in 11 on 14 Warnock Pro
by Cheshire Typesetting Ltd, Cuddington, Cheshire
Printed and bound in Great Britain by CPI Group (UK) Ltd, Croydon

The publisher has used its best endeavours to ensure that the URLs for external
websites referred to in this book are correct and active at the time of going to
press. However, the publisher has no responsibility for the websites and can
make no guarantee that a site will remain live or that the content is or will
remain appropriate.

Every effort has been made to trace all copyright holders, but if any have been
overlooked the publisher will be pleased to include any necessary credits in any
subsequent reprint or edition.

For further information on Polity, visit our website:
politybooks.com

War is the province of uncertainty . . .
Carl von Clausewitz, *On War*

Be wary, then; best safety lies in fear.
Hamlet, Act I, Scene III

Contents

Acknowledgments

On January 26, 2022, I received an email from Louise Knight, publisher at Polity. Louise introduced herself and asked if I'd given any thought to perhaps writing a "bold and incisive book of around 50,000 words" pulling together the many disquieting themes that appeared to be permeating global nuclear affairs at the time. That Louise chose to reach out when she did was serendipity: I had been giving precisely such a book careful thought at the time and essentially had an outline in mind already. From the Korean Peninsula to South Asia and the Pacific, my work on nuclear policy issues for the preceding years had persuaded me that the risk of nuclear war was rising. A month after my initial exchange with Louise, as Russia's brutal, full-scale invasion of Ukraine began, backed by implicit nuclear threat-making, I began to conceptualize the outline of this book, convinced that the world was entering a dangerous new nuclear era. Without Louise's initiative, however, I may never have written this book, and for that I owe her thanks – even if I exceeded her originally envisaged word count significantly.

Beyond Louise and her colleagues at Polity – especially, Inès Boxman, Olivia Jackson, and Aoibheann O'Flynn – I owe a debt of gratitude to several others for intellectually enriching me as I wrote this book. While the bulk of this book was written in Washington, DC, where I live and work, I was fortunate to be able to travel widely as I researched its contents, interviewing many officials, military planners, intelligence analysts, and nongovernmental experts to soak up their perspectives on the book's themes. While many of these individuals would prefer to remain unnamed, I owe them my gratitude for their time. I am further grateful to the anonymous reviewers who provided useful feedback on the initial concept note for this book and the draft manuscript. Their feedback helped tighten the screws and improved the final product. Finally, I am grateful to Sarah Dancy for her efforts copyediting the manuscript. Any and all errors that remain are my own.

Closer to home, I found myself constantly supported by my brilliant colleagues in the Nuclear Policy Program at the Carnegie Endowment for International Peace, where I have been fortunate to work since 2020. I worried initially that I may have trouble persuading the inimitable George Perkovich of the value of this book, but I was wrong to do so: George was immediately supportive and provided trenchant feedback on my conceptual approach, without which this book would have been quite a bit worse off. My Carnegie colleagues James Acton, Toby Dalton, Jane Darby Menton, Nicole Grajewski, Jamie Kwong, Eli Levite, and Tong Zhao, meanwhile, were constant sources of encouragement and motivation. I am particularly grateful to Anna Bartoux, Sueli Gwiazdowski, Kylie Jones, Lisa Michelini, and Mackenzie Schuessler for their research and logistical support as I worked through the manuscript. I can think of no better intellectual home for myself than the Carnegie Endowment as I worked on this book. I am also grateful to Tino Cuellar and Dan Baer for their support. Lastly, I acknowledge the Stanton Foundation, which has been an essential backer of my work.

As I wrote this book, I was fortunate to find constant inspiration and new ideas after enriching conversations and written exchanges with many friends and colleagues around the world, several of whom I encountered for the first time after years of separation due to the pandemic. The old cliché that writing is a lonely endeavor has been far from true, in my experience. I owe much to those who took the time – over meals, drinks, coffees, Twitter exchanges, DMs, and on the sidelines of various conferences – to ruminate with me on the disquieting content that characterizes much of this book. I am grateful to Rabia Akhtar, Nobumasa Akiyama, Alexei Arbatov, Andrei Baklitskiy, Darshana Baruah, Alex Bell, Eric Brewer, Elena Chernenko, James Crabtree, John Emery, Ryan Evans, Karl Friedhoff, Franz-Stefan Gady, Markus Garlauskas, Matt Gentzel, Camille Grand, Matt Harries, Shashank Joshi, Jeongmin Kim, Matt Korda, Hans Kristensen, Ulrich Kühn, Jeffrey Lewis, Oliver Meier, Steve Miller, Adam Mount, Vipin Narang, Michiru Nishida, Chad O'Carroll, Pavel Podvig, Joshua Pollack, Andrew Reddie, Phil Reiner, Wu Riqiang, Carl Robichaud, Christian Ruhl, Victoria Samson, Lee Sang-hyun, Lee Sangkyu, Markus Schiller, Manpreet Sethi, Dmitry Stefanovich, Aaron Stein, Bruno Tertrais, Jiang Tianjiao, Jenny Town, Ashley Townshend, Pranay Vaddi, Jane Vaynman, Tristan Volpe, Heather Williams, Amy Woolf, and numerous others.

Finally, I owe an enduring debt of gratitude to my closest friends and family, whose support remains essential to all I do. My friends have kept me laughing and motivated: Alexis Garby, Jeffrey Hodes, Claire Klobucista, Ben Krueger, Zach Laub, Kevin Lizarazo, James McBride, Alex Ogier, Sumit Poudyal, Danielle Renwick, Kynan Rilee, Angel Rubio, Arthur Safira, Mike Sobin, Nitin Viswanathan, Mike Wong, and many others. My parents Sanjay and Minati, my brother Aman, my mother-in-law Marina, and my sister- and brother-in-law Elissa and Harley have been unconditionally supportive of my work. While they might not read this until they're quite a bit older, I owe much to the little ones in my life: Ivan and Sabine.

They've been a tremendous source of joy. (Another little creature, my cat Cat, will never read this, but deserves my thanks, nevertheless.) Lastly, nothing I do, including this book, would be possible without the love, support, and care of my partner and editor since high school, Lindsay. She tolerated the long nights I spent writing sequestered away in my office, the weeks I spent overseas communicating by video call as I worked, and much more. This book is for her.

Abbreviations

ABM	Anti-Ballistic Missile (Treaty)
ADS	Arms Control, Deterrence, and Stability
AEC	Atomic Energy Commission
AI	artificial intelligence
CPGS	Conventional Prompt Global Strike
CRPF	Indian Central Reserve Policy Force
CTBT	Comprehensive Nuclear Test-Ban Treaty
ENCD	Eighteen Nation Committee on Disarmament
GMD	Ground-based Midcourse Defense
HCMs	hypersonic cruise missiles
HGVs	hypersonic glide vehicles
IAEA	International Atomic Energy Agency
ICBM	intercontinental ballistic missile
INF	Intermediate-Range Nuclear Forces (Treaty)
IRGC	Islamic Revolutionary Guard Corps (Iran)
JCPOA	Joint Comprehensive Plan of Action
JeM	Jaish-e-Muhammad
LAC	Line of Actual Control
LEU	low-enriched uranium
LLMs	large language models
LoC	Line of Control

MIRV	multiple independently targetable reentry vehicles
NATO	North Atlantic Treaty Organization
NCA	National Command Authority (Pakistan)
New START	New Strategic Arms Reduction Treaty of 2010
NMCC	National Military Command Center
NPR	*Nuclear Posture Review*
NPT	Nonproliferation Treaty
NTM	National Technical Means
SM-3	Standard Missile 3
TPNW	Treaty on the Prohibition of Nuclear Weapons
WPK	Workers' Party of Korea

Introduction

Thirty-odd years of relative nuclear stability in the aftermath of the Cold War have given way to a new and challenging era of multipolar nuclear competition against the backdrop of rapid technological change. Our world faces a novel set of pressing challenges – many unprecedented and some familiar – affecting nuclear deterrence and global stability that may well persist through much of the twenty-first century. The collision and intermingling of these complex dynamics has contributed to an environment of increased nuclear dangers. The first nuclear age was defined by bipolar superpower competition between the United States and the Soviet Union during the Cold War. The second nuclear age, after the conclusion of the Cold War, saw a transition to concern about stabilizing the former Soviet Union, preventing nuclear proliferation in South Asia and the Korean Peninsula, along with growing worries about possible nuclear or radiological terrorism. This period also coincided with the most rapid decrease in the nuclear stockpiles of the United States and Russia, which between them held, and continue to hold, more than 90 percent of the world's nuclear weapons, and created more hope than ever that gradual and total nuclear disarmament might be possible.

That hope gave way to greater pessimism as the 2020s began, and, in particular, as relations between Russia and China, on one side, and the West, on the other, have turned toward systemic confrontation. The decade beginning in 2020 marks a transition to a new, more dangerous, and more complex third nuclear age: a period that will be defined by the renewal of great power competitive dynamics, complex multipolar nuclear deterrence relationships, newly arrived and increasingly sophisticated actors like North Korea, and the anxieties introduced by the still-uncertain effects of a range of emerging technologies (such as hypersonic weapons, cyber-weapons/artificial intelligence, and possible space weapons). The challenges of this new nuclear age will intensify in ways that are unlikely to be fully foreseeable as so-called "great power competition" between the United States, Russia, and China intensifies. The task of averting nuclear escalation and mitigating the possibility that nuclear weapons may realize their longstanding latent potential to pose global catastrophic risks to humanity's long-term ability to grow and flourish will grow more urgent.

The very notion of nuclear "ages" is an artificial intellectual construct, of course, and one without any consensus or clear definition. Some have gone as far as to argue that the entire post-1945 era, in the aftermath of humanity's acquisition of the bomb, represents the start of a new epoch entirely for the human race: the Anthropocene.[1] The end of the Cold War and the collapse of the Soviet Union in 1991, however, marked a clear break point for humanity's initial dangerous coexistence with the bomb. The onset of the 1990s heralded a dissipation of the real, palpable, and even somewhat quotidian sense that the world as we knew it could end in a cataclysmic exchange of thousands of deployed nuclear weapons. As a result of bold, unilateral initiatives undertaken by the final Soviet leader, Mikhail Gorbachev, and his U.S. counterpart, President George H.W. Bush, thousands of nuclear weapons deployed outside the two countries' borders were repatriated, introducing new firebreaks and decreasing the likelihood that future conventional crises between the United States and Russia could quickly go nuclear. The bomb, with its attendant anxieties, fundamentally, did not disappear, but its grip over the relationship between Moscow and Washington did. It was due to these changes that some later came to dub the period between the United States' *Trinity* test in July 1945 and the moment of Soviet collapse "the first nuclear age." This was a period characterized by intense, bipolar superpower nuclear competition between Washington and Moscow, the discovery of nuclear strategy, the adoption of a diverse means of nuclear weapons delivery, and the invention of nuclear arms control. The lessons of the first nuclear age continue to bear relevance, even though they have been forgotten among many policymakers and military planners, who have had the luxury of turning their attention away from nuclear weapons to other global security challenges in the decades after the Cold War.

The bipolar superpower clash between the United States and the Soviet Union during the Cold War took place under the shadow of the tens of thousands of nuclear warheads that the two cumulatively built over the years. The idea of "victory" in a full-scale war between these two powers had little meaning in this world. As one U.S. top secret national security memorandum in 1977 put it, the "results of a major nuclear exchange between the United States and the Soviet Union are that both nations would suffer very high levels of damage and neither could conceivably be described as a 'winner'."[2] The memo continued: this was "true regardless of who strikes first, or whether the attack is a surprise or occurs after a period of warning." This two-player game was costly and dangerous, and held the potential to put an end to human civilization as we knew it – but Moscow and Washington were able to derive certain rules of the road to prevent a plunge into the abyss. After the fall of the Soviet Union, the Russian Federation became the Soviet successor state to inherit its nuclear arsenal. In the three decades that followed the end of the Cold War, however, a third major power, China, has quickly emerged as a major global player in its own right. From 1990 through the start of the Covid-19 pandemic in 2020, Chinese gross domestic product grew at an average of 9 percent per year, lifting hundreds of millions of ordinary Chinese citizens out of poverty and into unprecedented middle-class prosperity. As might then be expected, China's newfound national prosperity largely proportionately translated into greater spending on the country's military forces, commensurate with its growing status and resources. Chinese leaders authorized new programs of defense research and development, and began modernizing the country's armed forces along several axes. Xi Jinping, the Chinese leader who took over as general-secretary of the Communist Party of China in 2012, repeatedly called for the country to field a "world-class military."[3] This was a particular priority for Xi, who appeared to move away from every preceding Chinese paramount leader going back to the country's founder, Mao Zedong, on the appropriate role for China's military instrument as a tool of political influence on the global stage.

By the mid-2010s, the United States had come to view Chinese foreign policy ambitions with skepticism, and it became increasingly clear that Washington and Beijing were at odds over fundamental questions ranging from the nature of the international order to China's place within that order. While, in the 2000s, the United States had chosen to engage with China and encourage it to find accommodation in the existing post-Cold War global order as a "responsible stakeholder"[4] within that order, Beijing appeared to have more substantial ambitions to shape that order in ways inimical to the interests of the United States, its allies, and its partners. By the mid-2010s, China had started to behave in more assertive ways in its immediate neighborhood. Territorial disputes in the East and South China Seas with Japan and a number of Southeast Asian claimant states began to flare as Beijing constructed artificial islands, harassed civilian and military ships with its navy and maritime law enforcement vessels, and carried out unsafe aerial intercepts against U.S. and other military aircraft operating legally in international airspace.

Despite the growing confrontation between the United States and China in those years, there was still an element of compartmentalization in the relationship that allowed Washington and Beijing to collaborate on matters of global importance, such as climate change and nuclear nonproliferation. Most importantly, the economic relationship between the two countries remained on a strong footing; China manufactured and the United States consumed. This compartmentalization and generally positive economic relationship took a substantial hit beginning with the election of U.S. President Donald J. Trump in 2017. The Trump administration initiated a trade war against China and broadly sought to insulate the U.S. economy from Beijing. The administration more broadly took a far more openly hostile tone toward Beijing, going as far as to criticize the nature of China's communist political system and its leadership directly. By the time the Trump administration entered its final months in office, the Chinese leadership appeared concerned enough about a potential deliberately initiated conflict by the United States that the chairman of the U.S. joint chiefs of staff at the time, General Mark Milley, contacted his Chinese counterpart to offer reassurances to the contrary.[5]

It is against this backdrop that China's transition into this new nuclear age manifested itself in what is likely to be the most essential driver of enduring and new, global-scale nuclear risks. After decades of fielding a limited nuclear arsenal – comprising just a fraction of the warheads fielded by the United States and the Soviet Union at the height of the Cold War – China changed course and is now seeking a much larger force. Beijing's choice in this regard stands to shift the center of gravity in global nuclear affairs away from Europe and toward Asia, where six of the nine states that possess nuclear weapons have territory or regularly carry out substantial military operations. Substantial evidence suggests that China has shaken off its traditional preference for a smaller nuclear force, and that Beijing is pursuing an unprecedented quantitative expansion of its nuclear arsenal. U.S. intelligence assessments, as of 2024, estimated that China will build up to a force comprising some 1,500 nuclear warheads by the mid-2030s, although one senior U.S. military intelligence official involved in assessing Chinese nuclear modernization plans told me that substantial uncertainty still persists about the intentions of the Chinese leadership when it comes to the intended total size of this force.[6] While the 1,500 number will still see China field fewer strategic nuclear warheads than the United States and Russia in 2024, the combination of this change in the country's nuclear forces and possibly strategy, paired with the broader force of geopolitical contest that have Washington and Beijing at loggerheads, will contribute to a dangerous cocktail of nuclear risk in future crises and, if the event arises, war.

Historically, China's approach to nuclear weapons diverged considerably with that of the United States and the Soviet Union from its very origins. The day after China's first nuclear test in October 1964, the country's official Xinhua News Agency carried a statement noting that Beijing had sought nuclear weapons with the first objective of deterring attacks against its territory. The statement also included a statement that Beijing had "solemnly declare[d] that [it] will never at any time and under any circumstances be the first to use nuclear weapons."[7] This pledge, the first of its kind, introduced the idea of a "no first-use" nuclear weapons policy. A second important consideration for China in its original pursuit of nuclear weapons was to resist what its leaders perceived as unjust nuclear coercion by the United States. Mao Zedong,

China's first paramount leader, was particularly perturbed by Washington's brandishing of nuclear capabilities in the course of the final months of the Korean War, and the first and second Taiwan Strait Crises (1954–5 and 1958).[8] Before testing the bomb, the newly created People's Republic had no satisfying answer to American threats to potentially use nuclear weapons. Acquiring the bomb was meant to address this problem initially. From its very origins, however, China's approach to nuclear strategy diverged considerably from that of every other nuclear-armed state at the time. Beijing's declaration of a no first-use policy meant, in essence, that Chinese leaders were exclusively planning for a nuclear force that could absorb a first strike and still have a retaliatory capability to deliver what they believed to be sufficiently unacceptable damage as to have a deterrent effect on a prospective attacker. In the years after China's initial nuclear test, however, the country's scientists and engineers worked to develop better, more capable nuclear warheads and delivery systems. By the early 1970s, China had started to flight-test intercontinental-range ballistic missiles capable of reaching the U.S. homeland. In July 1996, China carried out its forty-fifth and last nuclear test, after which it signed the Comprehensive Nuclear Test-Ban Treaty (CTBT) and committed to cease all nuclear testing.[9] Despite this, it continued to modernize its broader military capabilities and adjusted its nuclear forces in ways to ensure their ability to meet the criteria for assuring "effective counterattack"; one example of this included the adoption of multiple nuclear warheads on certain missiles to cope with possible U.S. missile defense systems.[10]

Apart from its idiosyncratic approach to nuclear strategy privileging assured retaliation at the expense of nearly all other possible roles and objectives for nuclear weapons, China also kept the numbers of its nuclear forces rather modest. In 2020, for instance, the U.S. Department of Defense publicly released an authoritative assessment that Washington believed China had a nuclear force numbering warheads in the "low-200s."[11] This number actually was considerably lower than open-source estimates by independent researchers at the time, who had suggested that China had as many as 290–350 nuclear warheads.[12] By way of comparison, a single American *Ohio*-class ballistic missile submarine, if fully uploaded with nuclear warheads, could carry 160 nuclear warheads alone. (In practice, contemporary U.S. submarines deploy with far fewer warheads due to constraints imposed by arms control agreements.) Unlike the Soviet Union, which coped by building a massive nuclear arsenal that could not be disarmed effectively by a U.S. first strike, leaders in Beijing chose to tolerate unusually high levels of vulnerability to a disarming strike. This modestly sized Chinese nuclear force had a benefit for U.S. war planners, who were able to largely consider Beijing's nuclear forces as a so-called "lesser included case" of the targeting problems they faced vis-à-vis Russia. This phrase, used frequently by U.S. military planners, implied that the problem of Chinese nuclear weapons was largely insignificant for the purposes of U.S. force planning, given the substantially more complex, larger arsenal possessed by Russia – or, differently put, that any U.S. nuclear force sufficiently capable of holding at-risk targets in Russia could do the same for China.

The "third player" problem for the nuclear superpowers is meaningfully new, unprecedented, and a likely contributor to dangerous new risks. As I researched and wrote this book, I traveled to meet officials and thinkers around the world to discuss matters concerning the themes explored herein. Consistently, China's shifting nuclear posture raised great concerns – from Washington, to London, to Berlin, to New Delhi, to Singapore, to Seoul, and to Tokyo. In the United States, China's shifting nuclear posture has launched a new wave of thinking on nuclear deterrence in what many have come to call a "two-peer" (or "two near-peer") environment. While Beijing's arrival as a U.S. nuclear peer is contestable given the vast gap that will remain quantitively even if China should build up to the highest-end U.S. intelligence estimates of its intentions, the questions raised for the United States and its allies are significant. Finally, as U.S.–Russian relations enter their worst period since the end of the Cold War, exacerbated by Russian President Vladimir Putin's 2022 decision to launch an invasion of Ukraine, anxieties have surged in Washington about possible Russia–China cooperation on nuclear matters. Russia has already assisted China with developing an early warning architecture,[13] and the leaders of the two countries famously declared a "no limits" partnership just nineteen days before President Putin proceeded with his invasion of Ukraine without apparently having informed the Chinese president.[14] Despite their public exhortations, the two countries are far from allies, and mistrust lingers between them.[15] Leaked Russian military documents, for instance, have revealed that Russia continues to see China as a possible military threat itself and has carried out major military exercises to thwart a possible Chinese invasion of its territory.[16] Forging a stable nuclear balance in this emerging, difficult world will require new thinking, political courage, and, above all, prudence.

While dynamics between the United States, Russia, and China are central to this new nuclear age, the risks of nuclear proliferation and war implicate a far greater number of states. Increasingly, technologically sophisticated non-nuclear states may have the capability to raise the risk of nuclear escalation by threatening the nuclear forces of a number of countries. Some of these countries are allies of the United States and have started to domestically debate the possibility of seeking their own nuclear weapons, perceiving long-term political dysfunction in Washington as an unacceptable risk to the reliability of their chief ally. Regional nuclear tinderboxes, from South Asia to the Korean Peninsula, have continued to fester without meaningful guardrails or confidence-building mechanisms. Finally, military and policy planners across nuclear-armed

states bear anxieties about the potential role of rapid technological change on the nuclear balance – from emerging
artificial intelligence capabilities to the proliferation of new
missile defense and space technologies.

Cumulatively, these trends have rapidly thrust nuclear
weapons back to the forefront of international politics after
their general recession into the background in the three decades following the end of the Cold War. Not all matters that
will permeate this new nuclear age are "new" – old problems
concerning nuclear deterrence, limited nuclear use, and crisis
management are rearing their heads – but the intersection
and simultaneous culmination of these dynamics as the world
enters the middle of the twenty-first century present unprecedented risks. Across the six chapters that ensue, this book
seeks to answer a number of questions. First, what exactly
is meaningfully "new" about the nuclear age that appears to
be dawning in the 2020s? How much is this a resurgence of
old, long-forgotten problems? Second, what unique trends,
dynamics, and features characterize this new nuclear age?
Finally, what are the long-term implications for humanity, and
what steps might help mitigate the risks of nuclear war in an
era of unparalleled complexity? Ensuring that nuclear weapons
remain unused against this dangerous backdrop will become
increasingly challenging.

1

Slouching Toward a New Nuclear Age

In December 1942, the Italian American physicist Enrico Fermi watched in awe as the first manmade nuclear chain reaction was initialized. Fermi's experiment – part of the Manhattan Project that would lead to the creation of the first nuclear weapon – was an inflection point for humankind.[1] Fermi had experimentally validated what the Austrian physicists Lise Meitner and Otto Frisch had discovered four years prior. Fission, the phenomenon in question, involves the splitting of the nucleus of an atom. For two isotopes of two particular elements – uranium-235 and plutonium-239 – fission was found to release additional, excess neutrons. These excess neutrons, in turn, could trigger additional fission reactions – and so on. Engineered appropriately, this phenomenon presented a potential for weaponization unlike anything ever seen on Earth before. And so, under the auspices of the Manhattan Project, the United States built two designs: one based on a cylindrical formation of uranium-235 designed to be "shot" at an analogous target; the other based on a spherical plutonium-239 core surrounded by shaped explosive charges. Because scientists were practically certain the first design would work, but less so about the second, a test was carried out in the desert of the U.S. state of New Mexico. On July 16, 1945, under J. Robert Oppenheimer's guidance, the United States detonated the "gadget," an implosion-design plutonium bomb. This test, codenamed *Trinity*, marked the first nuclear detonation on Earth. The weapon worked. On August 6, the United States dropped *Little Boy*, the uranium-235-based bomb, on the Japanese city of Hiroshima, incinerating tens of thousands of human beings instantly. Three days later, the *Fat Man* device, based on the "gadget," was dropped on Nagasaki, another Japanese city, killing tens of thousands yet again. More than 100,000 people perished as the United States announced the power of atomic weaponry to the world.[2] The nuclear age had dawned and matters of war and peace between the major powers would never quite be as they were in the past.

After the Soviet Union broke the United States' initial few years of nuclear monopoly in the aftermath of the Manhattan Project and the Second World War with its first nuclear test in 1949, bipolar superpower nuclear competition came to define a new type of risk in global politics: a risk without precedent. In those initial years, leaders and military planners in Moscow and Washington didn't know fully what exactly to do about the bomb – or how to reap its putative political benefits – and the imperfect art of nuclear strategy hardly materialized overnight. Technological changes – the arrival of the intercontinental ballistic missile (ICBM), naval nuclear propulsion, and space-based intelligence, surveillance, and reconnaissance capabilities, to name a few – rapidly influenced the nuclear balance between the two. By the early 1980s, the arms race between the United States and the Soviet Union had led to their aggregate nuclear forces ballooning to nearly 70,000 nuclear weapons, driven by often perverse strategic logics mandating ever more nuclear weapons for the other side's growing array of targets. At this time, just a few hundred nuclear weapons – in total – were possessed by four other states that were thought to have developed weaponized nuclear bombs: the United Kingdom, China, France, and Israel. The aggregate megatonnage in the Soviet and American arsenals manifested in the early 1980s represented – and continues to represent – the greatest accumulation of manmade potential destructive energy ever amassed.[3]

The first nuclear age not only marked the discovery and evolution of nuclear strategy, including nuclear deterrence, but also its various necessary accompaniments, including arms control, a nonproliferation architecture to keep the bomb from spreading uncontrollably, and the development of collective security arrangements backed by nuclear weapons. The logic of nuclear restraint was not obvious at the dawn of this age, however. Over thirteen days in October 1962, the United States and the Soviet Union brought the world closer to nuclear Armageddon than at any point prior. The Cuban Missile Crisis, now unanimously recalled as the most dangerous moment of the Cold War and of the nuclear age writ large, was a rude awakening for American and Soviet leaders alike about the need to actively manage the risk of hurtling themselves – and the world – into nuclear apocalypse. The logic of nuclear deterrence could hardly be automatically relied on to prevent the occurrence of war, especially when leaders like U.S. President John F. Kennedy and Soviet Premier Nikita Khrushchev felt compelled to push their luck. In the ensuing years, Washington and Moscow – though they remained bitter, ideological foes with little in terms of a shared vision for the world – discovered arms control to be a useful means for addressing the problem of preventing a nuclear war that neither of their leaders wanted. Arms control had other benefits as well: it bounded the scope of what could otherwise have been an even more intense arms race. Finally, arms control would contribute eventually to the elimination of certain nuclear weapons entirely, reducing the risk of nuclear war and the damage that might ensue should deterrence fail.

It was also during this period that the United States entered the business of assuring other leaders that its nuclear weapons

could be relied on for the defense of their territory and interests. In 1949, the United States, Canada, and a group of West
European countries established the North Atlantic Treaty
Organization (NATO). At the core of NATO was the idea
of collective defense: that an attack on one ally equated to an
attack on all allies. The United States, having emerged trium-
phant from the Second World War as a global superpower and
now armed with nuclear weapons, ensured that its assurances
would be backed with nuclear weapons. As the Soviet nuclear
threat intensified and various crises emerged in Europe –
notably, over the fate of a divided Berlin – Washington found
itself adapting to new realities, first by brandishing its nuclear
weapons, and then by forward-basing those weapons on allied
soil. Eventually, the introduction of Soviet ICBMs further
intensified concerns among some allies that the vulnerability
of the American homeland to nuclear attack could dissuade
a U.S. president from coming through for NATO. In 1961,
French President Charles de Gaulle famously asked President
Kennedy if the United States "would be ready to trade New
York for Paris."[4] Washington failed to assuage French concerns at the time, prompting, in part, De Gaulle's decision to
leave NATO and pursue at full-bore an independent nuclear
deterrent.

Other allies – notably, West Germany – sought greater
input on *how* NATO might rely on or employ U.S. nuclear
weapons.[5] Washington and its NATO allies adapted by
expanding the scope of allied involvement in nuclear planning within the alliance, and even by adopting nuclear
sharing arrangements, whereby U.S. nuclear weapons – with
U.S. authorization – could be operated by allied European
forces. The Soviet Union tolerated this measure insofar as
it mitigated the risk of West Germany itself seeking the
bomb: Khrushchev himself, in 1963, internally justified the
Soviet position to members of the Warsaw Pact by suggesting that it would be tolerable "as long as the West German

revanchists' hands would be bound with regard to nuclear weapons by an agreement on non-proliferation."[6] Beyond NATO, Washington also forged alliances in East Asia, with South Korea and Japan. Neither state faced the same prospect of an imminent invasion by a nuclear-armed state at the time as frontline NATO states did, but North Korea maintained conventional military superiority in the period after the Korean War that eventually led the United States to deploy tactical nuclear weapons to South Korea beginning in 1958.[7] Washington continued to rely on its assurances to its allies as a nonproliferation tool; but in the mid-1970s, the United States detected a covert attempt by South Korean President Park Chung-hee to develop nuclear weapons. Washington coerced South Korea into refraining from pursuing the bomb and maintained forward-deployed conventional and nuclear forces to deter Pyongyang.[8]

While bipolar competition between Washington and Moscow characterized the central fulcrum of the first nuclear age, this was also the period that marked the proliferation of worldwide interest in nuclear technology and weaponry. Although only nine states possess nuclear weapons in the twenty-first century, at least twenty others flirted with the bomb to varying degrees through the latter half of the twentieth century.[9] Concern about the bomb's spread manifested at the very start of the first nuclear age and found global carriage. In 1959, the United Nations General Assembly adopted a resolution – put forth by Ireland – that called on any state possessing nuclear weapons at the time to refrain from sharing that technology with non-nuclear states.[10] Out of a shared concern that the bomb's spread would be detrimental to their interests, the United States and the Soviet Union came together to promote the development of a global treaty on nuclear nonproliferation. The Treaty on the Non-Proliferation of Nuclear Weapons, or the NPT, still stands as the cornerstone of the global nonproliferation regime. With 191 signatories, the NPT is the world's largest and most successful nuclear arms control treaty.

Order, proliferation, and growing malaise: The second nuclear age

When the Cold War ended, the bomb didn't go away, but the dark shadow it cast on the globe certainly receded. This recession was in one sense quite literal: reciprocal nuclear reductions by the United States and the newly formed Russian Federation in the first years of the 1990s resulted in the most dramatic reduction of deployed nuclear forces that the world had ever seen. What had been an undisputed arms race for many of the previous three decades came to be described by at least some observers as a "disarmament race."[11] Momentum on controlling and limiting nuclear arms carried over from the final years of the Cold War. The late Michael Krepon, a committed American practitioner and theorist of arms control, dubbed the period between 1987 and 2000 the "golden age of nuclear arms control."[12]

The nuclear age had made a turn and entered what one analyst termed in 2000 a "second act";[13] new themes came to define nuclear anxieties and hopes alike. The collapse of the Soviet Union, for instance, did lead to the drawdown of nuclear weapons, but it also resulted in significant concerns about the prospects for Soviet nuclear weapons that could go missing in the course of the political tumult that followed. A related concern was the matter of ensuring that nuclear weapons that remained on the territory of certain former Soviet successor states – Belarus, Kazakhstan, and Ukraine – could be effectively repatriated to Russia. The U.S. Congress appropriated billions to support these efforts in what came to be known as the Nunn–Lugar Cooperative Threat Reduction Program, named after the two senators from opposing political parties who came together to address the urgent risks stemming from Soviet collapse. In the end, the program successfully dismantled more than 7,500 nuclear warheads and more than 1,500 land- and sea-launched strategic nuclear missiles, and ensured that remaining weapons were accounted for and secured.

The relative nuclear optimism of the immediate post-Cold War period also manifested itself in significant advances in nuclear global governance and the related universalization of norms around nuclear weaponry. In 1995, those states that were party to the NPT agreed to indefinitely extend that agreement, reflecting what at the time was a real sense that general nuclear disarmament was tractable, possible, and desirable. (After all, the United States and the Soviet Union had just pulled back thousands of nuclear weapons that had previously been deployed.) This was also a moment for the five nuclear weapon states recognized under the treaty – those that had detonated nuclear devices prior to January 1, 1967 – to offer so-called negative security assurances to the world's non-nuclear weapon states.[14] The United States, Russia, China, France, and the United Kingdom committed, as a measure to buttress nuclear nonproliferation, not to threaten non-nuclear weapon states with their own nuclear arms. In 1996, the Comprehensive Nuclear Test-Ban Treaty was opened for signature, seeking to end once and for all nuclear explosive testing – another measure that came to be seen as a catalyst for disarmament. Other advances in this time were a function of negative developments. For instance, the International Atomic Energy Agency's failure to detect Iraq's work on nuclear weapons prior to the Cold War led to the introduction of an Additional Protocol to the Agency's standard Comprehensive Safeguards Agreement, which sought to monitor any diversion of peaceful nuclear material for possible weapons purposes. The subsequent adoption of these Additional Protocols by a number of states substantially strengthened the Agency's ability to verify that the full scope of nuclear activities within participating states remained of a peaceful nature.

As during the Cold War, nuclear proliferation continued to be a major concern in the early years of the second nuclear age. In 1989, South Africa, in the course of its post-Apartheid political transition to a majority-elected African National Congress-led government, abandoned its nuclear weapons program and voluntarily dismantled six nuclear weapons – the only state to date to have completely disarmed after assembling nuclear weapons.[15] Just as South Africa joined the NPT as a non-nuclear weapons state in 1991, the United States acquired strong intelligence indications that North Korea under leader Kim Il Sung was likely interested in developing nuclear weapons. This sparked a crisis that ultimately resulted in a 1994 agreement between Pyongyang and Washington to limit the former's potential pathway to the bomb through the reprocessing of spent natural uranium fuel from a reactor that had come online in 1986. That agreement would later collapse, leading to an acceleration in North Korea's sprint toward the bomb. In 2006, Pyongyang became the first – and, as of 2024, the only – new state to detonate a nuclear explosive device in the twenty-first century. After much attempted diplomacy, no effort to constrain North Korea's pursuit of nuclear weapons seemed likely to endure.

Iran presented another archetypal case of nonproliferation concern. Following the discovery of a covert uranium enrichment facility in the early 2000s, Iran and the major powers entered more than a decade of protracted on-again/off-again negotiations. Through a combination of deft, international diplomacy, secret backchannels activated by the United States, and a change of political circumstances with Iran, Tehran and a group of countries known as the P5+1 – comprising the five permanent members of the United Nations Security Council and Germany – made a breakthrough in 2013, agreeing to an interim agreement known as the Joint Plan of Action that set up the building blocks for an agreement that would later trade relief from national and international economic sanctions for Tehran in exchange for concessions relating to the country's civil nuclear program, including monitoring transparency. In 2015, the P5+1 and Iran cinched the Joint Comprehensive Plan of Action (JCPOA), which, over some 150 pages, codified a wide range of verifiable technical constraints of Tehran's programs and capabilities in exchange for sanctions relief. While the JCPOA represented a breakthrough on longstanding nonproliferation concerns pertaining to Tehran, it was heavily politicized in the United States. In May 2018, President Trump announced that he was withdrawing the United States from the JCPOA despite the United States having certified Iran's compliance with the agreement that same year. The JCPOA's unraveling came as the second nuclear age concluded, raising the uncomfortable prospect of a tenth nuclear-armed state: Iran.

Through much of the 1990s, the United States and other states remained concerned about the possibility of a nuclear breakout by South Asian neighbors and rivals India and Pakistan. India's decision to carry out what it called a "peaceful nuclear explosion" in 1974 had galvanized Pakistani efforts to build nuclear weapons in the final years of the Cold War. By the late-1980s, Pakistan was "two screwdriver turns" from a working nuclear weapon.[16] India, too, by the end of the Cold War had made significant progress and had started testing missiles intended to carry nuclear weapons. The two countries kept their nuclear capabilities in a non-weaponized state until May 1998. That month, India, under the nationalist leadership of Prime Minister Atal Bihari Vajpayee and the Bharatiya Janata Party, carried out its first weaponized nuclear tests, realizing what had been a campaign pledge. Pakistan responded days later with nuclear tests of its own. The nuclear age had thus arrived in South Asia, expanding the ledger of nuclear-armed states by two. One year after these tests, the two countries fought a war – the fourth since their independence in 1947. The prospect of a conventional conflict between South Asia's two new nuclear states escalating into a nuclear war was a prominent theme of the second nuclear age – particularly in the 2000s and 2010s.

Another prominent theme of the second nuclear age was the eruption of concern about acts of nuclear terrorism by non-state actors. In the aftermath of the September 11, 2001, attacks by Al Qaeda terrorists on New York and Washington, DC, the United States grew particularly concerned on this front. Counterterrorism, in all its forms, quickly acquired salience in Washington – much as nuclear strategy once did during the first nuclear age – as the George W. Bush administration's Global War on Terror took hold. Paired with proliferation in Pakistan, where concerns about nuclear weapons security were particularly acute, states were alert to the prospect of nonstate groups seeking to procure nuclear materials. The audacity and scale of the September 11 attacks suggested to many that this was not outside the realm of the possible. Even if terrorists did not successfully create a nuclear weapon, they might seek to sow mayhem through the detonation of a radiological dispersal device, a conventional explosive enriched with radioactive material – sometimes known as a "dirty bomb". Later, under the presidency of Barack Obama, the United States held global summits on nuclear security, seeking to ensure that all states in possession of sensitive nuclear material could adhere to best practices.

Despite the de-emphasis on great power nuclear competitive dynamics at the height of the second nuclear age in Washington and elsewhere, new sources of stress that would come to strain U.S.–Russia and U.S.–China nuclear relations began to emerge. In 1998, North Korea launched a satellite technology demonstrator, the Taepodong-1, over Japan, seeding in the minds of American policymakers the prospect that it may one day field a nuclear-armed ICBM. Disturbed by this possibility – and the prospect of a similar capability one day being fielded by Iran – the United States began moving toward the adoption of a homeland missile defense system. On December 13, 2001, President George W. Bush, citing "a vastly different world," withdrew from the 1972 Anti-Ballistic Missile (ABM) Treaty, which had limited the missile defense capabilities of Russia and the United States in a bid to stabilize their nuclear deterrence relationship at the height of the Cold War.[17] While the Bush administration's decision to withdraw from the treaty was taking place in a context where rogue states and nonstate terrorist groups were at the top of the United States' strategic agenda, the move became a festering wound in Russia, where it demonstrated, at a deep level, that Washington was simply unwilling to consider post-Cold War Russia's security concerns meaningfully in the course of its own national security decision-making. Although President Putin opposed the withdrawal in 2001, he did not overreact immediately, stating publicly that he believed Russian missiles could overcome any U.S. defense system. Years later, however, Putin would publicly cite the U.S. ABM withdrawal during a 2018 speech unveiling a range of exotic nuclear delivery systems – many of which were designed to bypass a missile defense system of the sort the United States built in the sixteen years that followed.[18] Meanwhile, in China, the U.S. ABM withdrawal prompted concern, too, with prominent security analysts expressing the view that Beijing would have to respond in its own way in due course.[19] The U.S. withdrawal from the ABM Treaty was, in a real way, the first domino to fall, indicating a shift away from the "golden age" of arms control toward a darker future.

By no means did the bomb disappear during the second nuclear age, but the prospect of nuclear war largely failed to permeate the public consciousness in the way that imagery of the mushroom cloud had done for many during the Cold War. Among academics and experts who thought about nuclear matters, research agendas shifted to reflect the changed environment: nonproliferation studies were in, and nuclear strategy, with some exception, was out.[20] One former U.S. official, involved in nuclear matters during the Cold War, reflecting on these shifts, told me that, once, "to be a serious foreign policy person, you had to know about MIRVs [multiple independently targetable reentry vehicles] and throw weights." The official added: "Then the Cold War ended, and the nuclear people got shoved to side because nuclear weapons stopped mattering in the way that they had."[21] A notable exception to this trend was South Asia, where the tests of 1998 sparked significant regional inquiry into nuclear deterrence. Both India and Pakistan continued to modernize their nuclear forces, command and control, and even postures well into the 2000s and 2010s. My own original encounter with the prospect of nuclear conflict and escalation came when I lived in New Delhi between 1998 and 1999 as a boy, through the tests and the Kargil War. After briefly being swept up in the excitement of India's acquisition of nuclear weapons, it dawned on me that these terrible weapons might actually be used (not that I had any appreciation for the supposed finer workings of nuclear deterrence at the time). I would later find, after arriving in the United States later in my life, that, for others in the millennial generation, terrorism – not nuclear war – was a more pertinent concern. Older Americans, who lived through the Cold War, however, recalled life under the prospect of Armageddon more vividly.

It bears repeating that what came to be known as the second nuclear age, while not free from sources of nuclear anxiety, was broadly a period of positive trendlines – at least at its immediate post-Cold War inception. The arms reductions by the United States and the Soviet Union – and then Russia – were deeply significant given that the two countries between them possessed, and continue to possess, the overwhelming majority of nuclear weapons in the world. The governance advances on nonproliferation, too, helped seal in a norm against the proliferation of these weapons – something that was once difficult to take for granted. At the height of the Cold War, President Kennedy famously predicted that by the 1970s as many as "25 nations may have nuclear weapons."[22] Instead, the twentieth century concluded with just eight nuclear possessors. Perhaps the apotheosis of optimism in the second nuclear age came in 2009 when Barack Obama, less than four months into his presidency, delivered a speech in Prague, Czechia, where he declared "clearly and with conviction America's commitment to seek the peace and security of a world without nuclear weapons."[23] Obama's idealism was punctuated with at least some realism: "This goal will not be reached quickly," he noted, adding that it may not even be reached "in my lifetime." In that same speech, he announced that the United States was working toward further strategic arms reductions with Russia. The new Strategic Arms Reduction Treaty of 2010, better known as New START, was agreed between Washington and Moscow the following year. To push the agreement through a skeptical U.S. Senate, the administration committed to a full-bore, multi-decade modernization of the U.S. nuclear triad of ICBMs, nuclear-armed submarines, and heavy bombers that would see those weapons last through most of the twenty-first century. As a new nuclear age dawns and relations between Washington, Moscow, and Beijing, in particular, worsen, that future alluded to by Obama appears to be increasingly out of reach in the near term. Instead of a world without nuclear weapons, we are due for a new, complex, and dangerous era of nuclear competition. Nuclear weapons, once again, demand our attention.

The new third nuclear age

In June 2021, a major U.S. newspaper ran a story with a stark headline: "China is building more than 100 new missile silos in its western desert, analysts say."[24] The story was accompanied by a neatly annotated satellite image, marking the locations of what a group of researchers had identified as 119 fixed missile silos – likely for the deployment of nuclear-armed ICBMs. A month later, two more analysts – at a separate U.S. research institution – found a second nuclear silo field, containing what appeared to be 120 more silos.[25] It didn't stop there: another month passed and yet another group of analysts – at yet another institution – found similar image signatures at a third site, showing a smaller, but still significant, number of silos.[26] A little more than a year later, the U.S. Department of Defense, in an annual report to Congress, assessed that China was in the process of the most significant expansion of its nuclear arsenal in decades, pursuing a likely quadrupling of a force that had numbered in the "low-200s"[27] as of 2019 to one constituting some 1,000 weapons by 2030. A year later, the U.S. military intelligence assessment went up further still, suggesting that if China continued to produce weapons-grade fissile material at the rates that it was apparently exhibiting that year, it may possess as many as 1,500 nuclear weapons by 2035.

China, since its first nuclear test in 1964, had exhibited a set of choices concerning its nuclear forces that set it apart from most other states – certainly the United States and the Soviet Union at the time. Beijing immediately announced a policy of "no first-use," noting that it would not be the first to use nuclear weapons under any circumstances and would only seek to retaliate after it had suffered a nuclear attack. China did build up a nuclear force over decades that was designed to be robust to the prospect of a disarming first strike, but did so largely by seeking survivability for its retaliatory capabilities through qualitative, rather than quantitative, means. Some of these choices included the adoption of intercontinental missiles armed with multiple warheads, the development of improved nuclear-armed submarines, and the development of countermeasures to stress and defeat missile defense systems.

The choice to maintain a nuclear arsenal numbering warheads in the "low-200s," even with the formidable United States as a notional adversary, was in a way an unusual acceptance of vulnerability by Beijing, but it reflected a deep-seated general devaluation of nuclear capabilities in Chinese defense strategy. Beijing had sought the bomb amid U.S. attempts to practice nuclear coercion in the course of the Korean War and the first and second Taiwan Straits crises in the 1950s.[28] At the time that news of China's new fields of missile silos became public, the United States regarded China as a "lesser included case" of the nuclear deterrence challenge it faced with Russia: the essential logic for American planners and policymakers was that any U.S. nuclear force that was sufficiently flexible, nimble, and survivable to deter Russia would, by definition, be capable of accomplishing comparable U.S. goals with regard to China.

Of the many topics discussed in this book that encapsulate the themes defining this third nuclear age, perhaps none is more important than the growing salience of nuclear weapons in the U.S.–China relationship. It is unknown how long Beijing had planned for the construction of these silos prior to their discovery, but their appearance in the deserts of western China followed the most precipitous decline in U.S.–China relations since the normalization of their diplomatic ties in 1979. Under the Trump presidency, Chinese leaders appeared to fear the possibility of war more than they had in decades.[29] One possible explanation for the appearance of these silos then simply concerns a possible assessment by Chinese leaders that more nuclear weapons were needed to deter American adventurism in East Asia in ways that could be detrimental to Beijing's interests. But, as of 2024, there was no clarity on China's intentions: unlike Vladimir Putin in Russia or Kim Jong Un in North Korea, Chinese President Xi Jinping is not too fond of delivering long, winding public speeches introducing and justifying changes to his country's nuclear force posture. Multiple hypotheses – from a search for national prestige, to underwriting aggressive revisionist intent toward Taiwan, and interest in limited nuclear war – might explain Beijing's choices, but Chinese leaders have made no public case for their build-up. Despite this opacity concerning intent, the matter has seized the attention of the U.S. military and nuclear policy community, which now frets about the arrival of an unprecedented "two-peer" nuclear environment, where Washington will, for the first time, find itself facing the prospect of deterring two nuclear-armed adversaries, each with a nuclear force numbering warheads in the four-digit range (at least, if the U.S. assessment of China's goals is correct).

The growing salience of competitive nuclear dynamics between the United States and China accompanies the most serious decline in relations between Moscow and Washington since the end of the Cold War. Vladimir Putin's decision to launch a brutal and illegal invasion of the former Soviet state of Ukraine in February 2022 has sparked a serious U.S.–Russian nuclear crisis, and has resulted in a near-complete meltdown of productive diplomacy between the two countries. In retaliation for U.S. countermeasures against Russia's invasion, including economic sanctions and material support to the Ukrainian armed forces, Putin has initiated a complete decompartmentalization of all aspects of U.S.–Russian ties – whereby nothing could be discussed independently of the United States' policy of supporting Ukrainian independence and sovereignty against Russian aggression. This included a proactive set of steps by Russia to dismantle the last remaining bits of meaningful nuclear arms control between the two countries. In February 2023, one year after the start of the war, Putin unilaterally announced that Russia was "suspending" its implementation of New START, the final legally binding limitation on the size of the U.S. and Russian strategic nuclear arsenals.[30] New START's fate followed that of other hard-negotiated arms control and confidence-building arrangements in the preceding years: under the Trump administration, the United States left the 1987 Intermediate-Range Nuclear Forces (INF) Treaty, which had banned an entire class of nuclear and non-nuclear missiles, and the 1992 Treaty on Open Skies, which improved transparency by allowing for unarmed surveillance flights over the territory of its participating states with short notice.[31] The course of Russia's war of aggression against Ukraine has been accompanied by disquieting overt and covert threats by senior Russian figures, including Putin, alluding to the possibility of nuclear escalation. While there is little certainty, as of 2024, regarding how Putin's war against Ukraine might conclude, Russia has all but completely severed itself from the world order favored by the West. Instead, it has doubled down on its relationships with Iran and North Korea, seeking their assistance with munitions for its war and, in turn, enabling their worst instincts. Moscow and Beijing, too, have deepened their strategic partnership substantially through the 2010s and 2020s. The consequences of these sharply negative trends in U.S.–Russia relations will have lasting ripple effects through the third nuclear age, and may herald a return to the sorts of intense nuclear war risks that existed between Washington and Moscow during the Cold War.

Elsewhere, familiar nuclear problems have taken on a new character. North Korea, once famously derided as a "fourth-rate pipsqueak" of a country by U.S. President Richard Nixon, is in possession of an increasingly capable and credible nuclear force, armed with thermonuclear weapons and ICBMs with ranges capable of reaching the entirety of the continental United States.[32] Under leader Kim Jong Un, the country has ceased to be a nonproliferation problem, as it was through the second nuclear age, and become a nuclear deterrence challenge for the United States. Even as the United States, South Korea, Japan, and much of the international community continue to call for the "denuclearization of the Korean Peninsula," the first principles guiding U.S. intelligence and military planning concerning Pyongyang largely acknowledge that Kim presents a new nuclear deterrence challenge.[33] These more advanced North Korean capabilities – notably, its ICBMs that are capable of ranging the U.S. homeland – have unnerved South Korea and Japan. Just as Charles de Gaulle once wondered whether Kennedy was ready to trade New York for Paris, so too have leaders in Seoul and Tokyo started to wonder whether current and future U.S. presidents would be willing to carry out their commitments in defense of their countries despite the potential vulnerability of the U.S. homeland to North Korean nuclear attack. Notably, since the collapse of diplomacy between the United States and North Korea in 2019 after two historic, leader-level summit meetings, Pyongyang shows little interest in diplomacy and has instead deepened its ties with Russia, in particular.

In South Asia, India and Pakistan, now more than a quarter-century into their mutual coexistence as nuclear-armed neighbors, are adapting to new realities. India's political leadership has grown less restrained in its willingness to employ military power against Pakistan, and both countries appear exceptionally confident in their ability to manage their differences under the nuclear shadow that prevails over them. A skirmish in 2019 between the two of them had the potential to escalate significantly, raising the risk of nuclear war, but was de-escalated largely due to luck and political judgment: an Indian pilot shot down by Pakistan in the course of a dogfight was apprehended and later exchanged, proving a useful off-ramp. (Incidentally, the skirmish marked the first time two nuclear-armed states had used conventional airpower against each other's territory.) Strategic anxieties in South Asia are increasingly being shaped by broader global dynamics as well. China's nuclear build-up – and investments in its own missile defense capabilities – have contributed to unease in New Delhi about its ability to deliver "unacceptable damage" in a retaliatory strike, as its nuclear doctrine professes. Meanwhile,

Pakistan, with increasingly acute fiscal constraints, feels a growing sense of pressure to render its nuclear forces more survivable against India. While neither India nor Pakistan has moved away from their respective preference for "minimum deterrence" (conceived idiosyncratically), strategic stability in South Asia is far from assured.

Interlinked multipolar nuclear dynamics present an obvious challenge to restraint in this new nuclear age. As the United States reacts to China, Beijing counter-reacts, prompting a response in India, which further unnerves Pakistan. North Korea, too, prompts changes to the U.S. and allied military posture in Northeast Asia that feeds into Chinese threat perceptions. Russia, meanwhile, has walked away from its prior restraint after its 2022 decision to invade Ukraine and may grow more reliant on its nuclear forces as its conventional military capabilities have been degraded extensively in the course of the war.[34] A preliminary condition for arms control is mutual interest in reducing either the probability of war, or the consequences of war, or the costs of preparing for war. While these may manifest within specific dyads – such as between the United States and China, or the United States and Russia – the largely uncharted territory of bringing third parties, or even multiple third parties, into these arrangements may leave future potential arrangements of negotiated restraint on thin ice.

Against this tense geopolitical backdrop, the new nuclear age is sure to see the maturation, proliferation, and wide deployment of a range of technologies – some meaningfully new, and some older – that may introduce new challenges for stability among nuclear powers. Old sources of tension such as missile defense will take on newfound relevance as established and newer nuclear powers alike move to develop and deploy these capabilities. Even if these missile defenses are somewhat ineffective in reality, they may create the perception for states seeking to assure nuclear retaliation that their means of delivery need to be improved. And so, as Russia, China, and North Korea have started to do, nuclear weapons may start to be placed on hypersonic glide vehicles – highly maneuverable systems that are specifically best suited to defeat missile defense systems designed to manage traditional ballistic missile reentry vehicles outside the Earth's atmosphere. Investments in hypersonic glide vehicles have, meanwhile, already prompted a counter-reaction in the United States, where missile defense development efforts have turned toward so-called Glide-Phase Intercept plans, seeking to render these missiles limited in their ability to threaten U.S. and allied territory. Aside from nuclear weapons and their means of delivery, advanced non-nuclear weapons, including precision conventional missiles, are likely to add further complexity. While many of the states with nuclear weapons possess substantial arsenals of such non-nuclear systems, several technologically advanced non-nuclear states are increasingly in possession of these capabilities, too. From South Korea to Japan to Poland to Finland to Saudi Arabia, more states will possess the ability to strike targets precisely and at long distances in ways that were unimaginable for much of the twentieth century. In many cases, these states may seek to strike the nuclear forces or national leadership of a state with nuclear weapons, introducing serious potential escalatory risks. South Korea is perhaps the archetype: Seoul seeks to reduce its vulnerability to nuclear attack from North Korea by threatening preemptive attacks with an impressive range of conventional missile systems. However, in choosing to do so, Seoul also gives Pyongyang powerful incentives to use its nuclear weapons rapidly in retaliation, as failing to do so could prove fatal for Kim Jong Un.[35] In this way, more states than ever will have a role to play in scenarios that could lead up to the use of nuclear weapons. In part, anxieties around precisely these sorts of scenarios contributed to the hesitation in many Western capitals to initially supply non-nuclear Ukraine with long-range strike systems as it sought to defend itself against Russia.[36] After Russia alleged that Ukraine had shelled Engels Air Base in Saratov Oblast in December 2022, destroying nuclear-capable bombers, the U.S. secretary of state publicly stated that the United States had "neither encouraged nor enabled the Ukrainians to strike inside of Russia."[37] Inherent in these concerns was the potential for a non-nuclear state to set in motion a series of events leading to nuclear war that could implicate the United States.

Adding further complexity, the nuclear balance could see disruption from the adoption of artificial intelligence (AI) technologies. These technologies could buttress practices to render an adversarial nuclear force more vulnerable – for instance, by enabling better data fusion for targeting in a war – or they could allow states seeking survivability the means to thicken the fog of war. Much concern around the intersection of AI and nuclear weapons has fixated, since the twilight of the Cold War, on the "Skynet scenario," famously depicted in director James Cameron's *Terminator* films – where a powerful artificial general intelligence chooses to largely eliminate humanity by using nuclear weapons. As a result of this familiar cultural touchstone of a computer-run-amok scenario, states – both those with and those without nuclear weapons – have started to give greater consideration to the role that computers may or may not play in nuclear weapons-related decision-making. AI systems could have a role to play in "decision support": helping the humans ultimately in charge make sense of a messy, complex, and uncertain world in the heat of a crisis. This, too, however, is not without risks.

Other technologies and domains still will contribute complexity to the task of seeking nuclear stability. Space, for instance, has been intimately linked to nuclear operations since the 1950s. Today, the major powers rely extensively on space-based capabilities to support both conventional and nuclear operations in times of war. Russia and China, in particular, have long recognized the United States' disproportionate lead in space-based military systems and have cultivated a range of counterspace weapons. These weapons, while largely non-nuclear, could in a time of war degrade or destroy U.S. satellites involved in supporting conventional military operations. If the affected U.S. satellite also played a role in a mission-critical mission – such as command and control, or providing early warning of incoming ballistic missile attacks against the United States – the attack could precipitate significant escalation. No agreement exists between these three countries on the steps that could best be taken to prevent these scenarios from playing out – nor are the means of communication in a crisis robust enough to deal with the risks. Another domain of growing concern is the cyber and information space, which encompasses everything from the execution of potent zero-day exploits against nuclear-critical computer systems in a time of war or crisis, to the deliberate use of bots and other measures to sow panic and uncertainty. These risks are likely to intensify as AI technologies grow more sophisticated. "Deep fake" videos of world leaders issuing nuclear threats or AI-enabled discovery of cyber vulnerabilities are just two ways in which cyber threats to nuclear stability could intensify.

Cumulatively, these technologies – and the above is a far from exhaustive list of new technologies that could have a bearing on global nuclear risks – present a wide range of challenges. While old strategic wisdom may still have utility in governing some of the most disruptive space and missile defense-related issues, AI, cyber, information operations, and other new technologies have little in the way of a tried-and-tested playbook developed during the Cold War. Two questions are fundamental in thinking through the potential impact of the many technologies that will be at play in the new nuclear age. First, will cumulative technological change abet or degrade the ability of nuclear-armed states to maintain the survivability of their forces and command and control? The consequences for stability diverge depending on the answer.

In the case of most technologies, there are opportunities on both sides of the ledger, making a simple answer infeasible. Second, to what extent will the proliferation of these technologies render traditional approaches to nuclear arms control *focused on nuclear weapons* less politically desirable or feasible? Given that there will be a greater blurring of the nuclear and the non-nuclear – for instance, as non-nuclear missiles grow increasingly capable of threatening nuclear forces – arms control efforts may have to grow in ambition and complexity in turn, which could simultaneously reduce the political feasibility and desirability of such agreements. Across the world, however, there is an unmistakable and growing sense of curiosity and apprehension among military planners – especially in the major nuclear-armed powers – about the potential for disruption ahead. While none of these technologies is likely to fundamentally upend or overturn the logic of nuclear deterrence, they will introduce new sources of complexity.

A most important task

For nearly eighty years now, humanity has been spared the sight of nuclear weapons being detonated in the course of warfare. Since the August 9, 1945, bombing of the Japanese city of Nagasaki by the United States in the final months of the Second World War, every subsequent detonation of a nuclear device has been in the course of testing, development, and the rare nuclear explosion for an ostensible nonmilitary purpose.[38] "The most spectacular event of the past half century is one that did not occur," noted Thomas C. Schelling in his lecture accepting the Nobel Prize in Economic Sciences in 2005, referring to the phenomenon of continued non-use of nuclear weapons.[39] Schelling, one of the doyens of the field of nuclear strategy, described this as "astonishing," but concluded ultimately that hope lay in the emergence of a "taboo" around the idea of nuclear use. A taboo, as a customary prohibition on behavior, is normally applied to matters considered sharply beyond the pale: in the sexual realm, for instance, incest and pedophilia are routinely, uncontroversially, and universally accepted as taboo. The nuclear "taboo" similarly manifests in a well-founded – and obvious – global revulsion at the idea of nuclear use and nuclear war.[40] In 1946, the American journalist John Hersey, in 1946, traveled to Hiroshima to record the effects of nuclear weapons not as abstract strategic and political tools, but as the means of inflicting harm to human flesh and bone – the consequences of fission that begins within the core of an atomic bomb. Hersey's testimony, widely regarded as one of the greatest works of journalism of the twentieth century, conveyed to a world that had already seen the effects of large-scale, unrestricted total war up close that this new weapon, based on the power of the atom, was something very different – and essentially abhorrent, by any measure.

Taboos exist because human beings are willing to express certain values and abjure others, and they must be reinforced. As this new nuclear age dawns, a growing concern among scholars who study the role of nuclear weapons in international politics is that the sense of a true, deeply ingrained taboo around nuclear weapons and their potential uses may be waning. Perhaps the most widely cited case evincing this tendency in the 2020s is found in Russia, where Vladimir Putin has resorted to wanton overt and covert nuclear threats and signaling to seek advantage during his war on Ukraine.[41] Putin's tendencies have led to once-respected and seemingly somewhat sober Russian nongovernmental analysts donning their threat-making hats, amplifying all sorts of nuclear threats – including preemptive nuclear attacks on NATO.[42]

Putin's loose nuclear talk has certainly unsettled a world largely unused to nuclear weapons in the foreground of international politics since the end of the Cold War, but he is not alone in resorting to these tactics. During his presidency,

Donald Trump threatened North Korea with "fire and fury like the world has never seen" – a statement widely interpreted, including by North Korea, as a barely covert nuclear threat.[43] (Kim Jong Un himself is no stranger to nuclear threat-making, either.) In India, on the election trail in 2019, Prime Minister Narendra Modi, in celebrating his decision-making in a skirmish earlier that year with Pakistan, waved away Islamabad's nuclear weapons, asking, "What do we have then? Have we kept our nuclear bomb for Diwali?"[44] More broadly, public opinion research, at least in the United States, has found little semblance of a taboo-like aversion to the idea of employing nuclear weapons.[45]

Above all, unlike matters that truly are considered taboos, nuclear weapons are routinely intellectualized, publicly discussed, and, among the states that possess them or depend on them for their defense, seen as useful and legitimate tools. In January 2022, a month before Russia's invasion of Ukraine backed by nuclear threats, the five NPT-recognized nuclear weapons states issued a joint statement reaffirming the famous 1985 statement once made by U.S. President Ronald Reagan and Soviet premier Mikhail Gorbachev: that "a nuclear war cannot be won and must never be fought."[46] In that same statement, they noted that, as long as nuclear weapons exist, they *"should serve defensive purposes, deter aggression, and prevent war"* (emphasis added). These objectives – all arguably moral, legal, and legitimate – underscored the tremendous utility that still permeate these weapons; the object of a taboo would hardly be spoken of in this instrumental way.

The most fundamental task facing humanity in this new nuclear age – with a special burden on leaders, advisors, and military planners in those states that possess nuclear weapons – is to ensure that Schelling's sense of astonishment, enunciated in 2005, continues hundreds of years into the future. The task of avoiding nuclear war remains paramount, and the sudden surge in the global salience of nuclear weapons should refocus attention on this. Any nuclear use, anywhere, will have global consequences: from the potential climactic effects of nuclear winter leading to massive famine, to second- and third-order economic, political, and social effects. While the world no longer lives under the shadow of some 70,000 nuclear weapons, amounting to several thousand megatons in potential damage, nuclear war remains all too thinkable. Maintaining the record of nuclear non-use since Nagasaki will be more challenging in a world of more players, more capable players in more places, new technologies, and growing loose talk around nuclear war. Doing so will require remembering the lessons the past holds, while approaching the new and unprecedented future with courage and aplomb.

2

From Terror, Peace

Whatever can humanity do about the bomb?

We have never been able to find consensus on this question, but its urgency has hardly been in doubt since the dawn of the nuclear age in the summer of 1945. In the immediate months and years following the *Trinity* test on July 16, 1945, and the use of nuclear weapons by the United States against the Japanese cities of Hiroshima and Nagasaki, the bomb and its implications for the future of war, peace, and humanity were hotly debated across the world.

Was the bomb – and the previously unimaginable destruction that could follow – such a unique affront to humanity itself that it required the abolition of warfare and the establishment of world government? Many believed so. The American physicist Arthur Compton, who worked on uranium and plutonium metallurgy in the course of the Manhattan Project that birthed the bomb, reflected in 1946 that nuclear weapons presented humanity with a "clear choice between adjusting the pattern of our society on a world basis so that wars cannot come again, or of following the outworn tradition of national self-defense, which if carried through to its logical conclusion must result in catastrophic conflict."[1]

Nearly a decade later, as the Cold War superpower competition between the United States and the Soviet Union went into full swing, the British philosopher Bertrand Russell and world-renowned physicist Albert Einstein issued a joint manifesto to underscore that nuclear weapons posed an existential threat to humanity itself. "We are speaking on this occasion, not as members of this or that nation, continent, or creed, but as human beings, members of the species Man, whose continued existence is in doubt," they wrote. "Shall we put an end to the human race; or shall mankind renounce war?" they asked, proffering the latter as a solution, even though it would "demand distasteful limitations of national sovereignty."[2] Their ultimate counsel was that the very survival of humanity and the avoidance of global catastrophic risks in the era of the newborn bomb depended on the prospect of world government.

Having witnessed the barbarism of the Second World War and the prosecution of indiscriminate total war by every major nation involved, these views were understandable, and many shared these instincts – if not on the feasibility of world government, then at least on the prospects for prompt disarmament and control of nuclear technology through internationalized means. In 1946, the United States itself mooted a failed – albeit audacious – plan to the newly formed United Nations Atomic Energy Commission (AEC) to bring under international control all aspects of nuclear technology that could result in the development of nuclear weapons. The Baruch plan, as it was known – named for Bernard Baruch, the AEC's U.S. representative – sought ultimately to internationalize the governance of this technology and seek its elimination. "Let us not deceive ourselves," Baruch said on June 14, 1946. "We must elect World Peace or World Destruction."[3] Despite this ambition, the spread of the bomb would not be so easily controlled. In 1949, the Soviet Union carried out its first nuclear test and the United States' technological monopoly came to an end as the systemic confrontation that would later be known as the Cold War intensified.

The abolition of war, the total internationalization of nuclear weaponry, and the prompt disarmament of the United States' weapons did not materialize as solutions to the problems posed by the bomb, of course. Neither could nuclear fission be unlearned by humanity. Instead, the terror inherent in the bomb and its awesome destructive power came to be viewed as *useful*. Historical debates continue to this day about the precise motivations behind the United States' decision to use the bomb against Hiroshima and Nagasaki in 1945, but by the late-1940s, the idea that the bomb's unique potential for terror could achieve significant political effects – in times of peace and warfare alike – was largely uncontroversial among military and political elites in the United States. In 1947, Henry Stimson, U.S. President Harry Truman's secretary of war at the time of the bombings, offered up what has since become conventional wisdom on the logic of the attacks: that Imperial Japan's surrender was not forthcoming at the time the decision was made and that the bomb was the preferred option to the alternative of a land invasion of Japan that would have resulted in significantly more American and Japanese deaths.[4]

This account is disputed – and Stimson was writing with his own legacy in mind – but even disputed accounts make the case for the bomb's putative political utility. The historian Gar Alperowitz, for instance, has argued that among the reasons for the bombing of the two Japanese cities was an American interest in demonstrating the awesome power of this new war-making technology to the Soviet Union, in a bid to seek influence in the period after the war's conclusion.[5] Beyond these debates about the circumstances of American nuclear use in the Second World War, prominent political leaders, including Truman's successor Dwight D. Eisenhower, saw the bomb as conferring substantial political power in the course of international statecraft. Through much of the 1950s, when

Washington enjoyed a decisive lead over the Soviet Union in the area of nuclear weaponry, the United States engaged in coercive nuclear signaling, seeking to compel the Soviet Union and the newly formed People's Republic of China in crises over Berlin and Taiwan.[6] Nuclear weapons were useful political tools; they could be "used," in effect, without being exploded.

Eisenhower, who once led allied forces during the Second World War, considered extending the utility of nuclear weapons further and went as far as to consider their use as substitution for other non-nuclear ordnance in the conduct of military campaigns. "Where these things are used on strictly military targets and for strictly military purposes, I see no reason why they shouldn't be used just exactly as you would use a bullet or anything else," he once said.[7] His secretary of state, John Foster Dulles, wrote in 1957 that advances in nuclear science and engineering were making apparent the possibility that it would be "possible to alter the character of nuclear weapons," and that "their use need not involve vast destruction and widespread harm to humanity."[8] Earlier in the 1950s, Dulles fretted too about the moral opprobrium associated with the bomb and the emergence of a taboo around nuclear weapons use.[9] During this broader period, the United States threatened to meet a large-scale attack by the Soviet Union against itself or its allies with massive nuclear retaliation. Dulles and Eisenhower were determined in casting nuclear weapons as yet another tool in the United States' warfighting toolkit.

Through all of this, however, the United States – and every other country that has gone on to successfully procure nuclear weaponry – arrived at essentially one answer to the question that began this chapter. *Whatever can humanity do about the bomb? Well, we shall seek to prevent its use through deterrence.* The bomb, in a sense, would continue to exist in order that it might never be used. The fundamental insight about nuclear weapons that so terrified Compton, Russell, Einstein, and countless others – their inherent capacity for never-before-contemplatable terror and destruction – would come to underpin the theory, theology, and practice of nuclear deterrence.

The very word deterrence is derived from the Latin word *terrere*, meaning to terrify or frighten: the visceral fear of nuclear Armageddon and destruction would be so potent that the threat of a nuclear response would dissuade an opponent from pursuing action adverse to one's interests. So went the theory, at least. Bernard Brodie, once a naval strategist, observed in 1946 that the advent of nuclear weapons had, in essence, introduced the "absolute weapon," one whose arrival was so meaningful that it had transformed the very essence of how the United States ought to think about the purpose of its military enterprise. "Thus far the chief purpose of our military establishment has been to win wars," Brodie observed. "From now on its chief purpose must be to avert them."[10] Nuclear weapons, in other words, were a revolution for the very enterprise of warfare: they provide for deterrence and, thus, defense of core national interests, not through their proactive use in the course of warfare, but through the mere possibility of their use. The Canadian economist Jacob Viner, writing in 1945, similarly hypothesized that the very prospect that the bomb may be used in the course of a war "may make statesmen and people determined to avoid war" altogether.[11] For Brodie, Viner, and others, the mere suggestion of possible nuclear use would imbue decision-makers with a prudence that was otherwise unimaginable in the pre-nuclear era.

These insights came to underpin the theory of the nuclear revolution, which posited that these terrible weapons, by dint of their unparalleled destructive power, would provide for defensive benefits not through their use, but through deterrence.[12] Some scholars posited that, whereas for centuries attackers and defenders would have had to invest heavily, and at great expense, in large armies, fortifications, and other capabilities to sustain intense conventional warfare, nuclear weapons should obviate this need.[13] As long as two opponents in a nuclear deterrence relationship each possessed a survivable and secure second-strike capability – i.e., that one of the two could not take the opportunity to disarm the other of his nuclear weapons with ease – stability would obtain. In this way, nuclear weapons could also become the great equalizer in world politics. As the theory of the nuclear revolution would have it, nuclear superiority would matter little; even a small state with a handful of survivable nuclear weapons could reap the benefits of deterrence against an adversary that possessed thousands of such weapons. At the center of the theory of the nuclear revolution and its prescriptions for stability is the idea of mutual vulnerability: nuclear deterrence can be most stable when both opponents accept the *condition* that they will remain vulnerable to the other's secure second strike.

The reality has been different, and states have been unwilling to readily accept the condition of vulnerability, even when it might manifest as a fact. From the U.S.–Soviet experience to the contemporary U.S.–China and U.S.–Russia experiences to South Asia and the Korean Peninsula, nuclear-armed states have seldom behaved as if they find the prescriptions of the nuclear revolution all too satisfying.[14] For starters, stable nuclear deterrence, if mutually recognized, could encourage rational risk-taking at the conventional level. This "stability–instability paradox," as scholars described it, has been a source of frustration and anxiety for nuclear-armed states and their allies. This insight was somewhat intuitive for political leaders even early in the nuclear age. Eisenhower, for instance, mused in 1958 that "mutual deterrence was an umbrella under which small wars could be fought without starting a global war – small wars even in the NATO area."[15] Moreover, as subsequent chapters will explore in greater detail, the allure of escaping the condition of mutual vulnerability has been a powerful motivator for innovations in nuclear strategy and technology alike. Bureaucratic politics, organizational pathologies, and even domestic politics conspire to undermine the prescriptions of the nuclear revolution, too – as do idiosyncratic political leaders. The nuclear revolution continues to hold salience in a weaker sense, however, in that the possibility of nuclear wars continues to largely induce sufficient caution in leaders, but just how long can this hold? The confluence of risks apparent at the dawn of this new nuclear age will surely continue to stress the logic of the nuclear revolution.

Nuclear deterrence: Unsatisfying, real, and risky

With the advent and spread of nuclear weapons, the world has not witnessed the sort of large-scale, unlimited conventional warfare between major powers that characterized the first half of the twentieth century. While the leaders of major powers may differ in their risk-acceptance and what they ultimately value, bounding the nature of their rationality, the idea that war between nuclear-armed states is ultimately too risky appears to have constrained their decision-making. Nuclear weapons, through their very presence in a crisis between states that possess them, would appear to introduce a degree of caution. War and skirmishes between nuclear-armed states are not impossible, however: two notable examples include the 1999 India–Pakistan Kargil War, fought just a year after both countries tested nuclear weapons, and the 1969 border conflict along the Ussuri river between the Soviet Union and China. But these are the exceptions rather than the rule.

The end of the Cold War dramatically reduced the baseline risk of global-scale nuclear conflict between the United States and Russia, but, as this new nuclear age dawns and U.S.–Russia relations nosedive, the risk of a direct clash grows. In October 2022, U.S. President Joe Biden, who was a nineteen-year-old when the world came to the brink of nuclear war during the Cuban Missile Crisis in 1962, said he viewed the risk of "Armageddon" to have grown substantially as a result of Russia's invasion of Ukraine and its attendant loose talk around the possible use of nuclear weapons. "We have not faced the prospect of Armageddon since Kennedy and the Cuban Missile Crisis," Biden said. While his comment may have overstated matters – there were certainly nuclear close-calls in the aftermath of the well-known Cuban Missile Crisis – he wasn't alone; 2022 marked a high watermark in the post-Cold War era in terms of global interest in the possibility of nuclear war. After three decades of general recession, the risk of a general, global nuclear war permeated the anxieties of ordinary citizens, decision-makers, and even military planners.

Anti-nuclear weapons advocates have pointed to the outbreak of the war in Ukraine in February 2022 as evidence showing that "nuclear deterrence doesn't work" and that the alternative must be global nuclear disarmament.[16] It is true that nuclear weapons did not prevent Russia from the prospect of invading Ukraine: after all, Ukraine had no nuclear weapons of its own with which to deter Moscow, and was not a party to an alliance backed by nuclear weapons, such as NATO. In the lead-up to the invasion, the United States and its NATO allies made no public claims to have an interest in risking nuclear war over Ukraine's territorial integrity and sovereignty. Biden himself was explicit in his State of the Union address to the American people: "Our forces are not engaged and will not engage in conflict with Russian forces in Ukraine," he said, unequivocally.[17] Nuclear deterrence thus had no particular role in influencing Russia's decision over whether to invade; that decision appeared to be a function primarily of Vladimir Putin's ideas about Ukrainian nationhood (or lack thereof) and his misplaced belief about the ease of a swift conventional victory over Ukrainian forces. What has been the case, rather, is that nuclear deterrence has worked to constrain both Russia and Ukraine's Western partners, including the United States and NATO.

Nuclear deterrence has done little to shape the brutal, day-to-day realities of the war: thousands of Russian and Ukrainian casualties attest to that. However, the conflict, from its earliest moments, saw nuclear deterrence providing two important boundaries or guardrails. First, NATO successfully deterred any deliberate Russian strikes on the territory of its member states, including on staging sites for arms and other materiel destined for Ukraine that would ultimately be used to strike and kill Russian soldiers and conquered territory. The robustness of this deterrence was not immediately apparent, however, resulting in a gradual, slow roll-out of ever more meaningful military assistance from NATO states to Ukraine. Ukraine's Western partners found much success in gradually implementing – albeit by accident – a strategy of salami-slicing: forms of assistance that seemed unthinkably escalatory at the onset of the war in 2022, such as long-range strike systems, were, a year later, being delivered routinely. For Western leaders, observed Russian behavior helped calibrate decision-making about increasing assistance to Kyiv under the shadow of possible nuclear escalation. For Russia, meanwhile, its nuclear weapons have successfully deterred the overt, direct involvement of NATO forces in the conflict on Ukraine's side.

This has been the key deterrence concern for Putin – from the very start of the war. In February 2024, after French President Emmanuel Macron noted that the direct involvement of NATO troops could not be ruled out, Putin reiterated the most fundamental nuclear deterrence signal that Moscow had sought to maintain through the war: "Everything that they are coming up with now, with which they threaten the entire world – all this really threatens a conflict with the use of nuclear weapons, and therefore the destruction of civilization – don't they understand this, or what?" During an annual state of the nation address just weeks before presidential elections, he added: "They must ultimately understand that we also have weapons – and they know about it, just as I now said – we also have weapons that can hit targets on their territory." Both NATO and Russia have been limited in their freedom of action and maneuver in ways that have been deeply frustrating as a result of the functioning of nuclear deterrence largely as intended by both sides. While this might be viewed as a "success," the central concern in the course of the conflict remains that the *failure* of nuclear deterrence remains a real possibility: through either a deliberate resort by Russia to the use of nuclear weaponry, or an inadvertent incident rapidly expanding the conventional war to NATO states, or myriad other pathways.

In this context, it is commonplace in Washington and European capitals to hear stalwart supporters of Ukraine and opponents of Moscow bemoan Russian "nuclear blackmail." What is often missing in these well-meaning exhortations, which often express unease with the consequences for the global order if Moscow's nuclear threat-making is allowed to constrain support for Ukraine, is that there is functionally no difference between nuclear deterrence and what is often described as nuclear blackmail. They are one and the same – both rooted in coercion. Or, put differently, nuclear blackmail is just nuclear deterrence with a value judgment applied: the deterree does not approve of the deterrer's values, desired ends, and means. That Russia has employed nuclear coercive signaling – the fulcrum on which deterrence rests – to pursue legally and morally unjust ends in Ukraine does not fundamentally turn nuclear deterrence on its head, or introduce a new category of coercive signaling that is better described as "blackmail."

Of course, Russia's unbridled brutality against Ukrainian civilians and the overt flouting of international norms, laws, and conventions in the course of the war leaves any well-meaning person sympathizing with those bemoaning Putin's "blackmail," but the matter remains that this is exactly a consequence of nuclear deterrence functioning largely as desired for

Moscow. The word "blackmail," in this way, is a term simply to describe the unpleasant experience of *being deterred* by the possibility of nuclear war – an unsatisfying, if rational, position. For the United States, in particular, the salience of nuclear weapons in international crises has become a somewhat distant, even alien, idea. After two decades of combating insurgencies in the broader Middle East and Afghanistan, the prospect of finding American freedom of maneuver limited by the presence of an adversary's nuclear weapons is disquieting, frustrating, and unfamiliar. For a certain generation of American national security professionals, the limitations imposed on the country's freedom for maneuver by nuclear weapons is the resurgence of an old problem: one that shaped Washington's approach to global affairs throughout the first nuclear age. But for a younger cohort of military planners, national security policymakers, and officials – many who came of age in a world defined by uncontested American unipolarity and the freedom it bestowed on Washington to exercise power fulsomely – this was unfamiliar territory.

These generalizations aren't universal, however. Notably, a former NATO supreme allied commander, Philip Breedlove, advocated vociferously in the early days of the war for the transatlantic alliance to implement and enforce a "no-fly zone" over Ukraine.[18] This call was echoed by U.S. lawmakers and others. Adam Kinzinger, then a representative in the U.S. House of Representatives from Illinois, took to social media to call for a "#NoFlyZone over Ukraine at the invitation of their sovereign [government.]"[19] Indeed, Volodymyr Zelensky, the Ukrainian president, had endorsed the idea, noting that Ukraine could "beat the aggressor" if its Western partners "do their part."[20] While others in the chattering classes – in Washington and European capitals – endorsed the idea, or a variant of it, the simple fact was that a no-fly zone was never going to be a serious consideration for anyone with influence over how the West chose to respond to Russia's invasion.[21]

In practice, a no-fly zone is more than a declared exclusion zone; it is to be enforced with airpower, which would bring the conventional military forces of the nuclear-armed NATO alliance into direct contact with Russian forces. Even under ideal circumstances, where NATO might have been able to gain Russian assent to enforce a partial no-fly zone over parts of Ukraine (a fantasy, by any measure), implementing such a zone would have required such a massive logistical effort and high sortie rate of fighters, refueling tankers, and airborne command and control aircraft that the risk of an inadvertent clash could not be ruled out. Ultimately, caution and prudence prevailed, and Biden ruled out any talk of such a zone.[22] He further outlined, in unequivocal terms, that U.S. forces would not be implicated in the fighting in Ukraine: "The idea that we're going to send in offensive equipment and have planes and tanks and trains going in with American pilots and American crews, just understand . . . that's called World War III, okay? Let's get it straight here, guys." Biden left little to the imagination on his theory on the controllability of escalation in a conventional war with Russia. He further added that "we will not fight the third world war in Ukraine."[23] These insights were seared into the minds of Cold War thinkers on similar matters. McGeorge Bundy, John F. Kennedy's national security advisor during the Cuban Missile Crisis, would write later in his life that the "most important thing that the United States and the Soviet Union can do to stay clear of the 'nuclear tornado' is to see to it that they have no war of any kind with each other."[24]

The dismissal of the no-fly zone idea was a consequence of Russian nuclear deterrence at work, in this case. Biden and his closest advisors correctly surmised that one condition that would substantially increase the probability of either deliberate or unintentional escalation to nuclear war is the prospect of direct military clashes between U.S., NATO, and Russian forces. As it once was for Kennedy and Khrushchev at the height of the Cuban Missile Crisis, escalation was front of mind for U.S. officials. Because a no-fly zone could not be imposed without accepting this unacceptable risk, it had to be ruled out. Breedlove would later voice his frustration at this caution: "We are almost fully deterred, while Putin is almost fully undeterred."[25] This perhaps was an expression of frustration less about the state of deterrence, per se, but more about the well-understood thresholds that Russia and NATO had already agreed to implicitly compete within when it came to Ukraine. Either way, it was good fortune that the possibility of nuclear escalation was at the forefront of those stewarding the United States and its allies through the early moments of the war. In August 2023, Jake Sullivan, Biden's chief advisor on national security matters, voiced his frustration with the recommendations offered by the chattering classes in Washington and in European capitals that sometimes appeared to wave away the possibility of nuclear war altogether: "[T]o be completely cavalier about escalation, to say that to even raise the question makes you a coward, that's easy to do from the outside, but when you sit in this seat you can't do that," Sullivan remarked.[26] "You have an obligation to the American people to consider worst-case scenarios," he added, voicing what may arguably come to describe the experience of many policymakers, military planners, and advisors concerned about the crises yet to come in Taiwan, Korea, and elsewhere.

The old debates about nuclear deterrence that were reignited in the wake of Russia's 2022 invasion of Ukraine emphasize the fundamentally disquieting and often frustrating nature of the entire enterprise. *Whom* do nuclear weapons *deter* and from *what* specific action are often left unsaid in arguments and debates on deterrence. Breedlove's exhortations that Putin is "almost fully undeterred" are true when referring to Russia's then ongoing conventional military campaign against Ukraine's southeastern territory, but that was never an objective for the United States and NATO's deterrence efforts once the conflict started – or in general in the years leading up to the

2022 invasion. Moreover, as was plainly clear in the lead-up to Russia's invasion, nuclear deterrence played no role whatsoever in influencing Putin's decision to attack. The confusion over the role of deterrence in this conflict is fundamentally also a reflection of the epistemic difficulty of observing deterrence in action: deterred actions are by definition unobserved counterfactuals, and, as such, cannot necessarily be attributed directly to capabilities, statements, and signals meant to deter. Despite all this, however, there is little doubt that Putin *was* deterred from crossing the most important threshold for NATO. As billions of dollars in military equipment poured into Ukraine from its territorially contiguous NATO neighbors, Russia found itself powerless to act in a way that would decisively deter NATO from such assistance. This remained true throughout the course of the conflict into 2024, gradually allowing for greater political will to manifest in various NATO states, leading to provision of increasingly lethal and advanced capabilities for Ukraine that had been unthinkable at the outset of the conflict.

Despite these observable consequences of nuclear deterrence, the prospects of both sides losing control and inadvertently entering a conflict appeared possible on several occasions. In 2022, a Russian fighter pilot fired missiles at a British surveillance aircraft over the Black Sea.[27] While both sides downplayed the incident in public – the Russians said it was a technical error while the British defense secretary said he did not "consider this incident to constitute a deliberate escalation" – a potential hit on the British aircraft would have potentially had disturbing consequences. In 2024, a Russian missile, fired in the course of the country's ongoing attempts to saturate and terrorize Ukrainian cities, struck just 500 meters from a convoy that carried Ukrainian President Volodymyr Zelensky and Greek Prime Minister Kyriakos Mitsotakis.[28] Mitsotakis, the leader of a NATO state, did not interpret the strike as deliberate, but, under different circumstances, a hit would almost certainly have sparked a major emergency within the trans-Atlantic alliance and potentially laid the groundwork for a conflict. In yet another incident of a missile going awry, in November 2022, a Ukrainian air defense interceptor crossed into Poland, striking a village and killing two civilians. In the fog of the moment, there was substantial confusion about what had happened, but given the war and broader NATO-Russia tensions, many in the alliance were primed to see the strike as a deliberate Russian attack. Making matters worse, the globally authoritative Associated Press released a wire report, attributed to an anonymous senior U.S. intelligence official, stating that "Russian missiles crossed into NATO member Poland."[29] By the time the truth emerged from NATO itself, multiple senior officials from the alliance's eastern member states had blamed Russia, and Poland had contemplated initiating formal alliance proceedings that could have been the prelude to war.[30] Wars, in general, do not start by accident, but, against a backdrop of crisis, inadvertent and accidental events have the potential to catalyze escalation.

As unsatisfying as the effects of nuclear deterrence have been for all in the course of Russia's war on Ukraine, a certain strain of analysis simply sets aside nuclear weapons altogether. Contemplating questions of how a nuclear war might begin and be fought is sometimes described, as the Cold War strategist Herman Kahn put it, as "thinking about the unthinkable."[31] With the exception of the American bombings of Hiroshima and Nagasaki, the bomb has not been used in war; the known terrible effects of nuclear weapons make their use unthinkable – or so it goes. In the course of the Ukraine war, several commentators found themselves drawn to simply dismiss the possibility of nuclear escalation – the unthinkable – altogether. The American essayist Anne Applebaum, for instance, offered up the assessment in May 2022 that there was "no indication right now that the nuclear threats so frequently mentioned by Russian propagandists, going back many years, are real."[32] This was only slightly more dismissive of Russian nuclear weapons than the occasional conspiracy theorist on social media who would insist – with utmost confidence – that the Russian military's conventional shortcomings in Ukraine were proof supreme that Moscow's nuclear weapons simply wouldn't work if called to the battlefield.

Nuclear deterrence rests on the real possibility that the inherent uncontrollability of war as a human enterprise will, at some unknowable point, cause its practitioners to irreversibly plunge into the abyss. The certain terror associated with the possibility of the plunge – and the unknowable, but non-zero probability that it may occur – helps manifest what Thomas Schelling, the seminal American nuclear strategist, once described as the "threat that leaves something to chance."[33] All it takes for caution to prevail – on both sides – is that the probability of Armageddon be non-zero. This is precisely how many U.S. and European policymakers involved in NATO policy deliberations on Ukraine described their own thinking about the risk of nuclear war in the course of Russia's invasion.[34] Ultimately, however much they might have been motivated to support Ukraine's righteous cause in its own national self-defense, European and U.S. officials *had to* consider that their interests in averting nuclear war diverged from the risks that Ukrainian leaders, already mired in an existential conflict, were willing to accept. It was largely for these reasons that many Western leaders, including Biden and his advisors, agonized about qualitatively new forms of military assistance that would manifest a potentially greater risk to Russia's nuclear forces, inviting a greater risk of potential nuclear use. Nuclear deterrence ultimately imposes a certain familiarity and shared sense of stake between bitter adversaries. Imagine two convicts, escaped from prison, but shackled nonetheless at the ankles, engaged in a bitter fistfight on the edge of a precipice: they may despise everything about each other, but, as they fight, they understand that one punch thrown too carelessly could send one of them careening off the edge, pulling the other along too. If they both value their own survival, punches may be more carefully thrown – or they may simply glare in contempt at each other, fearing the consequences of fighting at all. Just as these two convicts share a fear of the abyss, so too do American and Russian leaders share an interest in avoiding nuclear war. The shackles, in the above metaphor, allude to the odd intimacy that undergirds a nuclear deterrence relationship: the fate of each of them is very much intertwined with that of their adversary. As much as the other's nuclear capabilities frustrates their objectives, these leaders and decision-makers nevertheless choose to operate within the constraints imposed by deterrence – a form of perverse, if rational, cooperation with their opponent.

Nuclear deterrence is not and has not been a source of total paralysis. In the course of the war in Ukraine, Russia and the United States have sought to pursue their goals within acceptable levels of risk. For Russia, in particular, the *manipulation* of risk has been a critical component of its nuclear rhetoric in the course of the war. To return to – and refine – our analogy, the shackled convicts may not find themselves tussling on the edge of a cliff in bright daylight; instead, they may generally know that they're in the vicinity of a deep chasm, but the path to that chasm is shrouded in a thick fog. Schelling would describe the brink not as the "sharp edge of a cliff where one can stand firmly, look down, and decide whether or not to plunge," but as a "curved slope."[35] Leaders in a crisis under the shadow of nuclear weapons, then, can choose to walk along this curve, whose contours are discovered as they tread – slowly, and one step at a time. This is the dangerous practice of brinkmanship – the deliberate invitation of greater risk to seek bargaining advantage. Each of the shackled convicts might see advantage in taking one, two, or even three steps toward the chasm, but with each step comes a greater, palpable terror that the abyss will take them. Neither knows which step might be his last.

Vladimir Putin, a veteran Cold War spy and a man clearly interested in the role played by nuclear weapons in international statecraft for a number of years, appears to view nuclear threat-making and signaling in precisely these terms. In October 2022, during a period of heightened concern among global observers that Russia may resort to nuclear use, Putin was interviewed at the Valdai Discussion Club, a Russian think-tank and forum, about the war. Fyodor Lukyanov, a well-known Russian analyst, anchored the interview and alluded to comments the Russian president had made earlier about nuclear war. Lukyanov asked Putin to reassure him – and the audience present that day – that nuclear war was not imminent. Instead of responding right away, Putin turned his glance toward the floor and remained silent for some five seconds, prompting Lukyanov to observe that the president had "stopped to think" about this matter. Lukyanov added that Putin's extended silence was "disconcerting." Following this remark, Putin smirked and simply said "I did it on purpose to make you worry a little," followed by a self-satisfied smile. This moment encapsulated Putin's largely deliberate approach to manipulating "the threat that leaves something to chance" throughout the course of the Ukraine war – including in October 2022, which many Western analysts agree in hindsight was the most dangerous moment for possible Russian nuclear use.

The fundamental question for the great powers and their nuclear deterrence relationships comes down – as it once did between the United States and the Soviet Union – to the condition of mutually assured destruction. The famous pejorative of "MAD" is perhaps one of the better known absurdities inherent in nuclear strategy by the general public, but it is, above all, a condition – not a strategy. Despite popular misconception, neither the United States nor the Soviet Union adopted MAD as a strategy during the Cold War, but their leaders grew accustomed to the condition of MAD that was thrust upon them as

a fact of their adversary's capabilities. As described earlier in
this book, despite the dawn of a new nuclear age, there is much
that is unchanged about the fundamentals that underpin stable
deterrence. As a result, a paramount question will be just how
far from the stable ideal of MAD the three nuclear-armed great
powers will find themselves veering.

Deterrence and its discontents

The new nuclear age presents practitioners of nuclear
deterrence with fresh challenges even as the fundamental theoretical underpinnings of deterrence remain largely
constant. Fundamentally, these challenges will be especially
concentrated around the three great powers: the United States,
China, and Russia. China's abandonment of a "lean and effective" nuclear force, far quantitatively inferior to that of the
United States, has introduced concerns in Washington of
the implications of a possible "two near-peer" environment
for nuclear deterrence. Traditionally, the United States had
considered its nuclear deterrence problem vis-à-vis China as
a so-called lesser-included-case of the problem it faced with
Russia. In other words, any U.S. nuclear force sufficiently capable of deterring Russia and achieving U.S. objectives should
deterrence with Russia fail could do the same for China. Even
as China qualitatively modernized its nuclear forces in the
aftermath of the Cold War, Chinese nuclear forces were not
a primary or overarching consideration for U.S. nuclear deterrence strategy in the course of the second nuclear age.

In Washington, DC, it is not all too uncommon to hear
nuclear policy analysts from both the Republican and
Democratic parties express genuine concern that the United
States may soon have to contend with the possibility that both
Russia and China may cooperatively attempt a disarming first
strike on U.S. nuclear forces. The bipartisan congressionally

chartered Strategic Posture Commission, in an October 2023 report, noted that the possibility of Sino-Russian collusion in a possible crisis meant that the United States needed nuclear forces "capable of deterring two near-peer nuclear adversaries at the same time." They further counseled that the only response to this possibility should be planning for an expansion in the U.S. nuclear arsenal such that existing war plans can be adapted to hold at risk a greater number of targets, including those new nuclear-armed silos in China. What is left unaddressed is the logical reaction such a measure would beget from Moscow and Beijing, each of which would seek to further size up their own forces to ensure sufficient survivability. The prospect of a somewhat stable equilibrium of the sort that the United States and the Soviet Union eventually found between them during the Cold War appears elusive in this new three-player great power nuclear contest. Stability is not impossible in this context, but the intellectual underpinnings of how exactly it might manifest in this new nuclear age are not well-rooted. Admiral Charles Richard, a former commander of U.S. Strategic Command, likened the problem of strategic stability between three great powers to the famous three-body problem in classical mechanics.[36] In the three-body problem, unlike the two-body problem, solutions to describe the nature of interactions between the involved bodies are intractably chaotic. In the new nuclear environment among the major powers, so too may strategic stability be elusive.

From the American perspective, the severity of this two near-peer environment is due to its own nuclear strategy as well. Since the adoption of a nuclear deterrence strategy premised on counterforce targeting in the 1960s, the United States has seen it paramount to hold at risk the nuclear forces and command and control systems of its adversaries. In contrast to what nuclear strategists called countervalue, counterforce targeting would not deliberately pick out human populations or economic targets without military value per se. The purpose of this approach is to limit damage against the United States and its allies should deterrence fail, and to render nuclear warfare *somewhat* more compatible with the laws of armed conflict. While laypeople often recoil at the idea that there can be anything particularly lawful about global thermonuclear war, the United States is rare among nuclear-armed states for repeatedly publicly professing that it ensures that its nuclear war plans comport with the principles of distinction, proportionality, and military necessity. The Biden administration's 2022 *Nuclear Posture Review* (NPR), for instance, reemphasized, as previous reviews had, that "legal advice is integral" in the preparation of U.S. nuclear war plans, and that a process to "review . . . consistency with the Law of Armed Conflict" exists. (The United Kingdom, France, and Russia have asserted that international law could apply to nuclear use.[37]) In practice, this legal review is integral to limiting the "menu" of strike options that might be presented to the president of the United States in a nuclear crisis: the president, presumably, would select from one of a number of pre-vetted "legal" strike packages to limit damage against the United States. This could involve large-scale strikes against the known nuclear forces of Russia, China, or North Korea.

In practice, nuclear weapons are perhaps the furthest thing from a surgical scalpel and many so-called "counterforce" targets are located in the heart of major urban population centers in Russia and China. For instance, the political leadership of an adversary state might be a legally justifiable counterforce target with great military importance, but destroying such targets would entail massive nuclear strikes into the heart of Moscow and Beijing, killing millions of civilians. Counterforce – and the temptation to render targeting compliant with the law of armed conflict – represents something of a light "conventionalization" of nuclear weapons in the sense that it applies many of the precepts of conventional military strategy to nuclear warfare. For the bureaucrats and military planners who spend their time thinking through the unthinkable, this may render counterforce plans ultimately a less bitter pill to swallow than the inherently horrific enterprise of countervalue targeting (where the objective would be to deliver assured destruction of the adversary's nation and civilization by deliberately targeting industry and population centers).

Readers may have picked up by now that much of this discussion of counterforce is at odds with the fundamentals of nuclear deterrence discussed earlier in this chapter. Counterforce – and the aspiration to limit damage – is fundamentally at odds with the key prescription for stability that arises out of the nuclear revolution: that a secure, second strike capable of assuring the destruction of an adversary's most valued assets alone is sufficient for stable deterrence. Counterforce is not rooted in Schelling's idea that the "power to hurt is bargaining power," but in Albert Wohlstetter's observation that the balance of terror is "delicate."[38] For Wohlstetter, an American Cold War nuclear strategist, nuclear deterrence was a garden that required constant tending: deterrence, he wrote in 1958, was "not automatic," because the "technological race" mandates that competition is dynamic. Wohlstetter was writing at a time when the United States still adopted a deterrence strategy premised on massive retaliation, but from the late 1960s onward, mainstream U.S. nuclear strategic thought has come to fully imbibe the idea of a "delicate balance." Preparing for counterforce, after all, depends on an assessment of the adversary's capabilities and then considering the means necessary to limit damage to the United States. This obsession, in part, helped explain why arms control in the latter half of the Cold War became bogged down in arcane, technical debates about the throw-weights of particular large missiles, for example.[39]

Counterforce has faced other problems as well. U.S. adversaries, perceiving the United States to be substantially technically sophisticated in terms of the full array of technologies it might bring to bear to support a counterforce strategy, tend to react to Washington's moves. To paraphrase Robert McNamara, the U.S. secretary of defense who oversaw the transition to counterforce, the United States' damage limitation problem becomes the other side's assured destruction problem.[40] To render this less abstract, the basic idea here is that no matter the means the United States pursues to hold adversary nuclear forces at risk – be it with precise, ballistic missiles designed to kill ICBMs in their silos, or with missile defense interceptors designed to kill those same ICBM reentry vehicles outside the Earth's atmosphere once they've launched – the adversary will compete to ensure that his forces maintain a level of capability where the employment of those forces will result in the assured destruction of the United States as a functioning society and civilization. In other words, a nuclear deterrence strategy premised on counterforce targeting is the kindling for an arms race. It is this basic problem, for instance, that has led to a surge in interest in Russia and China in new and exotic types of nuclear delivery systems and basing modes. Moscow and Beijing maintain differing nuclear strategies, with Russia implementing counterforce targeting into its own nuclear war plans, but both prize their secure, second-strike capabilities. Whatever they – and the United States – may believe about just how "delicate" the balance of terror is, the *sine qua non* of stable deterrence continues to be the assured ability to retaliate.

It is easy then to see why, if the temptation that appears to be brewing in Washington is allowed through to its logical conclusion, the world may see a dangerous new nuclear arms race. Arguments in favor of a large-scale surge in the size of the U.S. nuclear force, among their proponents, seldom contend with the simple question of why Russia or China would simply watch as such a build-up played out and take no countervailing steps in response. It would appear that any U.S. nuclear sufficiently sized to enable a nuclear deterrence strategy premised on counterforce against *both* Russia and China, in tandem, would be large enough to prompt a reaction in both Russia *and* China. Neither Moscow nor Beijing would allow the vulnerability of their nuclear forces to rise substantially in the face of advancing U.S. nuclear capability. China, until before its build-up that began at the start of the 2020s, tolerated an unusually high level of vulnerability, but its political leadership appears now to have determined that this is no longer acceptable.

Beyond the risks of stoking a new arms race, counterforce is unlikely to work as desired in practice. Even if, under charitable assumptions, a nuclear war were to break out and escalate to such a level that would make the United States contemplate large-scale, damage-limiting strikes on the nuclear forces of either Russia or China, both states would likely find that a sufficiently large component of their forces had survived any American onslaught and, thus, were available to retaliate. Before choosing to authorize such a strike, a prudent U.S. president, in the real world, would be – or at least should be – deterred by such a prospect. After all, even a so-called small nuclear war can cause sufficient damage to the United States to limit its viability as a functioning society and country. Technological change has generated some excitement about the growing viability of counterforce, but, in practice, the uncertainties involved with crossing the nuclear Rubicon are so great that any American president seeking to limit damage would find him or herself dissuaded by the mere *possibility* that damage *cannot* be sufficiently limited. No amount of artificial intelligence, missile precision, or advances in intelligence, surveillance, and reconnaissance technologies is likely to change this psychological calculus for future leaders. (A particular tragedy here is that even if these technologies are unlikely to fundamentally change the balance, U.S. adversaries may react to the mere possibility of advances, further stoking a compulsion in the United States to arms race.)

If the United States does choose to build up its forces and also chooses to maintain a deterrence strategy premised on counterforce targeting, that could contribute substantially to a heightened risk of nuclear war. The damage-limiting logic that underpins current U.S. counterforce targeting strongly provides for preemptive attack incentives: if a U.S. president were to receive reliable intelligence that an adversary nuclear attack is either under way, or likely to be under way, the best way to limit damage – particularly to fixed, silo-based American ICBMs before they might be lost to incoming missiles – would be to use them. To be clear, the United States does not have a *policy* of nuclear preemption – or of launching its nuclear forces under attack – but it maintains this option. Fearing the United States' preemption of their nuclear forces in a crisis, Russia, China, and even North Korea could resort to nuclear use earlier than they might have in an alternate scenario where the U.S. did *not* maintain this option. Their strikes may or may not serve the end of limiting damage against their own societies – as noted earlier, damage limitation is a component of Russian targeting, but less so for China – but they could have other objectives, such as coercing the United States to stand down. As long as U.S. adversaries value their nuclear forces – and each of them universally does so to a high degree – counterforce targeting will contribute to a heightened probability of escalation to nuclear war in a serious crisis or conventional war.

There are alternatives to the status quo in U.S. nuclear strategy that may lower the risk of nuclear war and of an open-ended arms race in the new nuclear age. While it would be no small move for such a change – indeed, it would represent the largest fundamental shift in U.S. nuclear strategy since the 1960s – Washington could move away from a deterrence strategy based on counterforce toward one that relied on more limited targeting of assets that may be less escalatory, or less prone to stoking pressures to use nuclear weapons early. In 2023, three American scholars outlined an option, for instance, whereby the United States could deter by targeting "its adversary's economic and industrial infrastructure, including energy and communication systems, ports, and transportation nodes."[41] They underscored that the attractiveness of such a strategy was that, for it to work, "the relative size of countries' nuclear forces is irrelevant," and "all that matters for deterrence is the absolute size of their retaliatory capabilities and their ability to inflict damage." This was, in effect, a call to arms to take nuclear deterrence back to its fundamental origins and for the United States to fully embrace the logic of the nuclear revolution without opting for countervalue targeting once again. Alternatively, the United States could adopt substantially greater ambiguity in what it would seek to target, but fundamentally abjure the current language it adopts, indicating an intent to limit damage in a nuclear war: this would preclude the need to formally adopt morally odious and illegal countervalue targeting, but still support nuclear deterrence objectives. Perhaps nothing is more important, however, than what U.S. adversaries might expect the United States to choose to target *first* in a nuclear war: even under counterforce targeting, limiting the perception that the U.S. would seek to disarm adversaries or degrade their nuclear command and control at the outset of a war will be key to avoiding unwanted escalation. In an all-out nuclear war, however, the United States may still seek to reasonably limit damage as best it could; there would be no higher rung of escalation to fear or prevent, after all.

Separately, while the American impulse to render nuclear war plans compatible with the law of armed conflict is admirable, perhaps nuclear war should have been treated as a category of conflict unto itself. There is nothing noble or inherently moral in the terror that underpins nuclear deterrence, after all. Distinctions between countervalue and counterforce matter to nuclear strategists, but are merely intellectual dressing for the same fundamentally, ruinous outcome for mankind. So, while proponents of the status quo in U.S. nuclear strategy might paint advocates of change as callous and immoral in their disregard for the law of armed conflict, an approach that otherwise contributes to a lower chance of an open-ended, three-party arms race between the major powers, while also lowering the risk of nuclear war should a crisis erupt between them, may ultimately be the far more morally justifiable outcome. What is legal and what is wise, ultimately, may diverge. Importantly, while nuclear deterrence contributes to the security of the states that practice it and depend on it, it should not be valorized: this is essentially the business of seeking security through credibly threatening actions that amount to atrocities. Fortunately, the abstract, jargon-laden land of nuclear strategy obscures just enough to make intellectual sparring about these matters at least tolerably palatable. Nuclear strategists, after all, must sleep at night too.

Deterring limited nuclear use

In broad strokes, the fact that the total number of nuclear weapons in existence has declined precipitously since the end of the Cold War represents a deeply good turn of events for humanity. Should the precarity upon which nuclear deterrence rests give way, the scope of total damage – albeit catastrophic for mankind by any measure – would be significantly more limited than it might otherwise have been during the Cold War. Consider, for instance, that in 1961, the United States maintained the option to spasmodically resort to the total use of an arsenal encapsulating some 7,800 megatons of explosive yield against more than 1,000 pre-selected targets spanning Russia and China: the truest encapsulation of what the term Armageddon evokes.[42] The end of the first nuclear age heralded a substantial reduction in aggregate global megatonnage: nuclear weapons, in general, have trended toward lower yields in the last few decades. With the United States' 2022 decision to retire the B83 nuclear gravity bomb, a 1.2 megaton weapon, only China is known to possess a megaton-class nuclear warhead for its DF-5 intercontinental-range ballistic missile. "Strategic" weapons fielded in the United States, Russia, the United Kingdom, and France, however, are still capable of delivering massive amounts of damage, with explosive yields in the hundreds of kilotons range – several times the yield of *Little Boy* and *Fat Man*, the weapons used against Hiroshima and Nagasaki respectively. There truly is no such thing as a "small" or insignificant nuclear weapon or detonation, but the qualitative shift toward lower average yields is notable.

Lower-yield nuclear weapons – what some states consider to be nonstrategic or "tactical" weapons – are growing in salience among the nuclear-armed states at the onset of this new nuclear age, however. Countries seeking to deter territorially contiguous, conventionally superior adversaries such as Pakistan vis-à-vis India and North Korea vis-à-vis the United States/South Korea alliance have sought out these weapons to render more credible the prospect of limited use. A growing concern in Europe among NATO states – particularly frontline East European NATO members – is that Russia, given its conventional walloping in the course of the Ukraine war, may become substantially more reliant on its 2,000-plus nonstrategic nuclear weapons, too. Meanwhile, while China does not formally adopt the nomenclature of nonstrategic or tactical nuclear weapons, Beijing has invested substantially in regional nuclear options that could be employed to various ends in a conflict with the United States. Finally, the United States, too, has given thought to possible scenarios where limited nuclear use may be the way out of a conventional war that is headed for defeat – a reprisal of the offset strategy once employed during the Cold War when Washington relied on nuclear weapons to prevent defeat at the hands of conventionally superior Soviet forces in Europe. Compared to the force it maintained during the Cold War, however, the United States today maintains a far more limited array of nonstrategic nuclear options.

Together, these developments are likely to result in a sustained focus on the problem of limited nuclear use – and how to deter such use. Critically, there is a distinction between *nuclear use* and what used to be thought of and vividly imagined during the Cold War as *nuclear war*. The third use of nuclear weapons in war in human history, thus, may be enacted in service of a belief that it will communicate unshakeable resolve and avoid a general nuclear war. North Korea, for instance, may choose to employ a nuclear-armed missile against a strictly military target at sea in the course of a limited crisis; while this would mark a crossing of the nuclear threshold and constitute what American strategists would consider a "strategic deterrence failure," Pyongyang may choose to do so on the belief that South Korea and the United States may not rationally seek to retaliate in turn, fearing that subsequent nuclear strikes could escalate to hit their cities. In this way, Pyongyang and Kim Jong Un may hope to sue to terminate a conflict – and to live another day despite having used nuclear weapons. The coercive logic of limited use, thus, may have theoretical appeal for leaders. This problem is a particular focus for strategists in the United States who fret about an asymmetric initial resort to nuclear use by either Russia, China, or North Korea in a variety of contingencies. Military planners at U.S. Strategic Command, the military command overseeing U.S. global strike and nuclear operations, have spent considerable time thinking through possible limited use options and advocated vociferously for the development of new nuclear options for the United States as a result. But limited nuclear use is not a uniquely American concern by any means. Chinese nuclear policy experts have long expressed in expert dialogues and exchanges that the United States' growing conventional military inferiority in the Indo-Pacific region may mean that Washington could be inclined to become more reliant on nuclear weapons as an offset. I have heard these views firsthand from Chinese and Russian counterparts in dialogues as recently as 2024.

This concern is not theoretically or empirically ungrounded, either: during the Cold War, when the United States and its NATO partners faced a situation of conventional inferiority in central Europe, along the Iron Curtain, their military plans strongly emphasized the early use of nuclear weapons to degrade a potential invasion of West Germany by Soviet armor. The North Atlantic Military Committee, in 1957, observed that, "since NATO would be unable to prevent the rapid overrunning of Europe unless NATO immediately employed nuclear weapons both strategically and tactically, we must be prepared to take the initiative in their use," underscoring the offset value that nuclear weapons might provide.[43] By the late-1960s, NATO had adopted a flexible response posture, which nevertheless continued to dangle the possibility of limited nuclear use to deter Soviet conventional aggression.[44] These Cold War-era precedents are a source of concern for certain Chinese thinkers – particularly given sustained attention in Washington on the potential need for new, limited nuclear options for the United States, such as a proposed sea-launched, nuclear-armed cruise missile that the Trump administration endorsed, but the Biden administration refused to. (The U.S. Congress has since legislated a requirement to develop this missile.) India and even non-nuclear South Korea have similarly found their military response options to limited conventional attacks constrained by the possibility of their respective adversaries, Pakistan and North Korea, incorporating the threat of asymmetric nuclear escalation with the use of lower-yield weapons into their respective strategies. A broader concern for these states is that their adversaries might resort to conventional or even subconventional aggression to seek political or territorial gain, counting on the prospect of a limited nuclear attack to effectively deter a robust response in return.

The strategic problem of limited nuclear use appears to be growing in salience in a range of competitive relationships in the new nuclear age, but it is not a new problem unto itself. There are also several possible options – each with various drawbacks – that might inform how prospective defenders react to this growing problem. At the most basic level, limited nuclear use, or a limited nuclear war, might be deterred by the prospect of all-out nuclear escalation with existential stakes for a potential attacker. This is perhaps the simplest approach to deterring limited nuclear use, but it rests on the idea that both the defender and the attacker share a belief in the uncontrollability of nuclear escalation: that once a single nuclear weapon is used, both sides cannot help but escalate in turn to a limitless, spasmodic nuclear exchange. There's also the problem of credibility: it is simply not particularly credible for a defender to threaten to massively escalate to all-out general nuclear war after a single warhead has been exploded as a deliberate signal potentially against a purely military target on the battlefield. Here we return to Schelling and the "threat that leaves something to chance": a defender might seek to deter an attacker by clearly indicating that crossing the threshold into nuclear use would take both of them closer to the existential brink, and that the ability to forestall a descent into Armageddon could not be assured. Because this would not be a desirable outcome for a rational attacker, limited use might be avoided – or so goes the thinking. Despite the alluring simplicity of this approach, there are several problems in its practical implementation. None is bigger perhaps than the problem that many of the steps that nuclear weapons states might take to adopt such an approach in practice, such as deploying tactical nuclear weapons and delegating their use to military officers in the field, would also increase substantially the risk of accidental and inadvertent nuclear escalation.

During the Cold War, Soviet and U.S. thinking about nuclear strategy within their respective military establishments was somewhat strongly rooted in the idea that nuclear escalation could not be controlled. Some of the factors feeding this belief had to do with the state of technology at the time, which may be somewhat remediated in the new nuclear age. Soviet and American leaders feared the robustness of their ability to receive reliable warning of an inbound attack and the integrity of their nuclear command and control systems, to cite just two technology-driven motivators. As NATO relied on the early use of nonstrategic nuclear weapons to deter conventional attack, the Soviet Union adopted the view, expressed in a volume on military strategy in 1962, that "any armed conflict will inevitably escalate into a general nuclear war if the nuclear powers are drawn into this conflict."[45] In 1972, another Soviet text noted that the "logic of war" meant that a conflict would escalate "to the territory of the United States of America," and that strategic nuclear weapons could be used to this end.[46] The "threat that leaves something to chance," thus, was more easily manifested: the credibility of NATO's potential resort to the limited nuclear option to degrade a Soviet conventional attack was not particularly in question. The end of the Cold War, however, has resulted in the manifestation of different views in Russia, China, and North Korea on the automaticity of escalation given an initial instance of limited nuclear use by any party in a war.[47]

There are other ways to address the problem of limited nuclear use. An idea that repeatedly comes up in discussions on the matter around the world is that of a tit-for-tat, or proportional, response. Among its proponents, this approach has the allure of conveying one's resolve to cross the nuclear threshold in retaliation for nuclear use. In the United States, proponents note that existing U.S. commitments on rendering nuclear war planning as compatible as possible with the law of the armed conflict also should drive greater consideration of proportionate options. But proportionality in practice is far from obvious, and the risk of escalation may induce more caution still. Critically, given that the adversary gets a vote in interpreting the proportionality of a response, the unknowability of how an act of supposedly proportionate retaliation may be interpreted in the course of a war, where psychological and emotional stressors will be intense on leaders, is a problem. Moreover, given divergent nuclear capabilities across states, a proportionate response simply may not be available for certain scenarios, further muddying the nature of what exactly a tit-for-tat option might involve in practice. Military planners could choose to focus on a variety of characteristics to determine a proportionate response, such as the nature of the target struck, the type of weapon used, and the explosive yield. Finally, even with the intention to respond proportionately, it is eminently possible that a state could inflict damage that could be *perceived* as disproportionate, prompting an escalatory response in return that would take both parties closer to a general nuclear war.

In practice, proportionate response appears to be a consideration that is more attractive in the abstract than in practice. For instance, in the summer and autumn of 2022, Western debates on the appropriate response to the potential limited use of a nuclear weapon by Russia in Ukraine did not coalesce around a distinctly proportionate nuclear response. Instead, it appeared that major Western powers, including the United States, the United Kingdom, and France, communicated privately to Moscow that a nuclear attack would beget a massive conventional response.[48] While such a promise had the advantage of being credible, it appeared to set aside the literal nuclear option due primarily to concerns about follow-on nuclear escalation. Privately, one U.S. defense official told me that, in consultations, the nuclear response was not under serious consideration given that Ukraine was not a formal American treaty ally.[49] Broader concerns about escalation, however, were still a concern for the United States. This real-world preference might be contrasted with the outcome in a 2016 wargame involving U.S. National Security Council principals and their staff, reported by Fred Kaplan, an American journalist, in a 2020 book. In that game, the officials had to devise a response to limited nuclear use by Russia, but were concerned about the possibility of follow-on escalation in the aftermath of U.S. nuclear strikes on Russian soil.[50] In a bizarre turn – and in an attempt to find some roughly proportionate, but non-escalatory response – the principals determined that limited U.S. nuclear strikes on Belarus, a close Russian partner and former Soviet state, was an appropriate means of retaliating and communicating that the United States had the resolve to go tit-for-tat. Notably, some of the deputies involved in that same war game who chose *not* to respond with U.S. nuclear weapons held senior positions in the Biden administration in the months following Russia's invasion of Ukraine in 2022 and were present during subsequent debates on responding to nuclear use. (Part of the case against U.S. nuclear use in kind rested on normative and moral factors, for instance.)

A final approach to managing the problem of limited nuclear use has its origins in Cold War-era American nuclear strategy: seeking what Herman Kahn dubbed "escalation dominance" by maintaining the option of surpassing an adversary's escalation at every step – and communicating the willingness to do so. As long as a rational, somewhat risk-averse adversary perceives that one is willing to take a conflict past greater escalatory thresholds in the wake of limited nuclear use – and that this will is backed by real capabilities – limited nuclear use *should* be less likely. Or so goes the theory. In practice, this approach presents a range of risks. First, competitive risk-taking in a nuclear crisis of the kind that precipitates limited nuclear use by a more risk-acceptant adversary may not be usefully countered by communicating a willingness to escalate further. An adversary like North Korea, for instance, may perceive existential stakes after its potential limited initial nuclear use is met with nuclear or even massive conventional retaliation and then proceed to escalate to what Kahn dubbed a "spasm war," or unlimited war. (This would be especially true where, as is the case today, North Korea feared that its national leadership or nuclear command and control systems could be targeted.) Relying on an escalation dominance strategy may also add to the already intense arms-racing dynamics between the major powers in the third nuclear age. For instance, for the United States to rely on such a strategy to forestall the possibility of Russian and Chinese nuclear use, Washington would potentially have to pursue a quantitative expansion of its nuclear forces, and invest in a range of qualitatively new nuclear systems and enabling technologies. These steps would draw a reciprocal set of reactions from Russia and China that would mark the eruption of a mutually ruinous, unconstrained arms race.

As pressing as the problem of limited nuclear use is likely to be in the new nuclear age, the fact remains that the sustained record of nearly eighty years of nuclear non-use since Nagasaki means that *any* use of nuclear weapons again in war would be a strategic, world-shaping moment. Though not an idea central to debates on nuclear strategy among military establishments, the idea that the "nuclear taboo" and the related norm of non-use help reinforce the deterrence of deliberate, limited nuclear use remains popular among scholars.[51] If not deterrence, then the taboo on the use of nuclear weapons raises the threshold that might need to be crossed in the course of a conflict before nuclear use could be contemplated. If a single or handful of nuclear weapons were ever employed in a "limited" manner – and successfully – this taboo may fray entirely, and nuclear weapons may come close to being "conventionalized," as many in the United States once imagined possible in the 1950s. The importance of maintaining the unacceptability of *any* limited nuclear use is thus paramount in the new nuclear age.

3

Technology and Escalation

Nuclear weapons, in the eighty years that they have existed and proliferated since 1945, have done so against the backdrop of a rapidly changing world, marked by the arrival of a range of new technologies with military and civilian uses. Nuclear-armed states, since the dawn of the first nuclear age, have thus always had to contend with the possibilities and threats presented by these technological changes. Far from accepting stable deterrence at the hands of an adversary's assured retaliatory capability, as the logic of the nuclear revolution would counsel, nearly every pursuer of nuclear weapons has given tremendous credence to the promise of whatever advantage technological change might offer. During the Cold War, nuclear weapons were initially weapons that could exclusively be delivered by bomber aircraft. By the late-1950s, intercontinental-range ballistic missiles, for the first time, promised to reduce what used to be a precarious and slow process of nuclear weapons delivery – depending on the precise locations of weapons-equipped bombers – to a far more prompt capability. By the late 1950s, U.S. and Soviet planners realized that what had necessarily been a process requiring hours would now take just some thirty-odd minutes – and, unlike bombers, which could be called back to their bases, missiles, once launched, could not be recalled, making their use final. Before long, nuclear weapons had also moved to sea; the arrival of naval nuclear propulsion, in particular, made the basing of a survivable retaliatory nuclear force at sea an attractive means of assuring survivability. The pursuit of assured destruction by one side through technological means was often countered by the other's bid to seek an escape from vulnerability. Action was met with reaction, and the technological status quo around nuclear deterrence rarely persisted for long.

As the world enters a new nuclear age, anxiety about the implications of technological change for nuclear stability are high. In 2021, American officials marveled at the apparent demonstration by China of an unprecedented capability throughout the missile age: Chinese engineers successfully released a hypersonic glide vehicle from an orbital bus and managed to hit a target fairly precisely after an intercontinental-range flight.[1] General Mark Milley, then the chairman of the U.S. joint chiefs of staff, described the demonstration as something of a "Sputnik moment," hearkening to the United States' dismay at the Soviet Union's successful launch and insertion of the first manmade artificial satellite in 1957.[2] (In reality, the idea that the Sputnik launch was a strategic surprise to the United States is a myth; the Eisenhower administration had credible intelligence of Soviet preparatory efforts by the mid-1950s.) Meanwhile, in China and Russia, concerns have long persisted about the United States' longstanding efforts to develop increasingly more capable missile defense systems. Finally, the emergence of new AI systems, counterspace weapons, directed energy weapons, quantum sensing systems, and other technologies continues to receive significant attention by nuclear and non-nuclear states alike. Just what effect will these new technologies have on the stability of nuclear deterrence? Will crises have a tendency to grow increasingly unstable as military establishments forge forward with the unconstrained deployments of possibly destabilizing new military technologies, or does technological change instead present new opportunities for stabilizing deeply competitive relationships?

There is no simple answer to these questions, but the closest approximation is that it entirely depends. Beyond the practical effects of various technologies, human perceptions of the effects that certain technologies may have on nuclear deterrence matter quite a bit. For instance, despite all the hemming and hawing in Washington about China's demonstration of an unprecedented orbital-release hypersonic glider system in 2021, it's not clear that such a capability would be deeply destabilizing or disruptive to the nuclear balance between the two countries (despite its undoubtedly impressive nature from an engineering perspective). After all, China already has the ability to deliver devastating nuclear attacks against which the United States has no real hope of defending itself. Existing U.S. homeland missile defenses would be quantitatively overwhelmed, and their demonstrated real-world effectiveness is questionable against sophisticated ICBMs equipped with countermeasures. Even if Chinese leaders feel the need to invest in exotic, orbitally released hypersonic glide vehicles out of a perception that U.S. missile defenses are more capable – or may one day become exquisitely capable – the adoption of new technologies in pursuit of assuring a survivable second strike is hardly destabilizing.

But what about non-nuclear technologies that threaten the survivability – perceived or real – of retaliatory nuclear forces? This is a more concerning area for possible technological change. If strategic stability is built on the back of nuclear competitors seeing no advantage to nuclear use given the assurance that they will be met with unacceptable – possibly existential – destruction by an adversary's surviving forces after an initial attack, then any tools that might render an adversary's forces vulnerable to a comprehensive, disarming attack could be destabilizing. For example, if a sudden technological breakthrough were to enable high-fidelity tracking of nuclear-armed ballistic missile submarines – traditionally seen as the most survivable basing mode for retaliatory nuclear forces – then that could be hugely destabilizing. This "transparent seas" problem has been the subject of decades of concern, and is manifest even today in debates on U.S. nuclear modernization, for instance. Advocates of modernizing the U.S. ground-based ICBM force, for instance, allude to this bogeyman to argue that potential submarine vulnerabilities deserve to be hedged by new investments in ICBMs.[3] The United States, which has traditionally led in both anti-submarine warfare and in technologies design to enhance submarine stealth, observed in the 2018 *Nuclear Posture Review* that "there are no known, near-term credible threats to the survivability of the SSBN force."[4]

Concerns about assuring survivability amid technological change have animated the modernization efforts of several states with nuclear weapons. In the aftermath of the Cold War, Russia and China, in large part, modernized their nuclear forces amid broader concerns about U.S. technological advances. The First Gulf War in 1990–1, for instance, showcased the remarkable effectiveness of U.S. non-nuclear precision strikes against immobile targets in Saddam Hussein's Iraq, raising the possible specter of *non-nuclear* attacks against nuclear forces – what in the parlance of nuclear strategy could be dubbed non-nuclear, or conventional, counterforce. (Famously, however, the U.S. struggled to strike or destroy mobile missiles during that war.[5]) These concerns would later intensify after the George W. Bush administration authorized research and development efforts for a Conventional Prompt Global Strike (CPGS) program, whereby the United States would develop a capability to strike targets anywhere on Earth – nominally with the goal of attacking terrorist groups at short notice, or denying a "rogue state" like North Korea the ability to carry out a limited nuclear attack.[6] For Russian and Chinese strategists, U.S. interest in CPGS raised the worrying prospect of advanced American conventional missiles threatening their nuclear forces in a conflict – a meaningfully new problem. Alongside U.S. investments in CPGS, Washington had also, in 2002, withdrawn from a 1972 treaty limiting its pursuit of missile defenses and started to develop a limited homeland missile defense capability. This capability was nominally designed to safeguard the U.S. homeland against "limited" attacks from potential nuclear proliferators like North Korea and Iran, but similarly raised concerns in Moscow and Beijing about the potential for an American disarming strike. As it was often voiced, Russian and Chinese strategists had to worry about the possibility that U.S. conventional and nuclear strike capabilities could attrite their nuclear forces with a first strike and any remaining residual retaliatory capability could then be absorbed by the "limited" U.S. homeland missile defense system. Cumulatively, homeland missile defense and long-range conventional strike systems could potentially allow Washington to escape the stabilizing condition of mutual vulnerability – or so feared Russia and China. By the 2010s, these technologies had emerged as major pressure points in dialogues between the United States and Russia on the future of strategic stability, and Chinese strategists would write widely on these concerns.

Unsurprisingly, these perceived technological challenges to the survivability of Russian and Chinese nuclear forces were met with answers. In 2018, President Putin unveiled a series of exotic nuclear delivery systems and other capabilities designed to address some of these concerns. In a speech before the Russian Federal Assembly, Putin announced, among other things, a nuclear-armed intercontinental-range hypersonic glider known as *Avangard*, an autonomous thermonuclear torpedo system known as *Poseidon*, and a nuclear-propelled cruise missile, which he claimed had an effectively unlimited range, known as *Burevestnik*.[7] In discussing *Avangard*, Putin was flanked by a slide, showing the glider flying below and around hypothetical missile defense systems. As it happened,

U.S. homeland missile defense efforts in the 2000s focused on what was known as exoatmospheric midcourse defense. The United States, anticipating an ICBM threat from North Korea, sought to destroy incoming nuclear-armed missile reentry vehicles outside the Earth's atmosphere. These exoatmospheric interceptors had no capability to destroy cruise missiles or other targets that would fly largely within the Earth's atmosphere. *Avangard*'s arrival was largely an attempt to exploit this limitation. Even if the United States were to size up its missile defense capability, Russia would have a qualitative means of nuclear weapons delivery that would bypass any exoatmospheric defenses. (Hypersonic glide vehicles leverage aerodynamic forces within the Earth's atmosphere after reentering the Earth's atmosphere after separating from their rocket boosters.) In 2019, too, China, for the first time, paraded a medium-range hypersonic glide vehicle known as the DF-17. While this system was not capable of ranging the U.S. homeland, it nevertheless was the result of years of research and development efforts in China to develop missile systems that would be capable of penetrating missile defense systems optimized for ballistic threats. In the meantime, Chinese research and development on weapons resembling *Avangard* – intercontinental-range gliders – continued.[8]

Missile defense, precision strike, and their associated enabling technologies will all continue to be of relevance in the new nuclear age. However, alongside these older sources of technological malaise, a range of new technologies has already come into focus, with the potential to disrupt the status quo and potentially render survivable nuclear forces more vulnerable. Wohlstetter once worried that the endeavor of ensuring a secure second-strike capability would require constant effort, investment, and intellectualization in an environment of technological flux. Wohlstetter and many of his successors understood that the mere possession of nuclear weapons would not result in a stabilizing balance – what he described as a "presumed automatic balance" – because, in part, of the possibility of technological change introducing a capability previously unforeseen and unplanned for.[9] "Matching weapons" – particularly offensive weapons – was not the key concern for Wohlstetter, but, rather, the problem of "being able to strike back in spite of" an attack. Technological change remains endemic to the conditions under which nuclear weapons exist, and the sources of complexity are quickly growing. At the dawn of the new nuclear age, the fundamental question remains to what extent will technological change undermine confidence in second-strike capabilities and unleash destabilizing, escalatory impulses in potential future nuclear crises.

Missile defense

On November 16, 2020, in the open ocean northeast of Hawaii, the U.S. Navy *Arleigh Burke*-class guided missile destroyer, USS *John Finn*, launched a missile out of one of its ninety-six Vertical Launching System cells. The missile, a Standard Missile 3 (SM-3) Block IIA interceptor, accelerated straight upward, on its way out of the Earth's atmosphere. Several minutes prior to this launch, another missile had been launched out of Kwajalein Atoll, in the Marshall Islands in the southern Pacific. This missile was designed to emulate an intercontinental-range ballistic missile reentry vehicle target of the sort that North Korea might launch against the United States in the course of a nuclear war. Somewhere over the Pacific Ocean, outside the Earth's atmosphere, the SM-3 Block IIA's interceptor successfully struck and destroyed the target. For the first time, the United States had demonstrated a nominal ability to destroy an "ICBM-representative target" with a kinetic interceptor launched from a ship. Even though this might have otherwise passed as an anodyne technical development, it underscored a potentially destabilizing new advance for U.S. homeland missile defense efforts that could contribute to a new arms race with Russia and China, and possibly even increase the risk of nuclear conflict.

Intuitively, missile defense systems are an attractive technological solution to an unsavory problem. After all, which citizen would not want their government to invest in the means to protect them from possible nuclear attacks? The problem that these systems purport to solve is nuclear vulnerability. In doing so, strategic missile defenses undercut the logic of the nuclear revolution, which, as explained earlier in this book, underscores mutual vulnerability to attack as a stabilizing condition (when each side possesses secure second-strike capabilities). In 1967, in Glassboro, New Jersey, U.S. President Lyndon Johnson attempted to persuade Soviet premier Alexei Kosygin of the value of a ban for both the United States and the Soviet Union in deploying strategic defensive systems.[10] While Kosygin did not immediately reciprocate, insisting instead that Soviet ballistic missile defenses were purely defensive, the Soviet Union and the United States, in 1972, were finally able to agree to limitations in the form of the Anti-Ballistic Missile Treaty.[11] At the core of the treaty was a mutual acceptance of the idea that vulnerability to the other's retaliatory strike would provide some salve to the arms race incentives that both sides would otherwise perceive in a world of unbounded defenses.

In the aftermath of the Cold War, with the threat of nuclear Armageddon between Moscow and Washington having receded, the United States fundamentally reoriented its approach to missile defense. Starting in 1999, Washington began putting in place the building blocks for a missile defense approach fit for the threats of the second nuclear age. Amid concerns that so-called rogue states like North Korea and Iran might one day field limited nuclear-capable, long-range missiles, Washington began investing in a new homeland missile defense system, dubbed the Ground-based Midcourse

Defense (GMD) system. In 2002, the United States left the ABM Treaty under the Bush administration, in part to realize those ambitions (even though the treaty did allow for a limited number of deployed missile defense interceptors). In the intervening years, officials and experts from Russia and China consistently cited the United States' pursuit of a "limited" homeland missile defense plan as destabilizing and, in turn, invested in countermeasures that would ensure that their nuclear forces would have the ability to penetrate a sophisticated U.S. system.

In reality, U.S. homeland missile defense investments through the 2000s and 2010s yielded an outcome that might be described as the worst of all worlds. This was true in the sense that the Bush administration rushed the deployment of GMD, resulting in a technologically flawed system that exhibited real world performance on a per-interceptor basis amounting to something of a coin-flip in observed tests.[12] Despite this poor performance, the system *nonetheless* heightened the urgency of a response in China and Russia, adding to the United States' own perceived nuclear threats. While Iran did not develop an ICBM, North Korea *did*. Even so, while GMD might have been able to notionally defend against an incoming North Korean attack, the pace at which Pyongyang has been able to size up its ICBM force already suggests that the United States will be playing catch-up. As of 2024, the United States had just forty-four deployed interceptors, with twenty additional planned. In a scenario where North Korea launched ICBMs at the United States, the U.S. would likely employ three to four interceptors against each incoming reentry vehicle. Even under the most generous assumptions about the system's performance, North Korea could potentially saturate U.S. defenses with just fifteen ICBMs – or fewer if it starts adopting multiple warheads per ICBM, as Kim Jong Un has suggested he will. By 2024, Pyongyang had already demonstrated that it possessed more than fifteen launchers for ICBMs. It was in part due to these sorts of concerns that the United States Missile Defense Agency, at the behest of the U.S. Congress, carried out the November 2020 SM-3 test described earlier.

While the United States has disproportionately assigned the largest amount of funding and exhibited the greatest interest in missile defenses in the post-Cold War era, it is far from alone in doing so. A prominent notable change in conversations on missile defense in Washington in the early 2020s has been the frequency with which one hears growing expressions of concern about Russian and Chinese investments in new missile defense systems that could reduce the vulnerability of those countries to U.S. nuclear or conventional attack. In the two decades since the United States withdrew from the ABM Treaty, both countries have undertaken substantial research and development efforts into increasingly more advanced missile defense systems that, in technological terms, mirror the broad, area defense approach underwritten by kinetic interceptors favored by the United States. Systems such as the Russian *Nudol* and S-500 and the Chinese DN-3, for instance, can cover wide areas of territory and intercept incoming ballistic missile reentry vehicles. "China and Russia are developing increasingly capable and numerous missile defense systems, and integrating them into their defense strategies as they compete with the United States," a U.S. Department of Defense official noted in 2020, underlining this development as a growing point of concern for Washington.[13] Just as China and Russia have long been concerned about the possibility that U.S. missile defense systems could attrite their retaliatory nuclear forces and allow the United States to seek advantage in a nuclear crisis, so too might the United States grow increasingly concerned that its own ICBM and SSBN reentry vehicles could be limited in their ability to hold at risk the targets that the United States sees as essential for deterrence.

In this way, as it once did for the United States and the Soviet Union in the Cold War until the ABM Treaty was agreed, the three great powers might find missile defense systems lead to strong incentives to arms race. Just as the North Koreans have learned, it will be, on balance, far more cost-effective for even a resource-constrained attacker to size up his offensive force to saturate and defeat a missile defense system than it will be for a defender to invest in order to keep ahead of this threat. The incentive to exacerbate the arms race would, of course, also be affected by the many other competitive nuclear dynamics outlined in this book. But that fundamental principle of stable deterrence and the condition of mutually assured destruction – mutual vulnerability to the other's secure second-strike capabilities – does not appear to be any closer to materializing among all three major powers. Finally, even as current missile defense systems remain questionable in their efficacy, planners fret about possible technological breakthroughs that could revolutionize the strategic balance. Given the stakes, Russia and China have reasoned for years on the worst case scenario about U.S. missile defense investments, assessing them to be far more capable than their real-world test record would suggest. As a result, even if the existing U.S. homeland missile defense system has a little bit better than a 50:50 chance of destroying an incoming reentry vehicle in practice, Moscow and Beijing will be prompted to respond as if it is substantially more capable. During the Cold War, this type of pathology influenced how the United States' Strategic Air Command did its own nuclear targeting for sites located near missile defense sites – ascribing a probability of kill to the system that has been much higher than warranted, leading to absurdities such as sixty-nine nuclear warheads being assigned to a system capable of launching sixty-eight interceptors.[14] This sort of worst-case scenario thinking is partly why we've seen the adoption of novel types of nuclear delivery systems developed in these countries despite the questionable efficacy of strategic missile defenses; developing resiliency against area missile defenses has been a priority for these states.

Outside the competitive dynamics between the three major powers, missile defense systems are set also to influence regional nuclear dynamics on the Korean Peninsula and in South Asia. Starting in 2019, North Korea, for instance, started investing considerable energies in developing and testing a range of shorter-range missiles designed to stress deployed missile defense systems in South Korea and Japan. One such missile, known as the Hwasong-11A in North Korea and as the KN23 to U.S. intelligence agencies, maneuvers extensively within the Earth's atmosphere as it approaches its target at hypersonic speeds. In 2021, North Korea also, for the first time, introduced what it described as a "strategic" long-range cruise missile. Cruise missiles have been a particularly devilish problem for missile defense given their low altitude powered flight. Unlike ballistic missiles, which might rise high above the Earth's atmosphere and thus be tracked by radars at longer ranges, cruise missiles can be far more difficult to track and defend against. North Korea's investment in these capabilities has not dissuaded South Korea and its ally, the United States, from continuing to invest in missile defenses, but the Korean Peninsula offers ample evidence that even resource-constrained countries like North Korea will find the means to preserve their ability to hold at risk the targets they feel necessary for deterrence. In North Korea's case, many of these missiles may be used without nuclear warheads in a crisis to destroy radars and missile defense sites prior to an actual nuclear strike.

Meanwhile, in South Asia, missile defense is an increasingly relevant concern for both India and Pakistan. For Pakistan, fears about Indian advances in missile defense technologies has prompted continued modernization of the country's nuclear forces and delivery systems. In the worst-case scenario, Pakistani planners may consider missile defenses to be a potential enabler for an Indian move toward a strategy of conventional and nuclear counterforce.[15] Meanwhile, for India,

China's missile defenses are a growing source of concern. As China expands its nuclear arsenal, India will be increasingly hard pressed to ensure that its own, smaller nuclear arsenal can meet its doctrinal requirement of being able to inflict "unacceptable damage" on major Chinese cities in retaliation against a nuclear attack. As Chinese missile defenses proliferate, this grows more challenging.

While missile defenses will continue to be destabilizing at the strategic level, the world will likely see the continued proliferation of theater missile defense systems. This will largely be a response to the rapid vertical and horizontal proliferation of missile capabilities and the increased attractiveness and availability of long-range non-nuclear missiles around the world. One of the lessons that world leaders have taken from Russia's 2022 invasion of Ukraine and the subsequent warfighting is that long-range strike capabilities are instrumental to modern warfare.[16] As a result, missile defenses have an important role to play in deterrence and warfighting well below the threshold of nuclear war, and even for non-nuclear weapon states. For many wealthier states with the resources, particularly those allied with the United States, investments in missile defense will take on greater salience in the coming decades. This, too, could have downstream effects on nuclear stability. China and Russia, for instance, have long feared that U.S. allies could "network" their missile defense systems and associated enabling technologies, such as radars, with the United States, allowing Washington to improve the fidelity and performance of its homeland missile defense capabilities.

The means of delivery: Exotic and "fast" missiles

At the dawn of this new nuclear age, hypersonic glide vehicles (HGVs) have become all the rage. The term "hypersonic" itself seems to exude futuristic hype. News articles covering hypersonic weapons will often be accompanied by an image portraying a sleek, wedge-shaped projectile, covered in an evocative plasma sheath straight out of a science fiction film, as it heads toward its target at seemingly unimaginable speeds. These weapons have already started to see deployment. In 2019, Russia deployed its *Avangard* intercontinental-range HGV and China publicly announced the DF-17, a medium-range HGV.[17] The United States, too, has been accelerating its research and development efforts on regional HGV systems. Even North Korea, in September 2021, tested a prototype wedge-shaped HGV, the Hwasong-8.[18]

Are hypersonic glide vehicles really all that special – or are their implications for nuclear stability overhyped? And what about hypersonic cruise missiles (HCMs)? The place to start in answering this is to first understand that *speed* is *not* what makes these weapons remarkable. Nazi Germany's V-2 rockets, the first guided ballistic missile in human history, reached speeds approaching Mach 5, the threshold for "hypersonic" speed, as they approached their targets during the Second World War. A "hypersonic" projectile is one that travels at speeds in excess of five times the speed of sound in a given medium; this is a standard that is met by all ballistic missiles with a range of more than a few hundred kilometers. ICBM reentry vehicles, designed to range across the globe, can approach speeds in excess of Mach 22 upon reentry after their engines burnout. What does distinguish HGVs from ballistic missiles, rather, is their ability to maneuver in flight and their flight profiles. Unlike ballistic missiles, which are designed to elevate payloads to high altitudes outside of the Earth's atmosphere, relying mostly on gravity and atmospheric drag during the final moments of reentry from there on, HGVs spend most of their flight time within the Earth's atmosphere.

This latter feature presents several design challenges for HGVs, explaining in part why these weapons did not manifest outside experimental settings earlier in the nuclear age.

The aerospace engineering principles behind HGVs have been understood for decades, but the materials required to make longer-range, reliable HGVs plausible were out of reach as an economical or practical solution during the Cold War. (States, instead, invested in other countermeasures to cope with anti-ballistic missile systems.) Because these projectiles travel within the relatively dense atmosphere of the Earth en route to their targets (compared to the vacuum of near-Earth space), they must be robust enough to endure tremendous drag forces over, in some cases, tens of minutes. This can entail external heat loads amounting to thousands of degrees centigrade. To maximize their range and performance, however, they cannot be overly heavy, either. Finally, the physical shape of the glider must allow for a sufficiently positive lift-to-drag ratio to enable long-range gliding flight. This is often why HGVs resemble a triangular wedge, for instance. Optimizing for these requirements is not a trivial engineering task.

Despite these impressive engineering requirements, these weapons are unlikely to prove revolutionary. Their primary appeal, as alluded to earlier, is to stress and defeat the most sophisticated missile defense systems that have been developed over a number of years with primarily more traditional ballistic missile threats in mind. HGVs, by flying fast and "low" in the Earth's atmosphere, are particularly invulnerable to a set of missile defense interceptors operated by the United States and a handful of other countries that are exclusively capable of destroying objects outside the Earth's atmosphere. (Notably, the United States' homeland missile defense incorporates such a ballistic missile defense interceptor.) However, hypersonic glide vehicles may not be invulnerable to defenses altogether. Despite their speed, gliders are subject to the laws of physics and, as a result, drag forces and any maneuvering during flight will ultimately cost speed that could make them prone to being intercepted as they approach their targets. In the United States, there are efforts to explore the viability, too, of "glide phase intercept" technologies, which would seek to shoot down these missiles during their flight. This presents other challenges; for instance, tracking a hypersonic glider during its flight with sufficiently high fidelity may require the adoption of new space-based sensors. The U.S. Missile Defense Agency, in June 2024, tracked a hypersonic projectile for the first time using new, advanced missile-tracking satellites.[19]

Hypersonic weapons are both hyped and impressive feats of engineering. However, they are likely to remain niche capabilities in the new nuclear age. It bears stating that at long enough ranges, hypersonic missiles are actually *slower* to arrive on target than ballistic missiles.[20] Even at shorter ranges, ballistic missiles can be fired deliberately at shallow angles and to lower altitudes – what are known as depressed trajectories – to further shorten their flight times. The missile defense-stressing benefits of HGVs, while real, can be similarly taken advantage of by concerned states by simply investing in a larger force. Simply put, instead of better, more expensive missiles, attackers can more cheaply scale up their existing forces of ballistic missiles to saturate and overcome missile defense systems. In China, where a large-scale nuclear force build-up is under way, this may be an additional consideration, even as Beijing pursues HGVs as a supplementary capability.

Finally, hypersonic cruise missiles are also often described as "hypersonic weapons," but behave fundamentally differently. Like HGVs, HCMs fly toward their target within the Earth's atmosphere. Unlike HGVs, however, HCMs employ powered, sustainer supersonic combustion ramjet (or scramjet) engines. Like subsonic and supersonic cruise missiles, these engines are designed to combust oxygen present in the Earth's atmosphere with on-board fuel to produce tremendous thrust. Unlike HGVs or ballistic missiles, however, HCMs will be unlikely to exhibit speeds significantly in excess of Mach 5 in the real world. Nevertheless, these types of weapons will present challenges to missile defense systems in different ways.

For instance, because HCMs fly especially low, land-based radar systems designed to cue missile defense systems will often only see an inbound hypersonic cruise missile seconds before impact, providing a very short window for an intercept.

Hypersonic "hype" aside, a more substantial set of problems stems from the proliferation of good old-fashioned ballistic missiles and cruise missiles. In particular, unlike during the Cold War, *non*-nuclear missiles are growing increasingly capable of posing threats to nuclear forces.[21] Since the United States' successful use of precision conventional weapons during the First Gulf War (1990–1), states like Russia and China have grown increasingly concerned about the possibility of a disarming first strike either being carried out exclusively through the use of non-nuclear weapons, or potentially being supplemented with non-nuclear weapons. Under the Bush administration, the United States stoked up these concerns further by deliberately seeking a "conventional prompt global strike" capability – nominally with the interest of holding at risk terrorist targets anywhere on Earth in less than an hour.

At the dawn of this new nuclear age, these problems are likely set to intensify. Two factors, in particular, present risks in the U.S.–China and U.S.–Russia competitive relationships. First, the end of the 1987 INF Treaty has removed an important structural constraint on missile deployments by the United States and Russia. The treaty, which barred both Washington and Moscow from developing, testing, or fielding ground-launched ballistic or cruise missiles with ranges between 500 and 5,500 kilometers, irrespective of their payload type, was a landmark achievement of late-Cold War arms control negotiations. In 2014, the United States accused Russia of having violated that treaty and, in 2019, Washington withdrew – in part due to its growing concerns about China's missile capabilities. Beijing was unconstrained by the INF Treaty and, during the thirty-two years it remained in effect, significantly expanded its missile arsenal. The end of this treaty raises the prospect of new missile deployments in both Asia and Europe, by both Russia and the United States, that could influence the nuclear balance. The United States, in particular, has started to pursue a wide range of non-nuclear missile programs intended for deployment in Asia to better impose costs on China in the case of a conventional war in the region.[22]

A second, broader concern pertains to the potential role that non-nuclear missile systems may play in the United States' future approach to nuclear deterrence in a world where China fields a much larger nuclear force. In June 2022, U.S. national security advisor Jake Sullivan sought to rebut calls by proponents of a U.S. nuclear force expansion by alluding to the possibility of the United States potentially relying on its "cutting-edge non-nuclear capabilities," including "conventionally armed hypersonic missiles that can reach heavily-defended, high-value targets."[23] Sullivan made this case to suggest that the United States could maintain its nuclear deterrence of Russia and China without investing in a greater number of nuclear weapons. However, this remark may end up confirming long-held fears in Russia and China that advanced, precise, U.S. non-nuclear missiles could now be part of Washington's broader deterrence strategy, which incorporates counterforce targeting. The implications could be particularly destabilizing in a conventional war where such systems may be used for warfighting ends well below the nuclear threshold. For instance, U.S. long-range strikes on certain missile bases in China hosting both conventional and nuclear missiles could be interpreted by Beijing as the start of a potential disarming strike, leading to potential escalation to nuclear use. While this alternative path would mean that Washington would be able to resist the temptation to symmetrically set up an arms race with its two so-called near-peer adversaries on a nuclear-warhead-for-nuclear-warhead basis, it would introduce other risks, underscoring the difficult choices for the United States that will lie ahead.

Finally, a particularly concerning growing feature of the new nuclear age is the potential for missiles in the hands of non-nuclear states to drive serious nuclear escalation. During the Cold War, strategies of conventional counterforce were hardly prominent; nuclear weapons were largely to be targeted against other nuclear weapons – in both strategic and battlefield contexts. Today, resource-rich, technologically sophisticated, non-nuclear states, facing real and growing nuclear threats, are seeking to address these challenges in part by relying on an ability to combat an attacker's nuclear forces with non-nuclear weapons. This is especially the case in Northeast Asia where South Korea, in particular, and, to a lesser extent, Japan are seeking to hold at risk North Korea's nuclear forces, including its command and control system. On paper, this appears to be a sensible solution: faced with threats from a nuclear-armed Pyongyang, these states have a right to seek the means of self-defense and an obligation to their publics to address this potential source of existential risk for their societies. However, these aspirations could also drive escalation to nuclear use by North Korea during a war. To better manage these risks, political leaders and military planners alike in these non-nuclear states will have to better acquaint themselves with the logic of nuclear strategy and, particularly, how their adversaries might seek to preserve their nuclear forces against all odds.

All in the zeroes and ones

The term "cyber" is dated, lacks precision, and isn't even a noun unto itself, but is regularly used to describe anything and everything having to do with computers and computer networks.[24] For the purposes of our discussion here, consider "cyber" technologies to broadly encompass everything from the computerized systems that underpin nuclear command and control systems to the broader defense-relevant computer networks at play in a system and, at the broadest end, the general, critical infrastructure of the Internet at large. State-backed cyberattacks and cyberespionage became frequent and regular features of the global geopolitical landscape starting in the 2010s. Their intersection with nuclear weapons, fortunately, remains indirect to date: one of the best-known cyberattacks took place against Iran's civil nuclear program when the Stuxnet worm, built by the United States and Israel, caused significant damage.[25] In 2017, at the height of a crisis with North Korea, the Trump administration authorized an offensive cyberoperation into the computer networks used by Pyongyang's external spy agency, the Reconnaissance General Bureau, in what was likely intended as a shot across Kim Jong Un's bow.[26] Cyberattacks have also played a prominent role in wars well below the threshold of nuclear use; for example, as Russia prepared to invade Ukraine in 2022, hackers struck satellite communication modems associated with satellites operated by the U.S. firm Viasat.[27] In future crises, offensive cyberoperations, or even cyberespionage operations intended to scout for vulnerabilities, could prompt significant escalation, including possibly to nuclear war.

Any software designed with the goal of enabling degradation, damage, or unauthorized access to a given target system can be described as malware. This can take several forms – from self-replicating worms, to proliferated botnets, to ransomware, to control-seizing rootkits and trojans, to name just a few. In the context of nuclear stability, these capabilities present a challenge that is fundamentally distinct from those posed by physical weapons with kinetic effects. Unlike physical missile systems, which might be observed by a defender being readied in the course of a war and would exhibit obvious damage after use, malware – or "cyberweapons" more broadly – can strike without any warning, anticipation, or even obvious exhibition of effect. For a paranoid defender, concerned about the survivability of their nuclear forces, this is a significant source of stress. As with other technologies that may threaten the survivability of nuclear forces, generating incentives for nuclear use, we should not want a world where nuclear-armed leaders must wonder if they will be severed from their nuclear forces in the course of a crisis by some sort of exquisite, unrevealed adversarial cyberweapon (even if no such capabilities really exist).

Unfortunately, this may precisely be the world that is emerging. Almost universally, nuclear weapons establishments, including those that are fast modernizing their command and control systems, are anxious about the potential for escalation driven by cyberattacks, or even misinterpreted nondestructive cyberoperations during a crisis or war. Within nuclear-armed states, it may be the case that the military or intelligence organizations charged with carrying out cyberoperations – be it for destructive purposes, reconnaissance, or simply to sow confusion within adversary networks – are distinct from those managing nuclear operations. As a result, these operators could effectuate some actions with one intent, but potentially transgress a significant threshold for the adversary, prompting escalation. One example might be activity by Chinese hackers against the United States' National Military Command Center (NMCC) and associated networks during a conventional crisis near the Taiwan Strait. The hackers may simply seek knowledge of U.S. military tactics and plans in the course of the conventional war, but, should their intrusion be detected, U.S. leaders and planners could be highly alarmed given the instrumental role for the NMCC in enabling nuclear launches. In another case, the same hackers could seek to interfere with the communications capabilities of U.S. satellites charged with watching for ballistic missile launches to complicate regional missile defense efforts in Asia during a conventional war. However, because the United States relies on these same satellites to watch for incoming nuclear attacks, any degradation of these capabilities through a cyberattack could prove highly escalatory. Unlike kinetic weapons, whose collateral effects are limited by physical principles and geography, cyberweapons could behave or spread in unexpected ways, too, potentially delivering effects far greater than an attacker may have intended. In the United States, these sorts of anxieties around command and control and nuclear early warning systems have been deeply ingrained, even before the advent and popularization of cyberattacks. As a result, the U.S. nuclear command and control system is increasingly redundant and survivable – but the mere interpretation of an *intent* by an adversary to *potentially* attack nuclear command and control in a war could lead skittish, psychologically stressed leaders to take dramatic action.

Other distinct qualities, including attribution, were once thought to have been more serious problems than they have been in practice. Cyberattacks are often difficult to initially attribute to a particular source – and some hacker groups have attempted to mimic hackers based in other countries, by borrowing code snippets for instance – but far from impossible.[28] Attribution (who attacked), characterization (what happened), and damage assessment (what was damaged or destroyed) are all part and parcel of defensive cybersecurity efforts, including within large defense organizations today. However, it would be wrong to wave away the attribution problem entirely – particularly in the complex, multipolar context of this new nuclear age. For instance, in an environment of simultaneous global crises between nuclear states in different geographic regions, the detection and possible attribution of cyberespionage by one state within another's networks, if misattributed, could catalyze escalation. Worse yet, states could *deliberately* seek to catalyze escalation by carrying out cyberattacks bearing the hallmarks of operations by other states. This sort of a scenario may sound far-fetched, but Russian hackers, in 2018, impersonated North Korean hackers in a "false flag" cyberattack on South Korea.[29] Attribution, importantly, is not binary; in the aftermath of past cyberattacks and cyberespionage operations, time has been the most important variable affecting the fidelity of attribution.[30] In a nuclear crisis, time simply may not be available.

These risks probably cannot be fully eliminated, and so must instead be mitigating and managed. The opening of the cyberoperations Pandora's box presents likely irreversible and persistent challenges to nuclear stability. Political declarations on noninterference with nuclear command and control could have value, but this may not be feasible given the poor state of relations between the major powers and anxieties in the United States about North Korea. Regarding the latter, since 2017, U.S. intentions to disable North Korean missiles "left of launch" – i.e., before they can fly – with undisclosed cyberweapons have been talked about openly.[31] A leaked U.S. Department of Defense document that year described techniques that would have been "non-kinetic" and short of the United Nations charter definition of a "use of force" – almost certainly alluding to a cyberweapon.[32] For North Korea, U.S. talk of "left of launch" capabilities is simply old wine in a new bottle – and that old wine is counterforce. While North Korea punches well above its weight in cyberoperations, it likely does not feel confident in its ability to detect intrusions into its networks by U.S. operators. As a result, in a serious crisis, the mere *possibility* of a successful U.S. "left of launch" disabling attack could prompt Kim to use his nuclear weapons, lest he lose the ability to communicate with his nuclear forces entirely.[33]

Unilateral policy changes concerning cyberattacks could prove stabilizing. For starters, the United States could abandon its "left of launch" aspirations as part of its comprehensive missile defeat plans and invite other states – nuclear-armed and non-nuclear alike – to offer political commitments that they will not deliberately interfere with nuclear operations or command and control with malware. In the North Korea case, the United States might continue to rely on missile defense and other "right of launch" measures to manage risks. As discussed earlier in this chapter, even if missile defenses introduce their own flavor of instability, that is arguably less bad than the risks generated by articulating plans to preemptively destroy nuclear forces with cyberweapons. Most importantly, perhaps, states should be willing to practice restraint in cyberoperations against nuclear-armed states precisely because of the risks of unwanted nuclear war. Persuading leaders and military planners that the risks far outweigh the putative benefits, however, may not prove simple.

Technical solutions will also have their place. Though there is no such thing as a 100 percent safe, effective, and "unhackable" computer system, states should continue to invest in their nuclear mission sensitive systems by investing resources in systematic cybersecurity assessments. Awareness of cybersecurity risks has erupted among defense-critical organizations around the world in recent years, but that will be insufficient in tapering off the pathways to nuclear war described above. States could think creatively about what sorts of information they should maintain in electronic form and in real time during a crisis. For instance, for countries like Russia, China, or North Korea – all of which plan to deploy mobile missiles in a serious crisis – ensuring that the locations of these systems are not tracked in real time, by a centralized computer system, could reduce their vulnerability to cyberattacks. In the case of a cyberattack, too, military planners and decision-makers in these states would feel less pressure to use their nuclear forces if they could be assured that a breach would not meaningfully allow an attacker to discover the location of their dispersed missiles to destroy them. Of course, in the case of centralized, authoritarian systems, where assertive control of military forces may be a strongly ingrained norm, this type of adaptation may prove difficult.

The specter of potent malware will loom over the heads of military planners and decision-makers in future nuclear crises.

Beyond unilateral restraint and political commitments, arms control – at least, of the formal and verifiable sort – is unlikely to provide salve to states seeking relief from potential cyber-attacks and espionage against their nuclear mission-critical computer systems. Nuclear-armed states, however, should endeavor to surface their anxieties about cyberoperations and escalation risks in strategic stability dialogues with their adversaries. This should be the case in future dialogues between the United States and Russia, the United States and China, India and Pakistan, and even the United States and North Korea, should the conditions arise. What will be most important in avoiding a nuclear war born of cyberoperations gone awry will be for states to understand how their adversaries may perceive certain actions, if detected. An attacker's inability to assure non-detection and non-attribution, paired with the great consequences associated with potential nuclear escalation, ought to prompt caution. As this new nuclear age progresses, too, other technologies, including artificial intelligence, may expand the scope of non-kinetic technological influences on the course of crises.

Who's afraid of artificial intelligence?

In the course of this book being written, the promise and pitfalls of artificial intelligence (AI) technologies exploded in the global consciousness. The American AI research and development company, OpenAI, released ChatGPT in November 2022. By January 2023, ChatGPT had amassed 100 million monthly active users, making it the fastest growing consumer Internet application in history.[34] Shortly thereafter, Sundar Pichai, chief executive of global technology giant Alphabet, boldly declared that AI will "touch everything: every sector, every industry, every aspect of our lives."[35] While AI's novelty has seized global attention unlike any technological development since the smartphone, experts contemplating nuclear conflict have been considering the matter for a substantially greater period of time. In fact, intersections between AI computer systems and nuclear weapons had become a mainstay of science fiction and speculative fiction early in the Cold War. In the 1950s, the U.S. Air Force – at the time the most capable nuclear weapons-equipped military organization on Earth – sponsored research into computer-assisted decision-making and what might fairly be termed AI-adjacent research. Writing in 1958, the researchers Herbert A. Simon and Allen Newell, a political scientist and computer scientist respectively, writing for the journal *Operations Research*, declared that humanity was "poised for a great advance that will bring the digital computer and the tools of mathematics and the behavioral sciences to bear on the very core of managerial activity – on the exercise of judgment and intuition; on the processes of making complex decisions."[36] Their research had the backing of the U.S. Air Force, which was interested at the time in how the novel domain of computation could address new problems in military strategy, including nuclear strategy. Even earlier, the American mathematician Claude Shannon, in 1950, wrote the seminal article "Programming a Computer for Playing Chess," in which he suggested that theoretical work on complex decision-making by computers could lead to the development of "machines for making strategic decisions in simplified military operations."[37]

Before there was AI as we understand it today, military organizations relied on computerized statistical analysis to supplement their early warning systems. It was precisely this sort of a system that nearly caused a nuclear war at the height of the Able Archer crisis in 1983. That year, a Soviet computer system designed to warn designated watch officers of incoming American missiles pinged a warning. Stanislav Petrov, the officer on watch, reasoned that the computer was likely wrong and that no attack was inbound. He was right; the computer's false positive output was the result of a Soviet satellite-based missile-warning sensor interpreting solar reflections off cloud tops for inbound missiles. Petrov would later cite a "funny feeling in his gut" to justify his decision that day.[38] Petrov's example is now recalled in contemporary debates on the risks of AI integration with nuclear command and control system as an example of the virtues of maintaining a "human-in-the-loop" – both with regard to nuclear use decisions and attack assessments.

The American Cold War nuclear strategist Herman Kahn, in his opus *On Thermonuclear War* in 1960, raised the prospect of "doomsday machines," which might assure the ability of whichever state possessed such a contraption to fight a nuclear conflict even in the total annihilation of that state's functioning government and society.[39] Kahn's theoretical machines were further imagined to have the ability to assess large amounts of information about the course of a conflict or crisis and detect whether an enemy was about to attack and potentially even strike first to preserve the defender's advantage. The American filmmaker Stanley Kubrick famously parodied Kahn, among other early Cold War nuclear strategists, in his acclaimed 1964 film *Dr. Strangelove*. The fundamental conflict toward the climax of that film revolves around precisely such a Soviet "doomsday machine" having been put into operation without the knowledge of the American side. The Soviet side, having been informed by the American president that a nuclear-armed bomber bound for their airspace had been dispatched by a rogue general, is unable to decommission the device. Kubrick's point may have largely been to indicate the fundamental absurdities at the heart of nuclear strategy, but the Strangelovian doomsday machine was an idea steeped in some reality. "The most realistic things are the funniest," Kubrick said. (The idea to present the film as a dark comedy only struck Kubrick part of the way into the screenplay, when the apparent absurdity of nuclear strategy jumped out at him.[40]) *Dr. Strangelove* was far from the last depiction of the perils of nuclear weapons intersecting with automated systems; the *Terminator* films popularized the idea of a sentient, malicious AI system seizing control of nuclear command and control systems to launch devastating nuclear attacks against humanity. So sweeping was the influence of James Cameron's blockbusters that it remains all too common today to see news articles on nuclear risks and AI on many a website illustrated with an image of the iconic, crimson-eyed T-800 humanoid robot from the *Terminator* films.

The boom in interest around AI in the 2020s is new enough – and the pace of technological change rapid enough – that there remains substantial uncertainty about just how far AI technologies will truly go in penetrating every aspect of human society. Debates continue to persist about the nature of some of the most impressive systems that have captured human imaginations among the computer scientists, philosophers, and ethicists who study AI. For instance, experts dispute whether the large language models, or LLMs, that undergird applications like ChatGPT are truly "intelligent" in the vein of human beings, capable of adaptive and creative reasoning, or merely "stochastic parrots" – machines adept enough at mimicking human intelligence without necessarily grokking the substance behind their output.[41] These models also suffer from the black box problem, whereby the researchers and engineers who've built them are unable to reliably predict outputs because they simply cannot parse the processes at work within the LLM that lead to given outputs given an input prompt.[42]

The degree to which AI technologies might intersect with nuclear command and control systems, or with associated strategic situational awareness capabilities, is still unclear. Norms here are still light, though certain countries have taken first steps. For instance, at the 2022 Nonproliferation Treaty review conference in New York, the United States, the United Kingdom, and France declared that they will "maintain human control and involvement for all actions critical to informing and executing sovereign decisions concerning nuclear weapons employment."[43] This was a jargon-laden way of indicating that the decision to use nuclear weapons in time of war will not be automated, but will require the affirmative assent of human beings. The United States' 2022 *Nuclear Posture Review* reiterated this language, becoming the first document of its kind since the initial 1994 NPR to do so. Other nuclear states have not issued similar guidance, but are broadly seeking to govern AI technologies in other parts of their societies. China, in particular, has been proactive in setting up a robust set of internal governance mechanisms to manage AI technologies, including requiring that generative AI systems hew to the "core values of socialism."[44] For authoritarian states, in particular, there may be a reluctance to outsource decisions concerning nuclear weapons use to automated systems in all but the most catastrophic of scenarios. For instance, the Soviet Union implemented an automatic system, dubbed Perimetr, that was meant to serve as a fail-deadly mechanism of last resort: in the case that the Soviet leadership was eradicated fully in a first strike, Perimetr would have allowed for a retaliatory attack to take place with whatever forces may have survived.[45] North Korea, in 2022, indicated at least conceptual interest in a similar posture, though its mechanism for ensuring an automatic retaliatory response has not yet become clear.[46]

Few experts – within or outside governments – appear to think that the unconstrained marriage of AI systems and nuclear use decisions is a good idea. The few that do primarily see the potential for AI to help address the propensity of human beings to make poorly informed decisions under the tremendous time pressures that may exist in the course of a nuclear crisis.[47] In the case that an imminent first strike is detected on the United States, for instance, the president has the option to launch American ICBMs should he or she choose. The time available for the president to exercise this option is limited given that Russian and Chinese intercontinental missiles exhibit a total flight time of around thirty minutes to the continental United States, and the launch of these missiles can only be properly assessed after a few minutes. (Submarine-launched missiles might arrive at the White House in substantially less time – as little as fifteen minutes in some cases.) Might an AI system support presidential decision-making under such a circumstance? Or would any president be disinclined to trust the output of such a system under what would doubtless already be a highly stressful situation? In the course of several simulations and exercises that I've been involved in over the years examining how human decision-makers interface with AI systems, there's often a propensity for humans to second guess – or otherwise discount – machine-derived advice. (It turns out humans tend to rate their own intelligence and competence rather highly!) Decision-makers might, however, be less skeptical of the same assessment when presented by a human. In highly stressful real world scenarios, this could manifest in presidents and other nuclear decision-makers trusting advice or intelligence presented by trusted, known humans, including their advisors or even spouses, versus the less known, less understood output of an AI black box.

But even without being plugged into nuclear command and control directly, AI technologies could come to nip away at strategic stability in the third nuclear age. A major concern among researchers today is the potential for AI to render tractable military intelligence tasks that have previously been seen as infeasible or extremely challenging. Some of these tasks include the tracking of mobile missile launchers or interpreting a variety of inputs to determine the location of nuclear submarines. If secure second-strike capabilities can be rendered more vulnerable to preemptive nuclear – or even non-nuclear attacks – by means of more sophisticated data analysis and data fusion, abetted by AI systems, the risk of nuclear conflict could rise as defenders might feel immense pressure early in a crisis to use their weapons lest they be disarmed. Fortunately, this theoretical problem has yet to manifest, and may not do so for some time. While AI systems are excellent at recognizing patterns in large data sets, the availability and utility of such data – particularly in what might be a fast-moving crisis – may be questionable. Consider mobile missiles, for instance: an attacker might look to source data from a variety of space and air-based sensors (think satellites and drones) to cue their targeting. As this data is processed, the attacker will want to ensure that false positives are minimized: for instance, large commercial trucks should not be incorrectly characterized as missile launchers.

Depending on the fidelity of the inputs to the sensors, this may or may not be possible, but any attacker contemplating a potential disarming first strike – or other significant attack on a defender's nuclear forces – will seek high confidence that false positives can be managed. As one RAND Corporation study demonstrated in 2001,[48] even a fairly theoretically high-performing automatic target-recognition algorithm would struggle to generate a manageable number of true positives. Even under charitable assumptions about overall system effi- cacy, such a system may fall short. For instance, a false positive rate of 0.01 percent – indicating that a car or truck is falsely identified as a missile launcher only one in every 10,000 cases – may still result in a ratio of one hundred false positives to every one true positive in a country like China, where the ratio between missile launchers and civilian vehicles is significantly skewed.[49] An AI system could incorporate heuristics, such as looking for the proximity of a given candidate target to a known missile operating base; but getting to a small enough number – and at a high enough level of confidence – where target- ing could be done at scale, may simply be too challenging. A spectacular breakthrough in the state of the art of AI systems, including the development of an artificial general intelligence that far surpasses human intelligence, could change this. These technical realities notwithstanding, the mere perception that such systems were being built and incorporated into military planning could prove destabilizing. This is especially true for highly asymmetric deterrence relationships, such as that between North Korea and the United States. (As a practical matter, North Korea would exhibit a much more favorable ratio between military and civilian large vehicles than China, for instance.)

Beyond their effects on the delicate balance of terror that undergirds deterrence, AI technologies could infuse crises with other complications. LLMs widely available in 2023, for instance, were already capable of generating text that is not easily and readily distinguished as having been generated by a machine. States and nonstate groups alike could seek to manipulate the information environment by using such systems to generate misinformation at scale. Such misinformation could shape public opinion and create more permissive conditions for conflict escalation, particularly in democracies where leaders may be more sensitive to the general public's attitudes toward a particular crisis. This potential for AI to generate "useful disinformation," however, could paradoxically reinforce strategic stability. For instance, states concerned about a technologically sophisticated attacker disarming its nuclear force could rely on an AI system to release cues that would be designed to be specifically misleading to an attacker's AI systems. This could include generating military activity designed deliberately to mislead – for instance, deploying decoy missile launchers in a way that is designed to be seen and interpreted by the adversary while operating real missile launchers in less predictable modes.[50] It is far from obvious that an AI-influenced nuclear world will be more favorable to the offense rather than the defense. In the coming years, both "finders" and "hiders" will explore the possibilities inherent in these fast-changing technologies.

Other risks deserve consideration – particularly insofar as AI systems intersect with cyber domain risks. As AI systems are slowly but surely incorporated into defense planning, processes, and operations, including for nuclear systems, cybersecurity risks will be a major concern. For the foreseeable future, AI systems will rely on conventional computation and so will be vulnerable to compromise via cyberoperations. Given the black box problem, in particular, decision-makers in a crisis may be reluctant to trust AI system outputs given their inability to verify that a possible hack or breach had not resulted in the "corruption" of the system. Similarly, attackers could look to tamper with AI systems by poisoning the data on which these systems are trained. Such an attack could even take place during peacetime and reduce the reliability of a given AI system during a crisis or conflict.

Whether or not anyone likes it or is comfortable with the idea, the allure of AI will quickly seep into the military organizations around the world that manage nuclear weapons. At the inception of this technological diffusion, it is plainly clear that, handled poorly, AI technologies could substantially render nuclear stability more perilous and complex than in the past. The *Terminator* scenario, while evocative, is not likely to be the one that deserves the greatest contemplation by world leaders and their advisors. Rather, it is the possibility of AI technologies conferring false confidence during a time of crisis or war.

Space and nuclear escalation

In 2021, General James Dickinson, then head of U.S. Space Command, described a Chinese satellite, Shijian-17, noting that it possessed a robotic arm. He said that this arm provided a capability that "could be used in a future system for grappling other satellites."[51] He also drew attention to other counterspace capabilities under development in China, including ground-based laser systems, direct-ascent antisatellite missiles, and jamming and cyberspace capabilities. Partly in recognition of the United States' significant reliance on space to support a range of national security missions, China and Russia have invested heavily in counterspace capabilities that could be brought to bear in a serious conventional crisis or conflict to degrade U.S. warfighting efforts. A significant risk, however, lies in the fact that certain U.S. space-based capabilities support both conventional and nuclear operations. This entanglement between conventional and nuclear support missions for satellites presents a real risk that counterspace operations intended to degrade the United States' ability to support conventional military operations effectively could inadvertently degrade U.S. nuclear command and control or missile-warning capabilities.[57] This latter effect, even if unintended, could prove highly escalatory and raise concerns among U.S. military planners and political leaders that an attack on the country's nuclear forces may be imminent, prompting a possible escalatory response.

In recent years, space-based conventional war escalation has become a particular source of concern for American military leaders and strategists. In the 2018 NPR, the Trump administration specified that the "extreme circumstances" in which the United States might resort to the use of nuclear weapons included "significant non-nuclear strategic attacks," including attacks on "command and control, or warning and attack assessment capabilities."[53] In 2022, a senior military officer involved in U.S. space operations told me that he increasingly believed the "most likely start to a nuclear conflict may begin with an attack on our space assets."[54]

This concern is not entirely new, however. The space age began not long after the nuclear age, and early on in the Cold War the United States began to rely on military space assets for a range of purposes. Toward the end of that period, American planners had similar concerns about the potential escalatory effects of attacks on these assets. What is new today, however, is the general array of counterspace capabilities under development, the general lack of transparency around space capabilities and behaviors, and the broader transformation of the Earth's orbital environment. For instance, today, unlike during the twentieth century, it is commercial space firms – not governments – that operate the majority of artificial satellites across all Earth orbits. A further change concerns the disintegration of what used to be a relatively well-understood close link between national security space assets and nuclear operations. After the end of the Cold War, in particular, space-based systems involved in supporting nuclear operations – particularly in the United States – expanded substantially to play a greater role in supporting conventional military operations, general intelligence and surveillance, and attack assessments. Finally, as the space environment becomes more generally proliferated with a range of satellites to support various forms of human economic activity and welfare on Earth, states are exploring certain technologies that could primarily serve benign ends, but nevertheless exhibit a threatening dual-use nature as potential weapons. Shijian-17, for instance, has exhibited behavior that certain prominent nongovernmental space security analysts in the United States consider to be more broadly consistent with the demonstration of "[rendezvous and proximity operation] technologies for satellite servicing, space situational awareness, and inspection."[55]

What has been somewhat good news is that this potential pathway to nuclear war has largely, to date, been a problem nearly exclusively for the United States given its unparalleled reliance on space assets for critical nuclear and conventional military operations. This is, however, already changing. Russia and China are increasing their reliance on space-based assets. China, in particular, has started to deploy space-based early warning satellites designed to detect inbound ballistic missiles from the United States, or from sea-based launchers. Beijing is likely also growing more reliant on space-based command and control assets for its nuclear forces. While the United States has no publicly disclosed counterspace capabilities that would match the co-orbital or direct-ascent kinetic weapons available to and under development in Moscow and Beijing, Chinese and Russian leaders will be alert to the possibility of attacks on these assets in a crisis. (As an aside, while the United States does not officially field any direct-ascent antisatellite weapons, Russian and Chinese experts generally regard certain U.S. missile defense systems as having a latent capability to play this role.) This has been a longer-standing concern for Russia, which relies, like the United States, on space-based assets to enable an option to launch its nuclear forces under attack.[56] The high orbits of many of these satellites, too, means that they are out of the range of any currently deployed and likely soon-to-be-deployed direct-ascent anti-satellite missiles, which are capable only of ranging targets in low Earth orbit. As their name implies, these weapons launch from the Earth's surface to strike orbital targets and overlap considerably with missile defense interceptors, which are instead better suited to strike slower, suborbital targets (missile reentry vehicles).

These dynamics are concerning for other reasons, too. Consider, for instance, that space systems may malfunction rather spontaneously, and assessing the cause of a malfunction – or indeed, that anomalous behavior is a malfunction – can take significant effort for any space operator. In a conflict, where tensions on Earth may be high between two competing militaries, military planners may be strongly inclined to interpret any organic malfunction in a critical satellite as possible evidence of a deliberate non-kinetic attack. This could prompt an escalatory response even if no actual counterspace capabilities had been used, and even if attribution of such an attack would be difficult. (Just like offensive cyberattacks against Earth-based systems, cyber interference with satellite operations may be difficult to immediately attribute during a fast-paced crisis or war.)

As competitive nuclear dynamics intensify between the United States, Russia, and China, attacks on space systems present an under-appreciated pathway to nuclear escalation between them. Mitigating these risks is important, but far from straightforward given the many difficulties for states in fully understanding the nature of satellite operations by other countries and, in particular, the intention behind behaviors in space that may be perceived as hostile. As the example of Shijian-17, in particular, exhibits, dual-use space technologies present a particular challenge. Partly in recognition of this, the United States, along with the United Kingdom and other allied states, has started to favor an approach focused on "responsible behaviors" in space. Such an approach is designed to reduce the risk of inadvertent armed conflict or escalation in space, but also seeks to reduce the sources of deliberate space debris creation. As human space activities have exploded in recent decades, so too has the proliferation of debris from defunct satellites and satellites involved in collisions. Prominently, the testing of direct-ascent antisatellite missiles against live satellite targets – notably, by China in 2007, by India in 2019, and by Russia in 2021 – have resulted in a substantial increase in long-lived space debris. (Some debris from China's 2007 test, for instance, will persist for decades.) As part of an effort to generally dissuade the further development and testing of such weapons and to promote low Earth orbit sustainability, the United States, in 2022, adopted a unilateral ban on the destructive testing of direct-ascent antisatellite weapons and called on other countries to do the same. The effort has been largely successful in normative terms: in 2022, the United Nations' First Committee on disarmament adopted a U.S. draft resolution promoting the idea of a broader international norm banning such tests, with 154 votes in favor and eight against, with ten abstentions, suggesting broad global support.[57] Unlike other forms of space-based weapons restraint that would face verification difficulties, destructive direct-ascent antisatellite weapon testing is both easily attributable and detectable.

The growing international focus on direct-ascent antisatellite weapons, however, should be paired with broader efforts to understand the pathways to nuclear war on Earth that begin with attacks on space. The importance of the space domain is not going to diminish anytime soon – especially for the major powers. As the third nuclear age progresses, new players may seek to establish themselves with counterspace capabilities, too, adding further complexity to the task of maintaining stability in a crisis. Despite the negative trendlines for arms control in the early-to-mid-2020s, any future dialogue on strategic stability between, particularly, the United States, on the one hand, and Russia and China, on the other, will have to address the rising salience of nuclear escalation beginning with attacks on space capabilities.

Technology, flux, and stability

Predicting with any certainty the effects of technological change, as observed in the years spent researching and writing this book, is surely a path to longer-term embarrassment for any author. I have hopefully hedged any predictions sufficiently throughout this chapter. What is clearer, however, are human perceptions concerning the promise and pitfalls of new technologies. As I spoke to officials and military planners about many of these technologies – in the United States, in Europe, and in South and East Asia – several themes emerged. First, because this new nuclear age emerges against the backdrop of a fraying and decaying global nuclear order and its attendant arms control architecture, there is little optimism that the nuclear-armed states – and advanced non-nuclear states – will be able to seek robust and verifiable measures to enforce restraint. While some efforts, such as the United States' 2022 announcement of an effort to seek a new global norm banning destructive direct-ascent antisatellite weapon tests, may bear promise and set useful peacetime precedents, there appears to be little hope for many of the other sources of disruptive technological change.

Second, some policymakers – especially those without any particular expertise in any specific technology that may bear on the nuclear balance – appear to sense that an expectation of general technological flux may lead to an environment of greater caution, which could prove stabilizing. This is essentially the idea that their counterparts in other states, unsure themselves about the possible unbounded consequences of relying too heavily on a new, promising technology, may not choose to push the envelope. This may not apply to information operations and cyberespionage – both of which have become *de rigueur* for a number of states, including nuclear-armed states – but could affect the propensity for states to seek unilateral advantage or first strikes with non-nuclear weapons based on heroic assumptions about AI and missile defense, for instance. A third, contrasting, and perhaps most concerning view that emerged in many of these same conversations, however, was the possibility that technology would lead nuclear-armed states to the brink, and potentially beyond, given the intensification of time pressures for decision-makers in a world growing increasingly full of fast, nuclear and non-nuclear missiles, unobservable cyberweapons, and counterspace weapons.

Importantly, while it will be important for political leaders and decision-makers to understand the risks and opportunities posed by various technologies, it will be equally important for these leaders to be informed so as to be able to avoid magical thinking that could prove disastrous. If leaders believe, as former U.S. President Trump appeared to do in 2017, that U.S. missile defenses are nearly 100 percent effective, that could prompt dangerous and devastating overconfidence in a crisis, leading to a devastating nuclear war.[58] Similarly, the rapid advancements in AI technologies have heightened hopes in South Korea that, one day, it may be able to easily find all of North Korea's nuclear warheads and missiles to carry out a perfect, disarming strike – nullifying Pyongyang's deterrent.[59] Technological change will hardly play out in a simplistic or hermetic manner, allowing certain states to seek advantage at the expense of others. Practically, as during the Cold War and since, states will take measures to adapt to ensure the survivability of their nuclear forces. If sudden, unanticipated, and extraordinary technological shifts – be it the arrival of a truly omniscient suprahuman artificial general intelligence, a never-before-conceived-of sensor capable of rendering oceans practically transparent, or a kinematic breakthrough in the performance of ballistic missile defense interceptors – upend this, then all bets for nuclear stability are off.

4

The New Nuclear Disorder

The sources of growing nuclear risk are manifold in the new nuclear age. Earlier chapters describe the many drivers of growing inter-great power friction and competitive dynamics that have heightened the salience of nuclear weapons in national strategies. In parallel to these shifting geopolitical sands, the risk of nuclear war is growing as several measures of negotiated restraint, including critical arms control agreements, have atrophied and crumbled. The collapse of arms control most affects the nuclear relationship between Washington and Moscow. It has become almost clichéd to regularly hear nuclear policy analysts in Washington, Moscow, and European capitals alike exhort that "arms control is dead." Arms control as a tool to manage nuclear risk continues to bear relevance, but it is undeniable that critical arms control agreements have rapidly frayed and come undone as the second nuclear age transitions into a third.

Nuclear arms control has traditionally held many purposes, but none has been greater than its ability to lower the risk of a mutually unwanted nuclear war. Nuclear deterrence can address the problem of wanted wars, giving one's adversary sufficient reason to abstain from deliberate conventional and nuclear attacks, but it cannot wholly account for the possibility of misperception, miscalculation, or other shortfalls in reason in decision-makers that may lead to devastating escalation. Beyond this core function, arms control – primarily for the United States and the Soviet Union, and eventually Russia – helped bound the peacetime costs associated with preparing for the possible failure of nuclear deterrence. Central limits on strategic nuclear forces, for instance, ensured that, with sufficient verification, what might otherwise have been a calamitously ruinous arms race could be somewhat bounded. During the Cold War, arms control did not entirely eliminate the impulse for either side to arms race – primarily due to rapid qualitative technical changes in the means and modes of nuclear delivery – but there's little doubt that the counter-factual world where Washington and Moscow failed to agree to strategic arms limitations would have been substantially more costly for both sides, and dangerous as a result. As a supplement to this cost-limiting effect, arms control also has allowed for the adoption of measures providing for limitations on capabilities that various players within national defense bureaucracies were rather unenthusiastic about pursuing in the first place – or allowing for the elimination of capabilities that were otherwise seen as inessential, or more trouble than they were worth to sustain. Finally, nuclear arms control contributed to bounding the effects of nuclear deterrence failure. Instead of unbounded arsenals of tens-of-thousands of strategic nuclear warheads that, once used, would assuredly cause catastrophic global-scale destruction, constrained arsenals would be more limited in their destructive effects. (Of course, these are still nuclear weapons and no sort of massive use would be anything but a tragedy for humanity.)

The origins of nuclear arms control

Thirteen days in October 1962 brought the world to the door-step of nuclear Armageddon. On October 15, U.S. intelligence had analyzed incontrovertible evidence that nuclear-capable Soviet R-12 medium-range and R-14 intermediate-range ballistic missiles had arrived in Cuba, some 140 kilometers from the southern coast of Florida. In the ensuing days, U.S. President John F. Kennedy and Soviet leader Nikita Khrushchev maneuvered their countries dangerously close to the nuclear precipice. Neither leader entirely held the fate of the world in their own hands – even as it might have seemed the case to them at the time. Kennedy was informed in the course of the crisis, for instance, that an American U-2 reconnaissance aircraft, tasked with the collection of high-altitude radionuclide samples to substantiate possible Soviet nuclear tests, had inadvertently entered Soviet airspace. Kennedy, when informed of this turn of events, famously lamented that, despite the best efforts of much of the U.S. government, "there is always some son-of-a-bitch who doesn't get the word."[1]

While the severity of the crisis was apparent as it played out to officials in both countries, it was only decades later that the world at large learned of how close the two countries had come to a potential descent into uncontrollable nuclear escalation. In 2002, forty years after the crisis, historians learned that one of the Soviet submarines present in the waters of the Caribbean to protect their ships in those fateful days in October 1962 came remarkably close to firing nuclear-armed torpedoes. One Soviet *Foxtrot*-class submarine, the *B-59*, found itself under siege by U.S. destroyers firing depth charges, intended to force the submarine to surface and reveal itself. The submarine's first captain was convinced that the vessel's survival depended on the use of nuclear-armed torpedoes. "We're going to blast them now! We will die, but we will sink them all. We will not disgrace our navy," one officer on board the vessel, said, according to a declassified Soviet intelligence report.[2] Despite that officer's instincts, a launch depended on the concurrence of the vessel's three most senior officers. One of these three officers, Vasili Arkhipov, dissented, resulting in the B-59's eventual decision to surface. The vessel would later return to the Soviet Union, and Arkhipov and the rest of the crew were faced with contempt, with many viewing their decision to surface as tantamount to surrender. Only decades later, did Arkhipov's role in "[saving] the world" become known.[3] Robert McNamara, the U.S. secretary of defense during the crisis, would later reflect that the world was "very, very close" to nuclear Armageddon – certainly "closer than we knew at the time."[4]

The crisis was ultimately concluded by a secret political understanding and a bargain that addressed the origins of the Soviet missile deployments in the Western hemisphere: U.S. nuclear-capable Jupiter intermediate-range ballistic missiles that had been deployed to Turkey and Italy a year earlier were quietly dismantled, in exchange for a reciprocal Soviet pullback of missiles from Cuba. This was accomplished by April 1963.[5] However, sooner than this, the crisis had started to precipitate the start of a new moment in the course of the Cold War. Two months after the dust had settled from the crisis, the United States submitted a working paper to the United Nations-sponsored, Geneva-based Eighteen Nation Committee on Disarmament (ENCD) that contained a proposal to establish a "direct emergency communications link" between the leaders of the United States and the Soviet Union.[6] Earlier in 1962, the United States had received indication that Khrushchev was "very interested in the Washington–Moscow telephone set-up" and that the Soviets wanted to initiate "technical" discussions on implementation.[7] In the course of the crisis, Kennedy and Khrushchev found themselves improvising in a bid to have their concerns and positions understood by the other. As the historian Richard Smoke observed in a 1980s retrospective on the crisis, the normal means of transmitting diplomatic messages between heads of state that existed at the time were found to be "far too slow and formal for the nuclear missile age."[8] In April 1963, as the last of the U.S. Jupiter missiles were being dismantled in Europe, the Soviet Union announced that it was ready to immediately accept the U.S. proposal. Despite the earlier expression of interest by Khrushchev prior to the crisis, the United States did not expect the relatively quick Soviet acceptance of the December 1962 proposal, but by June 1963 Washington and Moscow had signed an agreement establishing the first ever bilateral measure of the nuclear age designed to intentionally lower the risk of nuclear war by facilitating direct communications. This "hotline" agreement – formally known as the Memorandum of Understanding Regarding the Establishment of a Direct Communication Link – proved to be the manifestation of several important ideas: that nuclear deterrence needed guardrails, that decision-makers would want the option of seeking clarity from their adversaries in a crisis, and that reducing the risk of unwanted nuclear war was a shared interest between two states that otherwise had little in common.

The last of these ideas proved instrumental to facilitating the emergence of what would become known as nuclear arms control. The 1962 U.S. working paper to the ENCD was titled "Reduction of the Risk of War Through Accident, Miscalculation, or Failure of Communication," and emphasized the many pathways to devastating unintentional nuclear war. While the United States remained reliant on nuclear deterrence, implicit in the content of the working paper – and in much of the post-Cuban Missile Crisis discourse on nuclear war risk – was the idea of mutually beneficial cooperative, negotiated arrangements with one's primary military adversary. The Soviet Union's reciprocity to this broader idea – beyond the desirability of a hotline to address some of the problems that had become apparent in the course of the 1962 crisis – was slow-coming. The two sides agreed to a treaty banning atmospheric nuclear testing in 1963 and supported a multilateral Outer Space Treaty to ban the emplacement of nuclear weapons in the Earth's orbit, but their first strategic arms control agreement would take nearly a decade longer to achieve.[9] In the final thirty years of the Cold War, the two sides would agree to several more such treaties. Arms control didn't eliminate the dangers inherent in the enterprise of nuclear deterrence during the Cold War, but it bounded the risks and provided a degree of predictability that both sides found beneficial as each pursued their own national interests against the other in their continuing global, systemic competition. To render arms control credible, the United States and the Soviet Union also undertook painstaking, detailed negotiations on the techniques and means that would be permissible for verifying the other side's compliance with negotiated agreements.

By the time of the Soviet Union's collapse in 1991, Washington and Moscow had substantial experience negotiating agreements with each other and had clinched a number of arms control agreements. Notably, in 1987, the two countries, for the first time, eliminated an entire category of nuclear delivery systems with the INF Treaty. That treaty eliminated destabilizing shorter and intermediate-range ballistic and cruise missiles launched from ground-based launchers. In the course of its implementation, the two sides destroyed more than 2,600 missiles. As the Soviet Union moved toward dissolution in 1991, U.S. President George H.W. Bush announced a set of unilateral measures to remove nearly all U.S. nonstrategic nuclear weapons that had been deployed overseas as a unilateral measure. Days after Bush announced these measures, which resulted in the removal of all forward-deployed nuclear weapons in Asia and almost all in Europe, Soviet leader Mikhail Gorbachev announced a reciprocal unilateral measure, calling for the withdrawal of a range of deployed Soviet nonstrategic nuclear weapons. These bilateral Presidential Nuclear Initiatives, as they came to be known, together represented the most stark, short-term reduction of deployed nonstrategic nuclear weapons in history.

A break for U.S.–Russia arms control

While the theory of arms control remains sound in its benefits for its practitioners, the arrival of this new nuclear age has cast the spotlight on the many sources of malaise chipping away at an otherwise positive legacy and trendline in efforts by adversarial states to control nuclear arms. The two most important traditional practitioners of nuclear arms control – the United States and Russia – have seen practically every meaningful agreement constraining their arsenals fall by the wayside. A February 2023 decision by Russian President Vladimir Putin to "suspend" Moscow's participation in the 2010 New Strategic Arms Reduction Treaty (New START) has pulled the rug out from under the last-remaining agreement constraining both countries' nuclear forces. The treaty's text did not formally account for a "suspension" mechanism, and so the United States deemed Russia's measure to be "invalid."[10] The treaty was set to expire in February 2026 after a five-year extension agreed in 2021, but its premature interruption was yet another casualty of Russia's war on Ukraine. In his speech announcing the suspension, Putin justified Russia's decision on the basis of ongoing U.S. support for Ukraine and further suggested that Washington would need to ensure that its allies, the United Kingdom and France, entered arms control talks.[11]

New START had a clear purpose: to verifiably impose limits on the strategic nuclear forces of the United States and Russia. Under the treaty, each country was limited to 1,550 deployed strategic nuclear warheads; these included all warheads deployed on land- and sea-based intercontinental-range missiles. Due to a technical quirk in how bomber-based warheads

were counted under the treaty – each nuclear-capable strategic bomber counted as a single warhead regardless of how
many nuclear weapons it could physically carry – both sides
possessed closer to 2,000 deployed strategic nuclear weapons.

Despite its suspension, Russia issued a declaration that it
would keep its nuclear forces within the treaty-codified central
limits. Moscow's decision did not reflect a reassessment by its
military establishment or leadership of the treaty's value for
Russian defense planning – after all, the Russians had substantial concerns about the United States' latent, rapid capability
to add additional warheads to nuclear submarines and ICBMs.
Instead, the suspension served the purpose of further manipulating nuclear risk in the course of the Ukraine war: at the
margins, a world in which both Russia and the United States
lacked greater visibility into the other's nuclear force was a
more dangerous one. That danger would suit Putin – at least
temporarily. The United States did not immediately reciprocate
Russia's suspension, but, in June 2023, did move eventually to
withhold data exchanges, notifications, inspection activities,
and telemetry exchanges on its missile launches to Russia.[12] At
the same time, U.S. officials asserted that Moscow could easily
return to compliance by allowing for inspections under the
treaty and meeting the United States at the treaty's implementation body – the so-called Bilateral Consultative Commission.
The two sides had ceased inspections in 2020 due to the Covid-
19 pandemic by mutual consent and, in the summer of 2022,
after the United States imposed a range of sanctions on Russia
following its invasion of Ukraine, Moscow insisted that it could
not resume inspections due to air space restrictions. (In reality,
Biden administration officials privately insisted that this was
a convenient excuse and that the United States would have
permitted the entry of inspectors despite the war.)

The uncertainty at the core of the U.S.–Russia arms control
question may hang over the two countries – and the world
– as the new nuclear age progresses. Much will depend on

Moscow's ability to once again decouple its own self-interest in avoiding unwanted nuclear war with the United States from its broader geopolitical mistrust of Washington and the West, as it once was able to do. But, more seriously, Washington and Moscow may simply find that a new generation of leaders, perceiving a more difficult and complex world, develop fundamentally divergent views of the purposes of arms control in a new strategic environment. Much could change still for the two of them as a result of how the United States resolves its own debates about how to deter an aggressive Russia in the short-term and the looming longer-term threat of a China armed with a substantially greater number of nuclear weapons than in the past. In the aftermath of New START, which will expire in 2026 irrespective of any diplomatic interventions, the three-player problem could impede realistic progress on arms control. Despite these realities, U.S. and Russian officials must be willing to at least enter the room to discuss nuclear stability between them; they may do so with a blank sheet of paper, and simply hear out the other's concerns and positions on matters of strategic concern. For the foreseeable future, with both of these countries possessing thousands more nuclear weapons than all other nuclear states combined, they will inherit this important burden. Their survival – and the world's – will hinge on an ability to rediscover adversarial cooperation through the process and practice of arms control.

The nonproliferation order

That nearly eighty years after the dawn of the nuclear age, only nine states possess nuclear weapons is a testament to the success of the treaties and norms that undergird the global nonproliferation architecture – primarily the Nonproliferation Treaty (NPT). The NPT was far from inevitable and, during the course of its negotiation, many leaders imagined a situation in which nuclear technology would inexorably spread, leading to a world with many nuclear-armed states by the turn of the millennium. U.S. President John F. Kennedy famously mused that by 1975 there may be "fifteen or twenty," nuclear states, later revising his estimate for the 1970s up to "twenty-five nations."[13] The NPT's success is a testament to the treaty's recognition of three fundamental realities about nuclear weapons and nuclear technology. First, the treaty acknowledged that global nuclear disarmament is a desirable long-term objective and that it would be worth committing nuclear-armed states to at least work toward this goal. Second, the treaty accepts the premise that a world where more states possess nuclear weapons is inherently a more dangerous one. Third, and most importantly, the treaty accepted what had become obvious by the 1960s: that states around the world would look to peacefully use nuclear energy and nuclear science to a variety of ends. These three insights form what have come to be called the three "pillars" of the treaty: disarmament, nonproliferation, and peaceful uses of nuclear technology.

The treaty has long had its critics and dissenters. India and Pakistan have refused to sign it – as has Israel. New Delhi argued for years that the NPT, at its core, was unjust in its effective legalization of the nuclear arsenals possessed by so-called 'N5' states. Israel's policy of nuclear opacity, meanwhile, meant it never confirmed (or denied) its possession of nuclear weapons and refused to sign the NPT as a non-nuclear weapon state. To make the treaty acceptable to the states that possessed nuclear weapons – and to incentivize them to champion a norm of nuclear nonproliferation – the treaty set January 1, 1967, as an arbitrary date beyond which any state conducting a nuclear test would not be granted legitimate status under the treaty as a nuclear weapon state. Because they had overtly tested nuclear weapons prior to that date, the United States, the Soviet Union, China, the United Kingdom, and France sealed in a privileged position under the treaty. (Despite this, Paris and Beijing neglected to join the treaty until 1992.) India, which tested its first nuclear explosive device in 1974, would never see its nuclear capability legitimated under the treaty. New Delhi's test that year instead galvanized an effort to establish export controls around sensitive nuclear technologies to reinforce the NPT's objectives. Beyond just India, however, this problem of treaty-codified nuclear "haves" and "have nots" has lingered well into the present. As non-nuclear states signed up to the treaty during the Cold War and in the 1990s, they were able to set aside this potential matter of injustice due to the treaty's sixth article, which committed the five states that had detonated weapons prior to 1967 "to pursue negotiations in good faith on effective measures relating to cessation of the nuclear arms race at an early date and to nuclear disarmament, and on a treaty on general and complete disarmament under strict and effective international control."[14] This obligation for the nuclear-armed states to work toward a world without nuclear weapons ultimately enabled the treaty's bargain – and the careful balance between its three pillars – to work. Non-nuclear weapon states, even some that had once covertly started work on nuclear weapons programs, ended up conceding that the benefits of joining the treaty would outweigh the costs of forgoing the nuclear option.

The end of the Cold War provided a great fillip to the treaty, which had been limited in its scope and effectiveness until then. The non-nuclear weapon states had a form of leverage on the nuclear weapon states under the initial text of the treaty, which noted that, at a conference of all states-parties to the NPT to be held twenty-five years after its initial entry into force in 1970, there would be an opportunity to fundamentally revisit the treaty's future direction. In theory, if at this occasion, a "majority" of non-nuclear weapon states concluded that the treaty wasn't working for them – either because the disarmament obligation was not being taken seriously enough by the nuclear weapon states, or because the benefits of the treaty were generally lesser than initially thought – the NPT could have been revised or revisited. In what in hindsight appears to be a happy historical coincidence, it just so happened that this date fell in 1995, four years after the collapse of the Soviet Union, and after the historic drawdown of nuclear weapons that ensued by the United States and Russia in the wake of the Cold War. If there was ever a period where global nuclear disarmament appeared tractable in the nuclear age, it was precisely this moment, where thousands of nuclear weapons deployed outside the borders of the United States and Russia had just been pulled back from Europe and Asia, and thousands of missiles had been destroyed in the course of the implementation of the INF Treaty.[15] As a result of this, and due to deft diplomacy at the time by the nuclear weapon states and others, the NPT states-parties managed majority support, agreeing to indefinitely extend the treaty.

At the dawn of this new nuclear age, many non-nuclear weapon states may look back to 1995 and perhaps wish that they had opted to work toward an alternative option, such as extending the treaty for "an additional fixed period or periods."[16] As this book has emphasized so far, the geopolitical winds, from Europe, to Asia, and the Middle East, are blowing away from nuclear disarmament and toward nuclear arms-racing and renewed competition. Perhaps understandably, starting in the mid-2010s, this has led to stewing frustration among non-nuclear weapon states – particularly those that do not benefit from extended nuclear deterrence assurances – that had once championed the NPT as evidence of the nuclear weapon states giving insufficient fealty to their obligations to seek "negotiations in good faith" on a world without nuclear weapons. The treaty's indefinite extension has thus come to be seen by many of these states as perhaps the greatest trick the nuclear weapon states ever pulled when it comes to the global nonproliferation order, depriving them ultimately of what had been a form of leverage in the original time-delimited applicability of the treaty.

Despite this growing frustration, non-nuclear weapon states – especially those that have no interest in the bomb themselves – are unlikely to leave the NPT anytime soon. As with most treaties, the NPT contains a withdrawal provision, which has to date been exercised by just one country: North Korea, in 2003. Citing "extraordinary events," any state could withdraw from the treaty, but this is not an appealing option. Beyond an established norm against nuclear nonproliferation that has taken hold in the decades since the NPT went into effect, withdrawal fundamentally imposes other costs on states. For instance, without participation in the NPT, states cannot reliably access global markets for peaceful nuclear technologies, including for nuclear energy. Treaty withdrawal would terminate states' Comprehensive Safeguards Agreements with the International Atomic Energy Agency (IAEA), which are implemented under Article III of the treaty. (There have been proposals to encourage such agreements outside of the NPT, however.) Nonparticipation in the NPT, more broadly, would have other ripple effects. For instance, laws in the United States, the European Union, and elsewhere would likely result in sanctions on such states, harming their economies in ways broader than the loss of access to peaceful nuclear technology. Finally, in the decades since the treaty's opening for signature in 1968 nuclear nonproliferation has emerged as a global norm; proliferators could expect to be treated as controversial, global pariahs, sharing the ignominy of having left the NPT with just North Korea alongside them.

While, cumulatively, the credibility of the NPT has come under pressure from these dynamics, there are other stressors that may take on growing relevance as the twenty-first century progresses. In September 2017, after years of campaigning by nuclear disarmament advocates and weeks of negotiations in the United Nations General Assembly, another treaty, the Treaty on the Prohibition of Nuclear Weapons (TPNW), was agreed on and opened for signature. The TPNW shared an important goal with the NPT: a world free of nuclear weapons. However, as its name implied, its primary and exclusive goal was to fundamentally render nuclear weapons unacceptable as a class of weaponry for possession by any states and, by extension, to delegitimize nuclear deterrence, which necessarily depends on the existence and possession of nuclear weapons, as a basis for any state's national security. In this way, unlike the NPT, the TPNW was closer in philosophy to the Biological Weapons Convention and the Chemical Weapons Convention, two multilateral arrangements that seek to govern a class of weapons of mass destruction given their widely agreed abhorrent effects on human beings. However, unlike those conventions, the TPNW functioned largely as a political commitment, lacking comprehensive verification measures. Even among those who agree that nuclear disarmament is desirable, debates have raged for years on how to effectively verify a world where states once possessing nuclear weapons had disarmed and would not rearm. At its center, however, the TPNW endeavored to raise a norm stigmatizing nuclear weapons and nuclear deterrence – something the NPT emphatically does *not* formally do.

Between its opening for signature and by 2024, the TPNW had gained seventy parties – all without their own nuclear weapons. Not one nuclear-armed state – be it an NPT N5 state or otherwise – has endorsed the treaty, nor has any state that receives nuclear extended deterrence assurances from the United States signed up. Still, the growing appeal of the TPNW among states in Latin America, Africa, Southeast Asia – regions considered part of the "global South," or "global majority" and long viewed by the nuclear "haves" as peripheral to global debates on nuclear matters – has raised anxieties about the future of the global nuclear order and the NPT. For these states, all of which are NPT states-parties, the decision to endorse the TPNW was in many cases born of frustration with the state of progress toward global disarmament.[17] Despite the potential corrosive effect on such a treaty in a world where the NPT had long set the benchmark, TPNW proponents argued that the treaty was designed to complement the NPT – building fundamentally on that treaty's Article VI language on disarmament. (The TPNW's preamble mentions the NPT explicitly.) While the TPNW has arguably succeeded in raising anxieties among the states that strongly oppose it and favor the NPT, its long-term success remains questionable. With seventy parties already signed up, one could point to political science research suggesting that a new norm emerges in international politics when it has been endorsed by roughly one-third of the states in the international system.[18] The TPNW meets this threshold. But without the support of nuclear-armed states and their allies, the treaty will ultimately fail to fundamentally achieve its objective of delegitimizing nuclear weapons as tools of statecraft. What could alter this for some states that remain critical of the TPNW is a world in which nuclear use – or broader nuclear war – occurs, but such an event could just as easily precipitate nuclear proliferation and break the NPT's back through other means.

For supporters of nuclear nonproliferation, the central question in the new nuclear age may focus not at all on the tensions between the NPT and the TPNW, but on other challenges to the global nuclear order. Following Russia's invasion of Ukraine in 2022, for instance, Moscow has relegated all of its traditional objectives in international diplomacy, including nuclear nonproliferation, to its short-term geopolitical interests in the course of its war.[19] While the NPT would likely not have been able to come into existence during the Cold War without Moscow's cooperation, Russia's post-2022 international behavior has strained many of the core shibboleths that undergird the NPT system. For one, in attacking Ukraine while issuing covert and overt nuclear threats, Moscow arguably violated its own general negative security assurances. These assurances, which assert that the states with nuclear weapons will never use them to attack or threaten non-nuclear weapon states, were issued by the NPT N5 prior to the treaty's indefinite extension in 1995. In addition to its general assurances, Russia violated a similar negative security assurance it endorsed for Ukraine specifically in the Budapest Memorandum of December 1994. By the time of the 2022 NPT Review Conference, which was originally scheduled for 2020 but was delayed two years because of the Covid-19 pandemic, Russia's dangerous and deliberate attacks against Ukraine's Zaporizhzhia Nuclear Power Plant were also a central concern.[20]

In this dark environment, which had already raised the serious possibility of nuclear war in Europe for the first time since the Cold War, the NPT states-parties met in August 2022 to work toward producing a final outcome document at the fifth review conference since the indefinite extension decision in 1995. While almost everyone anticipated that conference to crash and burn, with little hope of reaching the consensus required among all 191 states-parties, deft diplomatic maneuvering actually made that consensus somewhat within reach by the final day of the meeting. At the last minute, however, Russia refused to endorse the draft text, deeming any references to what was transpiring in Ukraine to be unacceptable.[21] For pessimists, the Russian decision to break consensus at the review conference was a dark omen of a world to come, where the great powers would choose to ignore nonproliferation goals in pursuit of their interests. Russia was hardly the first major power in the post-Cold War era to subjugate nonproliferation to its strategic interests, however. The United States' willingness in 2005 to conclude a civil nuclear cooperation agreement with India, effectively granting New Delhi a bespoke and exceptional status as a nuclear weapons possessor outside the NPT, remains an archetypal case. Additionally, the September 2021 decision by the United States and the United Kingdom to share nuclear naval propulsion technology based on highly enriched uranium fuel with Australia to shore up its conventional defense capabilities drew sharp, albeit technically questionable, criticism from China on nonproliferation grounds.[22] At the time of the 2022 NPT Review Conference, a "rogue" Russia, deciding to trample nuclear norms along several axes, was hardly a far-fetched idea. For optimists, however, the fact that 190 states reached a consensus at all was an unexpected and welcome surprise. Most importantly, however, for pragmatists, who continued to see the benefits of a world with a functioning, if strained, NPT, another failed review conference was hardly a fatal event for the global nuclear order. (Before the 2022 conference, the 2015 conference similarly failed to achieve consensus.)

Beyond a rogue Russia, the United States' future political direction may have greater consequences, in practice, for nonproliferation. The United States plays a particularly unique role in reinforcing the norm against nuclear proliferation out of its own self-interest. Beginning in the years immediately after the dawn of the nuclear age, Washington has built up, over decades, alliances that are backed by the full range of its military capabilities, including its nuclear weapons, if necessary. In theory, this *extended* deterrent, offered to many of the United States' closest allies – countries that just happen to be, in many cases, wealthy, scientifically sophisticated, and, in some cases, proficient in nuclear technologies – is designed to keep them non-nuclear. In the idealized practice of extended deterrence, allied leaders and publics should be able to go to sleep at night with the assurance that U.S. nuclear weapons are practically as good as their own. In reality, this ideal form of extended deterrence has been far from the reality. As many of these non-nuclear allies perceive a more dangerous world, their interest in nuclear weapons has started to grow. Most fundamentally, however, the polarization of national politics in the United States and the emergence of a significant strain of alliance-skeptical political thinking – personified in none other than Donald Trump – has likely raised anxieties that are likely to persist in the long term. As a consequence, U.S. allies will be more prone to thinking about seeking the bomb and more skeptical of Washington as this new nuclear age develops. Some already are.

Alliances and extended deterrence

On January 20, 2021, Joe Biden stood before thousands in Washington, DC, to deliver his inaugural address after being sworn in as the forty-sixth president of the United States. Biden's speech sought to communicate to the world that his election and inauguration were evidence that "America is back." After four years of uncertainty for U.S. allies under the idiosyncratic, chaotic, and unorthodox foreign policy instincts of the outgoing president Donald J. Trump, Biden pledged to restore U.S. leadership, and to "repair our alliances and engage with the world once again." However, the incoming U.S. president knew that trust had to be earned back. "I know the past few years have strained and tested the transatlantic relationship," Biden said, zeroing in on U.S. allies in Europe. "The United States is determined to reengage with Europe, to consult with you, to earn back our position of trusted leadership."[23] The sentiment was appreciated in Europe. European Council president Charles Michel, less than a month later, punctuated his keynote remarks at the prominent Munich Security Conference on global challenges with a poignant "Welcome back America," and similar sentiments flowed freely from supporters of a once-again globally engaged United States in Japan, South Korea, Australia, and elsewhere.

Despite Biden's pledges at the outset of his presidency to "repair" alliances, the Trump presidency had sown a deep-seated malaise in virtually every capital city of every foreign state in a treaty alliance with the United States. Behind every publicly stated variant of Michel's welcoming remarks were private concerns that Trump's election happened once and it could happen again – both literally, with the second-term-eligible former president making a return in 2025, or in the form of an alternative "America First" fellow traveler candidate. More fundamentally, U.S. allies had, by 2021, found time to process the consequences of the shockwave that was the U.S. 2016 presidential election and understood that the inward-looking political forces favoring retrenchment that resulted in Trump's election were now an endemic feature of the American political landscape. And so, while Biden's election provided temporary salve to allies that had been disturbed by Trump's propensity to extort, ignore, and, at worst, threaten American allies, it was temporary. The consequences of this revised view of the United States among U.S. allies stand to have potentially far-flung consequences in the new nuclear age.

Among all nuclear-armed states, the United States has been unique since the 1950s in its proactive efforts to communicate to other states around the world that it would come to their defense – including with nuclear weapons, if necessary. In this way, the United States *extended* its nuclear deterrent to states beyond its own borders. The reasons for this were hardly altruistic: the extension of U.S. assurances to allies in Europe and Asia was seen as a stabilizing force against the intense systemic geopolitical confrontation with the Soviet Union that characterized the Cold War. Preserving regional status quos was often in the U.S. interest and Washington was willing to run the risk of nuclear conflict to do so. More importantly, however, extended nuclear deterrence came to underpin another important U.S. interest: nuclear nonproliferation. By the 1960s, the United States had come to the conclusion that a world with scores of nuclear-armed states – even friendly ones – was less safe for U.S. interests. Nuclear-armed allies could even escalate or initiate nuclear wars that the United States would have to then finish. As a result of these concerns, the United

States took measures to actively frame its nuclear assurances to allies as a nonproliferation incentive. Doing so meant that the United States would enjoy greater room for geopolitical maneuver. The success of this approach was far from assured at the time. In the mid-1960s, for instance, Washington agreed to implement changes to NATO's approach to nuclear policy to assuage West German concerns about the sufficiency of extended deterrence.[24] This resulted in the establishment of the Nuclear Planning Group, which continues to serve as a key organ for nuclear policy consultations within the transatlantic alliance. In the 1970s, Washington detected a clandestine effort by its ally, South Korea, to build nuclear weapons. In the 1970s, coercive U.S. threats paired with assurances caused Park Chung-hee, the South Korean dictator at the time, to change course.[25] Washington similarly walked Taiwan back from seeking the bomb (though it would end its formal security assurances for Taipei following diplomatic normalization with China in 1979).[26]

Crucially, extended deterrence was never a straightforward or simple enterprise for the United States. One of the most frequently quoted bits of Cold War truisms on the matter is attributed to Denis Healey, a former British defense minister, who observed that while it "only takes a 5 percent credibility of American retaliation to deter an attack [from the Soviets] . . . it takes a 95 percent credibility to reassure the allies." Put simply, for Washington, the matter of deterring nuclear-armed adversaries is a comparatively simpler task than assuring its non-nuclear allies, which can seem like an endless task. In the new nuclear age – and the post-2021 Trump era in American politics – a fundamental, and perhaps irreparable, fissure has torn through decades of hard-fought American efforts to build credibility with allies. Following Biden's election, during travels to European and East Asian capitals alike, I would find myself contending with concerned statements about long-term American reliability. What made Trump's election a rude awakening was not merely the experience of the four years between 2017 and 2021, which certainly strained American alliances, but the unshakable feeling in allied capitals that political forces in the United States would steer Washington away from the broader approach to alliances that had remained generally consistent across administrations since the end of the Second World War.

The idea of absolute consistency in American alliance management before Trump is, however, an oversimplification and ahistorical. U.S. presidents before Trump contemplated – and in some cases executed – prominent changes to how Washington interacted with its allies. In 1969, President Richard Nixon, in declaring what would later come to be known as his eponymous doctrine, noted that while the United States would observe its treaty commitments and "provide a shield if a nuclear power threatens the freedom of a nation allied with us," lesser forms of aggression would require threatened allied states to "assume the primary responsibility of providing the manpower for its defense."[27] Later, Nixon would enact the most substantial reduction of U.S. troops deployed to South Korea; between 1969 and 1971, U.S. forces were reduced from 63,000 to 43,000 in Korea. Incidentally, this series of events partially stoked fears of U.S. abandonment that led President Park in Korea to contemplate the acquisition of nuclear weapons. President Jimmy Carter, a Democrat, meanwhile, campaigned on a promise to pull U.S. troops out of South Korea, citing Park's poor human rights record. Following his election, Carter moderated his position and reduced the U.S. troop presence by an additional 3,000. Part of Carter's change of heart was motivated by his discovery, upon assuming the office of the president, that his belief that South Korea could defend itself at the time against North Korean attack without U.S. assistance was mistaken.[28]

American alliance management had also for years sought to carefully balance allied fears of abandonment with concerns about entrapment. When it came to abandonment, the United States feared during the Cold War that perhaps several of its allies would come to the conclusion that France had arrived at by the late-1950s. Paris found the idea of relying on U.S. extended deterrence to safeguard against existential threats deeply unpersuasive. Charles de Gaulle, in a meeting with John F. Kennedy in 1961, a year after France's first nuclear test, posed the question of "whether [the United States] would be ready to trade New York for Paris."[29] This problem of allied "decoupling," as it came to be known, emerged toward the latter years of the 1950s with the arrival of the ICBM. As discussed elsewhere in this book, the acquisition of ICBMs turned what had been a fundamentally hours-long lurch toward nuclear war to a matter of tens of minutes. The perceived ease with which the once nigh-impermeable continental bastion of the United States could be pierced by the Soviet Union was deeply disquieting to several allies, but, for de Gaulle's France, it was especially intolerable. France's status as an independent nuclear power in its own right could not be reconciled with American assurances at the time. For the rest of the United States' transatlantic allies, Washington had to make credible its promise to run the risk of nuclear attacks against its homeland in the course of a conventional war in Europe. This was a moment of conventional inferiority for the United States and its allies vis-à-vis the Soviet threat in Europe, and forward-deployed nuclear weapons were seen as a crucial offset for the alliance. Through the 1960s, the United States met allied concerns through several approaches – some successful and some less so. In the latter category was the ill-fated idea of a Multilateral Nuclear Force, which would have seen European allies operate an array of nuclear-armed submarines and warships. As the risks and complications associated with this idea became apparent, the alliance instead settled on the adoption of a modified nuclear strategy for coping with the threat of Soviet attack known as Flexible Response and introduced the Nuclear Planning Group.

For many in the Biden administration contending with the alliance management challenges in the post-Trump era, much of this Cold War history has become somewhat instructive amid new challenges. While the future of U.S. alliances and extended deterrence in the new nuclear age remains fundamentally uncertain, the most important test case for the enduring ability of extended deterrence to stem the impulse toward nuclear proliferation will be South Korea. Public opinion surveys in the country for a number of years have shown consistent support for the acquisition of an independent nuclear deterrent, even as the country has remained a stalwart U.S. ally with more than 28,000 American military personnel stationed on its territory.[30] A 2021 survey found that support for nuclear weapons acquisition transgressed partisan affiliations in the country and had a broad base of support at 71 percent – and many other surveys have consistently reported similar numbers.[31] This support also appeared to be positively correlated with support for the alliance with the United States, suggesting that the pull of nuclear proliferation was more about the perceived intrinsic benefits of nuclear weaponry than concerns over U.S. commitments, per se. In January 2023, Yoon Suk Yeol, a conservative South Korean president, became the first leader since the country's transition to a democracy to publicly moot the acquisition of nuclear weapons. Yoon, in a wide-ranging, somewhat rambling speech to South Korean bureaucrats, underscored the country's technological sophistication and suggested that Seoul could "acquire our own nuke."[32] Yoon premised this possibility, however, on a conditional, noting that Seoul would only consider this dramatic step "if problems become more serious."

On the one hand, South Korea's interest in nuclear weapons acquisition is unsurprising. Its neighbor to the north withdrew from the NPT in 2003 and sprinted to a substantial nuclear weapons capability by the end of the 2010s. Longstanding scholarship on the causes of nuclear proliferation interest points to a state's security environment was one among several variables influencing a decision to seek the bomb.[33] While Yoon had his reasons for supporting this possibility, progressives in the country see benefits in the bomb for different reasons. While South Korean conservatives largely see value in developing nuclear weapons as a deterrent against North Korea, progressives in the country largely operate on a more de Gaulle-style logic, seeing an independent nuclear deterrent as a sovereign imperative that could reduce Seoul's reliance on the United States and enhance its autonomy. Both sides, meanwhile, acknowledge South Korea's considerable technological sophistication, but, crucially, Seoul lacks an indigenous, industrial-scale uranium enrichment or plutonium reprocessing capability – either of which would be a *sine qua non* for a credible short-term sprint to the bomb. As a result of this limitation, South Korea's ability to credibly threaten rapid proliferation has been somewhat limited; with sufficient political will, this could change.

Yoon's remarks created global headlines and rattled several senior policymakers in the Biden administration, even if they knew better than to state openly the degree of American concern over the leader of a treaty ally publicly mooting the acquisition of nuclear weapons. A little more than three months after Yoon's remarks were reported, the South Korean president traveled to Washington and the two countries announced a historic document known as the Washington Declaration.[34] The declaration was a two-way exchange of reassurances between the United States and South Korea. It included language from South Korea reaffirming its legally binding nonproliferation commitments. It also featured new assurances from the United States, including an aspirational commitment for the U.S. president to consult with his South Korean counterpart in a nuclear crisis prior to the use of nuclear weapons, and the establishment of a new consultative body on nuclear policy matters, dubbed the Nuclear Consultative Group. I traveled to Seoul in the weeks after the declaration was announced and encountered numerous South Korean observers – including proponents of an independent nuclear capability for the country – who were perplexed by the inclusion of language affirming Seoul's nonproliferation commitments. Expectations in Seoul had coalesced around the idea of a steady, reliable flow of assurances from the United States, but the growing interest in nuclear proliferation had prompted many in Washington to dust off the old Cold War playbook on allied proliferation and seek assurances of forbearance in kind from Seoul.

While both elite and public opinion interest in South Korea have grown clearer in the 2020s, what remains fundamentally uncertain is whether the country has a credible proliferation *strategy*. In 2024, a little more than a year after he first mooted the prospect of seeking the bomb, Yoon alluded to the costs associated with proliferation for his country, suggesting that a decision to seek nuclear weapons would devastate South Korea's heavily globally integrated economy.[35] "If we develop nuclear weapons, we will receive various economic sanctions like North Korea does now, and our economy will be dealt a serious blow," Yoon told a South Korean journalist. He was right. South Korea would also face automatic U.S. sanctions, many of which could not be waived even by a U.S. president motivated to see Seoul get the bomb.[36] As a result of these constraints, Seoul could seek to hedge strongly until the moment it perceives an irreconcilable breaking point in its alliance with the United States. Part of Seoul's strategy, too, may continue to revolve around using threats of proliferation to bargain with the United States – a strategy that other U.S. allies have employed in the past with varying degrees of success.[37]

While South Korea represents the most acute test case for proliferation by U.S. allies in the new nuclear age, it is far from the sole case of an American ally disquieted by the long-term potential consequences of political drift and discord in Washington. In Europe, the debate on the continent's nuclear future cracked wide open in the aftermath of the twin shocks of the Trump presidency and Russia's 2022 invasion of Ukraine. Consider, for instance, that Joschka Fischer, a former German federal foreign minister and committed member of the nuclear and NATO-skeptic Greens, in 2023 suggested that the European Union "needs its own nuclear deterrence."[38] Fischer, in 2020, had signed an open letter supporting the TPNW, underscoring just how quickly views in continental Europe had shifted.[39] In February 2024, European observers watched in shock as Trump, on the campaign trail in the United States, told an agitated crowd of supporters that, if reelected, he would "encourage" Russia "to do whatever the hell they want" against any European allies that he considered to be spending too little on their national defense.[40] As he had during his presidency, Trump appeared to continue to believe that NATO's so-called "2/20 guideline" amounted to something akin to binding dues on its member states: that allies somehow owed 2 percent of their GDP to the United States for the benefit of their protection. In reality, the alliance, in 2006, agreed to set a benchmark whereby member states would work toward increasing their defense spending to 2 percent of their national GDPs. This was reiterated after Russia's illegal annexation of Crimea in 2014 and because most alliance members had lagged to keep up with the 2006 goal; the 2014 iteration also outlined a goal of ensuring that 20 percent of defense spending should go toward defense equipment by 2024.[41] Whatever Trump's views may have been, the reality within the alliance quickly shifted as a result of Russia's war against Ukraine. In 2024, twenty-three out of thirty-two NATO states met the 2 percent guideline, a twofold increase compared to 2020.[42]

While European states may move to recalibrate longer term as the United States' perceived reliability remains a problem, the continent continues to face pressing short-term questions around conventional defense and deterrence as well. Despite Russia's significant nuclear capabilities, including its more than 2,000 nonstrategic nuclear weapons, NATO's European members collectively see reason for confidence in the alliance's conventional deterrent. Russia's woeful conventional military performance against the Ukrainian armed forces in the immediate aftermath of its February 2022 invasion punctured many of the pre-war assessments of its military strength and organizational competency. Despite this, the fundamental problem for NATO as it stares down the possibility of a long-term future either without the United States, or with a fundamentally uncommitted United States, is that recalibration will require time. While political will to increase defense spending has grown – alongside public perceptions of a more threatening Russia in many key capitals – the continent faces real constraints with its ability to marshal resources for a surge in defense-industrial output and production. As a result, it is all too common to hear European leaders and analysts call for patience as the continent charts an alternative.

However, as the most significant land war on the continent since the Second World War takes place on Europe's eastern frontiers, these same voices grew all too aware that time may be a luxury that the continent simply does not possess. Several NATO allies – particularly those on Russia's frontiers – took the threat from Moscow seriously in the aftermath of the illegal 2014 annexation of Crimea from Ukraine and increased their defense spending. In Poland, what were once whispers about nuclear weapons have turned louder. In February 2024, Radosław Sikorski, the Polish defense minister, told an audience in Washington that his country would rather "eat grass before becoming a Russian colony again."[43] That choice of words – alluding to eating grass – would be instantly recognizable to any student of the history of nuclear proliferation.

It was the precise turn of phrase that was famously used by Pakistani Prime Minister Zulfikar Ali Bhutto after India's 1974 nuclear test prompted Pakistan to go all-in on seeking the bomb – whatever the economic costs may be for the country. Germany, the wealthiest large non-U.S. NATO ally – albeit one traditionally seen as a laggard in defense matters – has started to see a debate on nuclear weapons against the backdrop of a broader conversation around defense and security. Despite declaring Russia's decision to go to war against Ukraine the catalyst for a *Zeitenwende* – or "watershed" – moment for Germany and Europe, Berlin has been fundamentally slow to place resources behind its intentions. Two years after German Chancellor Olaf Scholz first announced the *Zeitenwende*, questions persist around the urgency of Germany's timeline for increasing its defense spending, the seriousness of German lawmakers to commit to legislature and funding, and, most critically, the implementation of an industrial plan to realize a real sea change in the country's defense spending. German defense minister Boris Pistorius, in 2024, articulated that he saw the country's defense spending potentially surging to an unprecedented 3.5 percent of GDP, but conceded that funding this surge would prove difficult.[44] The German debate on seeking nuclear weapons – be it for Berlin independently, Brussels, or sharing with Paris – however, remains largely inchoate and aspirational.[45]

European debates have also centered around the viability of the European Union as a future organizing institution for the continent's defense needs in a world where the United States has retreated. This, however, ignores several realities that will especially inhibit the EU's ability to meet actual or perceived defense needs in the short term. For instance, while many EU states also participate in NATO, as Jens Stoltenberg, the Norwegian former secretary-general of the alliance, has noted, "Eighty per cent of NATO's defence expenditures come from non-EU NATO allies."[46] In part due to these practical barriers to augmenting conventional deterrence vis-à-vis Russia, European strategists have begun to look to solutions in possible new extended deterrence arrangements. These center around France and the United Kingdom, the two main European nuclear powers, both of which have idiosyncratic relationships with NATO and the EU: France does not participate in NATO's nuclear policy deliberations, and the UK now sits outside the EU. Neither country, meanwhile, has articulated a clear willingness or pathway to pick up the role currently played by the United States.[47] French strategists reject out of hand suggestions that the country's deterrent could be extended to EU states in exchange for funding; this appears to undercut the very central idea of autonomy and independence that are more or less foundational to French nuclear strategy and identity. One French analyst describes the possibility of accepting such a proposal as tantamount to "[discarding] the political heritage of Charles de Gaulle" – a political nonstarter, in other words.[48] Neither a "Eurobomb" built out of the existing French and British nuclear forces, nor new, bespoke European extended deterrence arrangements appear all too likely – even if debates on the continent on these matters have quickly chipped away at post-Cold War taboos around nuclear matters.

The specter of a permanently unreliable United States has served as an accelerant in Europe for debates on strategic matters that would have seemed largely unimaginable throughout much of the 2010s. At the dawn of this new nuclear age, the continent is fundamentally reckoning with vivid concerns about nuclear and conventional threats from Russia and fears of abandonment by the United States. Seen from Europe, the entirety of the post-Cold War security architecture on the continent is in tatters. In the lead-up to the 2024 U.S. election, some European observers in private would suggest that, while Trump's return to the White House would augur poorly for the continent, his campaign trail rhetoric on alliances should not be taken literally. "It's good red meat for his base, and he may just be seeking to frighten Europe into increasing its defense spending," one European analyst told me, suggesting that Trump's words – including his indication that he would encourage Russia to attack allies failing to meet the transatlantic alliance's defense spending benchmarks – needn't be fatal for NATO. This view, however, hardly appears to be the basis of short-term policy planning in European capitals. But, given the real limitations on what Europe can and can't do to defend itself, it may be for the best that Europeans choose to focus on the matters they can control and rather than on those they cannot.

Writing on these matters from Washington, DC, it is difficult to offer an informed and authentic expression of faith that the American endeavor of projecting reliability to the world can soon be restored. As much as the diplomats and bureaucrats tasked with interfacing with allies for the Biden administration might wish it, they are fundamentally unable to answer the most fundamentally important question posed by any allied counterpart: "How can you assure us that Washington will stay the course under a future Republican presidency?" As distasteful of a reckoning as it may be, the political realignment that played out in American politics in the second half of the 2010s has ended seven decades of broad continuity in the United States' effective approach to alliance management. Alliance management crises of the past pale in contrast to the fundamental inability of U.S. allies today to trust that the United States might still, against all odds, "do the right thing, but only after exhausting all other options," as British Prime Minister Winston Churchill once observed. The sinews of trust within any alliance or collective defense arrangement rest ultimately on political solidarity. Trump and, more broadly, the Trumpist impulse driving so-called "America First" politics and foreign policy have proven sticky enough at home that other countries depending on a reliable United States simply have to consider their options. While the prospect of proliferation by U.S. allies in the new nuclear age still remains highly contingent on a range of political, geopolitical, and technical factors, the long-term consequences of political dysfunction in Washington may truly be dire.

5

Nuclear Flashpoints

The practice of nuclear deterrence rests on the real possibility of catastrophe. Without the risk in a crisis that everything might get out of hand and that nuclear weapons may be used, nuclear deterrence fails to function. In other words, the risk itself is central to the benefit from nuclear weapons that leaders and decision-makers often seek. It is why, for instance, Russian President Vladimir Putin felt it necessary to pair his implicit threat to the leaders of the United States and other NATO states prior to his invasion of Ukraine in 2022 that their direct intervention in the conflict would be met with possible nuclear Armageddon with the announcement of an order to place the "Russian army's deterrence forces to a special mode of combat duty."[1] Nuclear signaling, including the issuance of nuclear threats, is an old practice. The United States, when it enjoyed peerless nuclear superiority in the 1950s, brandished its nuclear capabilities openly to deter, coerce, and compel, for instance. Soviet leaders, similarly, alluded to the prospect of nuclear warfare. Prior to Russia's avalanche of nuclear loose talk in the aftermath of its 2022 invasion of Ukraine, North Korea was particularly known for its frequent nuclear threats – threats that grew more credible as Pyongyang advanced its capabilities.

As nuclear weapons take on renewed salience in national defense strategies, the prospect of nuclear escalation increases. The old problem of unwanted nuclear war that once led Cold War-era American and Soviet leaders to discover the importance of crisis communications, arms control, and strategic stability is back in a world of relatively unconstrained great power nuclear competition. Regional nuclear powers, like India and Pakistan, too, have seen their competitive relationship and capabilities evolve in dangerous new ways. Finally, the arrival of new nuclear states like North Korea presents new challenges and pathways to nuclear use. The prospect of deliberate nuclear escalation – long set aside in the post-Cold War period by military planners and theorists as a problem largely solved by nuclear deterrence – has reared its head again, too. Russia's remarkable lack of conventional military success against NATO-backed Ukrainian forces, for instance, has raised concerns that Moscow may deliberately seek to employ nuclear weapons to offset catastrophic conventional defeat – particularly if Ukrainian forces attempt to retake Ukrainian territory in Crimea that Moscow annexed in 2014. Longer-term, Russia's substantially weakened conventional military forces may force a greater reliance by Moscow on its substantial arsenal of nonstrategic nuclear weapons. While Ukraine will likely remain a nuclear flashpoint for some time, the prospect of NATO-Russia confrontation concurrent to or in the aftermath of Russia's war against Ukraine will be a central feature of the new nuclear age.

The Taiwan flashpoint

Perhaps no potential nuclear flashpoint is growing faster in relevance at the dawn of the new nuclear age than the Taiwan Strait, where the unfinished business of the Chinese Civil War threatens to spark a conflagration with global consequences.

The Communist Party of China views the self-governing island as part of its sovereign territory and, despite a temporary *modus vivendi* under previous Taiwanese governments, the political underpinnings of cross-strait relations have soured significantly since the mid-2010s. A confluence of factors – including demographic and political change in Taiwan, the deepening of an inherently "Taiwanized" identity for the citizens of the island, and Beijing's own heavy-handed application of pressure against Taipei – have raised the prospect of a conflict. China maintains that any steps toward formal independence by Taipei would transgress a red line that would leave open the possibility of seeking unification with Taiwan through force. Meanwhile, the United States and China remain in the throes of a dangerously spiraling security dilemma, with each seeking to buttress its conventional military locally in East Asia. As described earlier in this book, the remarkable increase in the size of China's nuclear forces has sparked worst-case-scenario thinking in many parts of the United States' national security apparatus about the potential for deliberate nuclear escalation by Beijing in a Taiwan conflict. Similarly, Chinese nuclear policy experts privately express concerns about a possible resort to nuclear weapons by the United States. These experts note, for instance, that the United States may seek to offset its potential conventional military inferiority in East Asia as it once did in Central Europe during the Cold War: by resorting to the early use of nuclear weapons as an asymmetric capability. Taiwan has not been a formal treaty ally of the United States since 1980, but the fate of the self-governing, democratic island has become a core U.S. strategic priority with bipartisan support in Washington. Critically, President Biden repeatedly expressed the view that he believes the United States has a commitment to come to Taiwan's defense, even if unarticulated in any formal treaty.[2]

For years in Washington, war games and table-top exercises at major research institutes and think-tanks simulated how a

U.S.–China clash over Taiwan might play out. Over the years, as these simulations accounted for advancing Chinese military capabilities – and, essentially, local military superiority for China in East Asia vis-à-vis the United States – the implications for the United States appeared dire.[3] Many of these wargames would terminate at the point of nuclear use, or simply leave nuclear weapons out altogether. Gradually, as the military balance shifted, the salience of nuclear weapons – including "theater nuclear [capabilities]" – took on greater relevance. The temptation, as existed in Europe in the 1950s and 1960s, to reach for a nuclear offset was growing in Washington.[4] Fundamentally, it is unserious to raise the prospect of a U.S.–China conventional war over the fate of Taiwan, which China treats as a "core interest," without accounting for the possibility of nuclear escalation. Such escalation could be initiated by either side to seek tactical advantage or strategic coercive benefits, or to communicate resolve. Chinese military leaders appear to have internalized this possibility a long time ago. At the height of the third Taiwan Strait crisis in 1996, one senior Chinese military official told an American interlocutor that times had changed in the U.S.–China nuclear relationship. "In the 1950s, you three times threatened nuclear strikes on China, and you could do that because we couldn't hit back," this officer reportedly said at the time, alluding to the frustrations that drove Mao Zedong to seek the bomb in the early years of the Cold War. "Now we can. So you are not going to threaten us again because, in the end, you care a lot more about Los Angeles than Taipei," the official added.[5] Any war between the United States and China would implicate nuclear weapons from the start, and there would be no precedent in modern history for the kind of conventional military clash that this would represent; both the United States and China would bring the most modern, networked, and lethal set of non-nuclear capabilities to such a conflict. Given the tyranny of geography, the United States would face the difficult task of projecting conventional military power across the vast, watery expanse of the Pacific Ocean. While its regional bases in Japan, the Philippines, and Australia may play a role in supporting conventional operations, interdicting a vast Chinese amphibious landing force would not be a straightforward endeavor. A war of conquest – what unification with Taiwan through force would represent for China – would require the movement of tens of thousands of People's Liberation Army troops across more than 150 kilometers of water. The Taiwanese, too, have invested readily in their own defense and would seek to ward off an invading force with the goal of granting the United States and its allies sufficient time to offer support.

There is much disagreement among defense analysts and experts about the probability and timeframe of a full-scale conventional war between the United States and China over Taiwan. Many, especially in Washington, are persuaded by an almost fatalistic logic that Xi has made his mind up and plans to go to war by some arbitrary deadline; the years 2027, 2035, and 2049 are often brought up by those who hold these views. Senior U.S. military officials, including those involved in military planning in the Pacific, have reiterated the case for urgency because their resourcing depends on a motivated U.S. Congress and public treating the possibility of this conflict as a priority.[6] While Xi himself has described unification as an inevitability, he will likely have ample cause to kick this can down the road.[7] First, despite Xi's orders to the Chinese military to be ready by 2027 to invade Taiwan, if necessary, senior U.S. intelligence officials have indicated that China's leadership harbors doubts about the actual ability of the People's Liberation Army to prevail in such a war of choice.[8] Vladimir Putin's miscalculation concerning the Russian military's odds of swift success against Ukraine may, in some way, have provided a reminder to Xi that, as Carl von Clausewitz once observed, war will remain the "province of uncertainty." Second, throughout his tenure,

Xi has appeared to exhibit – rather openly – a lack of confidence in senior political and military leaders, including those
hand-picked by him for senior positions. In 2023 alone, China's
defense minister, foreign minister, and much of the leadership
of the People's Liberation Army Rocket Force, the branch of
the Chinese military overseeing its land-based nuclear forces,
were purged.[9] Xi, as a profoundly ideologically oriented leader,
appears to lack the same neoliberal drive that influenced his
predecessors going back to Deng Xiaoping. In this way, the
economic costs associated with a war of choice against Taiwan
may be less of a concern, but Xi would still fundamentally
have to contend with the possibility of a Taiwan-war-gone-
wrong posing an existential concern for his personal control of
the Communist Party of China, or the broader survival of the
Communist Party itself.[10]

Without treating a U.S.–China war as an inevitability, it will
be incumbent on leaders, military planners, and their advisors
on both sides to contemplate the risks that could manifest in
nuclear escalation. Optimistically, both countries may believe
that the obvious nuclear shadow that exists between them
will be sufficient to bound the scope of a conventional conflict, but this would be Pollyannaish and naive. The kind of
high-intensity conventional warfighting that may ensure in a
Taiwan conflict could quickly see conventional weapons used
against Chinese bases housing nuclear-armed missile units, or
attacks against U.S. satellites involved in nuclear command and
control operations.[11] Leaders may also be prone to take risks
competitively based on a misreading of the other side's stakes
in a conflict. For instance, while unification with Taiwan may
be a "core" interest for China, it is substantially less of a key
national priority for the United States, which views the maintenance of the status quo in the Taiwan Strait as fundamentally
more important than Taiwanese independence (which the
United States has opposed as a matter of policy). In a scenario
where China may be losing a conventional conflict, however,

the prospect of issuing threats to use nuclear weapons – or actually using nuclear weapons in a limited way – could be tempting as a means of viscerally conveying the stakes as perceived by the Chinese leadership in the conflict. Meanwhile, as one former U.S. official involved in defense policy planning noted, the United States would similarly feel a pull to rely on limited nuclear use to destroy a concentrated Chinese landing force on Taiwanese shores.[12] As I explored in Chapter 2 of this book, such limited use by either side would create pressures to respond in ways that could start the two countries down a dangerous path to a general, mutually ruinous nuclear exchange. Though Chinese and American leaders might be wary about war under the nuclear shadow, their advisors may believe that limited nuclear use provides a useful opportunity to seek strategic advantage.

Related to these nuclear escalation possibilities between the United States and China is a growing concern for Washington in the era of two nuclear near-peer adversaries related to the problem of opportunistic aggression. U.S. military planners have started to increasingly wrangle with the nuclear and non-nuclear challenges that may arise when the United States seeks to simultaneously deter both Russia and China in potentially unrelated, simultaneous crises in Europe and Asia. Because the United States, despite its overwhelming global military superiority, cannot reasonably mass sufficient non-nuclear forces in *both* Asia and Europe, its leaders may be more tempted to take military advice recommending nuclear use at a lower level of conflict in *either* theater. In private settings, concerns about this are used to support calls for a larger U.S. nuclear arsenal, but more creative thinking may abound to allay these concerns. First, despite the understandable concern among military planners concerning these matters, the United States can avail a broader toolkit of national power, including diplomacy, to seek arrangements, offer assurances, and negotiate arms control agreements that could attenuate the pressures that might otherwise manifest to seek nuclear use. Second, even failing to change the contours of the international environment, the United States may instead choose to rely on its superior conventional qualitative edge to address perceived shortcomings. Fundamentally, however, this problem may be one of scoping U.S. interests appropriately for a new nuclear age that collides with the evaporation of uncontested American unipolarity and hegemony as it existed in the immediate post-Cold War period. A relatively weaker United States may be more prone to reach into its nuclear holster, but Washington must understand, too, that, wish as it might, shaping the course of major crises in multiple hemispheres simultaneously may be out of reach. Muddling through while avoiding calamity may be the best option on offer.

The South Asian tinderbox

A little after 3 p.m. on February 14, 2019, outside Lethapora in India-administered Kashmir's Pulwama district, a large convoy of vehicles carrying a couple thousand Indian Central Reserve Policy Force (CRPF) personnel was suddenly and unexpectedly approached by a minivan. The minivan accelerated and rammed one of the buses in the convoy. Instead of running the bus off the road, the minivan exploded, killing forty CRPF personnel, marking the deadliest attack in the disputed territory in some thirty years. The minivan was a vehicle-borne improvised explosive device and was packed with hexogen, or RDX, explosives. In a video that appeared on the Internet shortly afterwards, an 18-year-old from India-administered Kashmir, identifying himself as Aadil Ahmad Dar, said he had joined the Pakistan-based terror group Jaish-e-Muhammed (JeM) and claimed responsibility for the attack. A day later, Indian Prime Minister Narendra Modi pledged that India would retaliate for the attack. "The sacrifices of our brave security personnel shall not go in vain," Modi said in a statement, leaving the precise nature of India's retaliatory plans ambiguous.

This attack was the latest manifestation of a problem that had vexed India for years: Pakistan-based terrorist organizations carrying out suicide attacks against Indian military and paramilitary personnel, either across the border or by recruiting Indian citizens. In the lead-up to the 2019 attack, Pakistan-based militants had carried out significant attacks in January and September 2016 on an Indian Air Force base in Punjab and an Indian Army base in Kashmir, respectively. In July 2015, gunmen who had infiltrated across the international border into India attacked a police station in Punjab. After the September 2016 attacks, Modi authorized, and the Indian government later publicized, a retaliatory "surgical strike" carried out by Indian Special Forces in Kashmir. These forces crossed the Line of Control (LoC) demarcating India and Pakistan-administered territory in the disputed region; while this wasn't the first such operation, the apparent scope and the Indian government's voluntary public disclosure were a notable departure from earlier practice. New Delhi had long exercised what various commentators had deemed "strategic restraint" in the aftermath of attacks by Pakistan-based terror groups, including, most notably, after large-scale attacks on civilians in the Indian metropolis of Mumbai by Lashkar-e-Taiba terrorists, which killed 166 and injured more than 300. India, then under different leadership, did not mobilize for war, despite its suspicions that the attackers were covertly assisted by Pakistan's military and intelligence apparatus. In the aftermath of the Pulwama attack, Modi's pledge to retaliate and his reputation for risk-taking in the aftermath of the 2016 "surgical strike" suggested that New Delhi's traditional restraint might not hold: not only had Modi promised that the death of the forty CRPF personnel wouldn't be "in vain," but he'd pledged retaliation "with interest."[13]

Twelve days after the attack, early on the morning of February 26, Pakistan's military public affairs branch released a statement that Indian military aircraft had entered Pakistani airspace, but retreated after a "timely and effective response from [the] Pakistan Air Force," which scrambled fighters.[14] The Indian side later noted that it had deliberately carried out an airstrike on what it said was a JeM outpost near the village of Balakot in Pakistan's Khyber Pakhtunkhwa. This was the first use of conventional airpower by India against Pakistan since 1971 and the first deliberate airstrike by one nuclear-armed state on the territory of another in history; Modi had demonstrated a substantial departure with past Indian practice and significantly upped the ante. Even if many in Pakistan knew that Indian retaliation would be assured given the exceptionally high casualties in Pulwama, few would have expected India to respond in this manner. In the aftermath of India publicizing the claimed strikes, Pakistan's military indicated that it was convening the country's National Command Authority (NCA), the apex military decision-making body in the country that would allow for consultations on a response. Its military spokesperson, in what was likely a plausibly deniable nuclear signal, told the world in a press conference: "I hope you know what the NCA means and what it constitutes."[15] The next day, the Pakistan Air Force retaliated in what the country's military apparently deemed a proportionate response that was unlikely to invite further escalation: it carried out strikes near to, but not at, Indian military installations.

In the first signs that matters were starting to spiral, however, the Indian Air Force's scramble in response to the Pakistani retaliation – which, no doubt, had been anticipated by New Delhi – resulted in the loss of a MiG-21 Bison in an air-to-air exchange and downing of a Mi-17 military helicopter in a friendly fire incident amid the fog of what was at the time not-quite-war. The pilot of the downed MiG-21 Bison miraculously ejected and survived, landing in Pakistan-controlled territory, where he was captured. The fate of this pilot, Wing Commander Abhinandan Varthaman, quickly became the fulcrum upon which the course of the crisis came to rest.

The Pulwama/Balakot crisis was a remarkable escalation of long-simmering bilateral tensions between India and Pakistan, two nuclear-armed neighbors. It marked the first use of conventional military force by India on undisputed Pakistani territory (as opposed to disputed, Pakistan-administered Kashmir), the first-ever deliberate air-to-ground strikes by one nuclear-armed state on the territory of another, and the first use of military airpower by India against Pakistan since the two had fought a major war in 1971. India's greater tolerance for risk was inherent in the decision to proceed with the strikes and the de-escalation of the crisis – as with an uncomfortable number of crises through the nuclear ages – largely came down to luck. That an Indian Air Force pilot was downed in an air-to-air engagement over Pakistan-held soil, survived his ejection, was not killed afterwards, and proved the key to de-escalation could not have been planned by either side. For India, its behavior in the aftermath of the Pulwama attack served as a "reputational reset," of sorts, communicating to Pakistan that its erstwhile propensity to act with restraint had evaporated.

Despite this, both India and Pakistan, judging by official statements and prevailing public narratives, appeared to observe that the crisis suggested that escalation could be bounded and controlled in crises: both countries employed conventional airpower against the other and lived to tell the tale. Nuclear weapons lingered in the foreground and the background of the crisis. At its original press conference on the Indian Air Force's initial strikes, Pakistan's chief military spokesperson announced that the country's NCA was due to meet soon, adding that India knows "what that means." The NCA is responsible for authorizing use of Pakistan's nuclear weapons. The statement was an unsubtle reminder that the nuclear sword of Damocles was hanging over the two countries and sending a possible catalytic signal to external powers, including the United States, which had previously played a role in de-escalating South Asian crises. India, too, appeared concerned about the possibility of nuclear escalation. The Indian Navy acknowledged that "nuclear *submarines*" (emphasis added) had been deployed during the crisis;[16] at the time of the crisis, India had just one conventionally armed, nuclear-powered submarine and one nuclear-powered, nuclear-armed ballistic missile submarine, INS *Arihant*. The reference to *submarines* in the plural implied that both had been deployed, suggesting a real concern in New Delhi that the crisis could have escalated to significant heights. Modi, while campaigning for India's general elections, which were due later that year, emphasized that he was ready to seek a "night of murder" had the Indian pilot not been returned.[17] Nearly two months after the crisis, Modi, still on the campaign trail, asked a crowd rhetorically whether India had "kept our nuclear bomb for Diwali,"[18] referencing the Hindu festival of lights that regularly involves fireworks demonstrations.

In May 1998, India and Pakistan announced to the world their arrival on the scene as nuclear powers days apart. In a series of underground nuclear explosive tests – first, *Pokhran-II* in India, and then *Chagai-I* and *Chagai-II* in Pakistan – the two South Asian neighbors ended a period of furtively nurturing the technological wherewithal to develop nuclear weapons and removed any doubt about their respective capabilities. For years prior, both countries had maintained what scholars have described as a non-weaponized deterrent posture, whereby both countries had undertaken great efforts to develop their expertise in nuclear science, metallurgy, warhead design, and missile development. The South Asian tests of May 1998 heralded the start of the nuclear age in South Asia and established a new dangerous dyad. While India had carried out a so-called "peaceful nuclear explosion" in 1974, its design at the time was impractical for weaponization and New Delhi made every effort to publicly portray that effort as a scientific endeavor. Pakistan gave little credence to those claims, however, and galvanized its own efforts to seek the bomb.[19]

Since their joint arrival as nuclear powers in 1998, India and Pakistan have seen no shortage of major incidents, including the Pulwama/Balakot crisis. A year after their breakout, in 1999, the two even fought an all-out conventional war – albeit with limits on the use of airpower and other escalatory capabilities. More than twenty-five years on, their nuclear relationship continues to evolve – as do their respective nuclear and non-nuclear military capabilities. The nuclear balance in South Asia is perhaps not as precarious as it once was; both countries, for instance, have built up experience in stewarding their respective nuclear forces, improving force survivability, and establishing workable nuclear command and control procedures and practices. Despite this, the India–Pakistan dyad is far from stable and the prospect of nuclear escalation between the two neighbors remains. In the quarter-century since their 1998 tests, South Asia has seen diversifying and expanding nuclear capabilities, supplementation of nuclear forces with new non-nuclear strategic technologies, and even evolving strategies.

Somewhat like the Soviet Union and the United States in the first two decades of the Cold War, prior to their discovery of strategic arms control, India and Pakistan are seeking advantage over each other – or, at least, aiming to limit the extent of their vulnerability vis-à-vis the other. While their competitive relationship has not manifested in a quantitative arms race in the same vein as the Cold War, both countries have serious concerns about the other's strategic intentions. India faces the prospect of early, asymmetric escalation past the nuclear threshold by Pakistan, which has deployed low-yield nuclear weapons for use on the battlefield, threatening to nullify India's conventional military advantages. India, which has since 2003 professed a nuclear policy of "no first use" (with a carveout for biological and chemical weapons attacks on its forces), has developed an increasingly diverse array of non-nuclear capabilities, including missile defenses and precision, conventional missiles that may be capable of threatening Pakistan's nuclear forces. Both countries have also started to move their nuclear forces to sea; while survivable, second-strike capabilities like nuclear-armed submarines are traditionally thought of as stabilizing, command and control vulnerabilities and technological shortcomings introduce new risks in the South Asian context.[20]

The nuclear balance in South Asia doesn't begin and end with India and Pakistan, of course. Multipolar nuclear dynamics are central in the new nuclear age, and, more so than in the past, factors exogenous to South Asia, such as nuclear competition between the United States and China, stand to influence the region. The nuclear "trilemma," as some analysts in the region have described it, between India, Pakistan, and China had been somewhat stable along the India–China dyad, but that may stand to change as Beijing pursues a build-up in its nuclear forces.[21] In private exchanges, prominent Indian strategic thinkers have begun to express concerns that the country's assured destruction criteria vis-à-vis China could also be affected by Beijing's pursuit of a growing arsenal of increasingly precise conventional missiles paired with more capable missile defense systems. These same concerns once colored Chinese perceptions of how an increasingly capable United States could undermine Beijing's deterrent. Other factors, such as potentially undisclosed offensive cyber capabilities, have further raised Indian anxieties.

The salience of Sino-Indian confrontation has surged as the new nuclear age dawns, too. Beginning in May 2020, the two countries saw the start of what would mark the most serious set of confrontations at their disputed border along the Line of Actual Control (LAC), the demarcation line corresponding to the status quo along their frontier after the 1962 war. The clashes were precipitated by Chinese forces moving across the LAC to obstruct the construction of a road by the Indian side, interpreting this as an unacceptable change to the status quo. After weeks of close proximity, troops on both sides brawled in a brutal physical melee in June 2020, resulting in the death of an unknown number of Chinese soldiers and twenty Indians. Due to their compliance with two prior bilateral agreements concerning the disputed border in 1996 and 2005, troops on both sides did not have firearms available, resulting in this peculiar clash between two nuclear-armed neighbors that was fought with fists, sticks, and, most brutally, barbed wire-laden clubs.[22]

The clashes of June 2020 resulted in a prolonged standoff along the LAC. Although the two sides managed to disengage to some extent that year, Indian and Chinese forces remained on high alert. In New Delhi, the clashes prompted a significant rethink of the country's allocation of national defense assets. India, despite its professed commitments to the vast maritime commons to its south and the broader Indo-Pacific, remained fundamentally tethered to the obligations that came with its key perceived national security threats to the north from both Pakistan and China. The Indian Army was tasked with substantially increasing its strength along the LAC with China. The Army's One Strike Corps, comprising four brigades, a mountain division, and an armored brigade, was assigned to the Chinese border in 2021, away from its traditional focus on the Pakistan border, which had remained consistent since the wars of 1965 and 1971. Prior to this, only the XVII Mountain Strike Corps had been dedicated to the Sino-Indian border. This corps received 10,000 additional troops and new equipment to bolster its capabilities.[23] By the end of 2023, both India and China had substantially buttressed infrastructure – both civilian and military – along the disputed border. Beijing, too, had buttressed its positions along the LAC. Conventional war between India and China remains the most likely catalyst to a position where either country may rationally contemplate nuclear use and the post-2020 status quo along their disputed border raises the prospects of possible escalation in a limited crisis.

For Pakistan, meanwhile, this apparent reallocation of Indian resources and attention has not provided substantial respite from longstanding concerns about New Delhi's conventional and nuclear capabilities. Pakistan's influential military has grown particularly concerned about a more risk-acceptant India. While this is based in real concerns about New Delhi's proclivity to carry out cross-border strikes, as the 2019 Balakot skirmish demonstrated, they also contributed to a broader anxiety about Indian intentions. At 6:43 p.m. on March 9, 2022, just days after Russia invaded Ukraine, the Pakistan Air Force's Air Defense Operation Centre detected an object traveling at supersonic speeds from within India. Seven minutes later, the object crashed within Pakistani territory. Pakistan's Inter-Services Public Relations, its military's communications arm, publicized the incident immediately, noting that Pakistan had tracked a "supersonic flying object, most probably a missile, but it was certainly unarmed."[24] About two days passed without any official Indian response, during which time speculation on social media in both countries ran amok. Finally, the Indian Ministry of Defense issued a statement claiming that a "technical malfunction led to the accidental firing of a missile," which New Delhi considered to have been "deeply regrettable."[25] Though India did not confirm the type of missile that had been launched, the only candidate was New Delhi's sole operationally deployed supersonic cruise missile: the BrahMos. In the past, India has maintained a degree of ambiguity about whether this missile is capable of accommodating nuclear payloads, but Pakistani analysts largely see the system as nuclear-capable.

The incident was a remarkable first between two nuclear-armed states; despite a long list of near misses during the Cold

War, the United States and the Soviet Union never launched missiles accidentally into each other's territories – perhaps partly as a function of their geographic distance. Although wars seldom begin by accident, accidents could prompt serious escalation during more challenging times. Pakistan's relatively sober response to the incident was a function of the fact that background conditions between New Delhi and Islamabad were anodyne in March 2022; had the incident taken place during the February 2019 Balakot clash, the outcome could have been substantially different, with Pakistan's military perhaps psychologically primed to view any violation of its airspace as a significant threat. To this day, despite India claiming a technical malfunction, several Pakistani observers have raised the possibility that the incident was orchestrated by New Delhi to test the limitations of Pakistan's air defenses against non-ballistic missile threats. While this is unsupported by any available evidence, it does speak to the deep sense of insecurity that permeates Pakistan's threat perceptions vis-à-vis New Delhi.[26]

Despite this remarkable, and unprecedented, instance of one nuclear-armed state accidentally firing a missile into another nuclear-armed state, the incident hardly emerged as page one news outside of South Asia. Much of the world's attention remained transfixed on Russia's invasion of Ukraine, which at the time had turned into a debacle, depriving Putin of his likely pre-war goal of swiftly overrunning Kyiv and ousting the Ukrainian government. Overlooking South Asia in the face of new anxieties in Europe amid an intensifying confrontation between the West and Russia may be something of a bellwether for the salience of South Asia as a nuclear flashpoint in the new nuclear age. Crises between India and Pakistan were at the forefront of the second nuclear age, but as global attention now focuses on the return of competitive nuclear dynamics among the major powers, the South Asian tinderbox may receive comparatively less attention. This would be a mistake. India and Pakistan, despite more than twenty-five years of coexistence as nuclear-armed neighbors, are far from having found a sustainable status quo. The world can't afford to focus its attention on South Asia solely when the next major crisis – an inevitability – rolls around.

North Korea's arrival as a nuclear power

On a cloudy night outside an industrial warehouse in the town of Pyongsong, some thirty kilometers northeast of the North Korean capital Pyongyang, a group of Korean People's Army engineers were readying a missile for its first flight test. Kim Jong Un, the North Korean leader, observed the preparations closely over a number of hours. At around 3 a.m. that night, the missile roared into the sky as Kim watched. This missile, known as the Hwasong-15, was at the time the largest ballistic missile North Korea had ever flight-tested. If it worked, it would demonstrate that North Korea had the ability to range the entirety of the continental United States with a nuclear warhead. To avoid overflying Japan, the missile flew on a deliberately steep trajectory into the Pacific Ocean; its two stages worked as intended, fully burning out the available fuel and oxidizer. The next day, Kim declared North Korea's nuclear deterrent "complete" – punctuating what had been a years-long search for sufficient nuclear deterrence that began with his grandfather in the 1990s.

Kim's statement was an observation about the qualitative requirements of nuclear deterrence as North Korea appeared to perceive them. For years, North Korea's pursuit of nuclear weapons had been brushed off as unserious – and even laughed off. After North Korea's fourth nuclear test in January 2016, the *New Yorker* magazine taunted Kim Jong Un by depicting him on its cover as a toddler playing with missiles.[27] North Korea's missile development efforts were similarly mocked on

U.S. late night comedy talk shows. The tendency to under-rate Pyongyang's competency, seriousness, and capability was somewhat chronic in U.S. and broader popular culture: after all, give North Korea's inherent strangeness as a polity and society, the idea of it successfully acquiring nuclear arms seemed largely unthinkable to very many people. Not everyone dismissed North Korea, however: U.S. intelligence agencies, in particular, tracked Pyongyang's nuclear and missile development efforts closely and with concern. Over time, North Korea's push for effective deterrence led to an inexorable pursuit of credibly demonstrated capabilities. For a country that had once been derided by U.S. President Richard Nixon as a "fourth-rate pipsqueak," it seemed that nothing less than the demonstration of undeniably awesome capability would help it sink in for the United States that North Korea had arrived as a nuclear power.[28] And so North Korea launched missiles – and detonated nuclear weapons. To date, it remains the only country to have tested nuclear weapons in the twenty-first century, having carried out six underground nuclear tests. Its sixth test, a little more than two months prior to Kim's observation of the Hwasong-15's maiden flight, was claimed as a fully staged thermonuclear device, yielding some two hundred kilotons of explosive force – likely the largest nuclear explosion on Earth since a May 1992 underground test by China.

Perhaps no nonproliferation problem permeated the second nuclear age quite like North Korea did: Kim Il Sung's initial efforts reprocessing spent nuclear fuel for weapons-useable plutonium were picked up by U.S. intelligence shortly after the collapse of the Soviet Union, and Pyongyang repeatedly negotiated with the United States and its allies over nearly thirty years to address concerns over its nuclear capabilities. As this new nuclear age dawns, however, it is apparent that North Korea is no longer appropriately taxonomized as a non-proliferation problem; it is, rather, a nuclear deterrence and disarmament problem. Since that fateful November night in

2017, North Korea tried its hand at diplomacy with the United States one more time, seeking concessions amid its development of greater nuclear capability, which it hoped would have conferred a certain degree of leverage. That diplomatic process culminated in two historic leader-level summit meetings between President Trump and Kim – first in Singapore and then in Hanoi, Vietnam. Trump, an unconventional American president by any measure, engaged North Korea without any particular emphasis on nonproliferation outcomes personally. By the time the two leaders met for their second summit in Hanoi, Vietnam, Kim was hoping for a capacious package of relief from international sanctions in exchange for relinquishing part of his fissile material production complex. The United States rejected North Korea's request outright, prompting an angry, disappointed, and humiliated Kim to head home and reevaluate his approach.[29] The two leaders met one more time in person informally at the inter-Korean Demilitarized Zone in June 2019, and their envoys convened in October that same year to see if further progress could be made. But Kim had largely made up his mind about what had to come next in the weeks immediately following the diplomatic implosion in Hanoi.

After a brief pause in missile launches during the diplomatic engagement with Washington, Kim turned back to testing in May 2019. At the end of 2019, he voiced his aspiration to seek a "new way" going forward,[30] obliquely implying that whatever this path entailed would have little to do with engaging with the United States. In January 2020, an already insular North Korea indicated that it would take its isolation further, declaring news of an unknown novel coronavirus reported in China as a potential threat to its "national survival" given its anemic national healthcare capabilities.[31] North Korea has reacted with similar fervor to other public health threats, including Ebola, avian influenza, and SARS. The country locked down and Kim continued to develop his capabilities further, carrying out regular missile testing and exercises throughout 2020.

In January 2021, North Korea's ruling Workers' Party of Korea (WPK) held a party congress, the apex political event on the country's political calendar. Party congresses had been a mainstay during Kim's grandfather Kim Il Sung's time, but had fallen into disfavor under Kim Jong Il, his father, who cared little for the institutionalized practices of yore. Kim Jong Un, ever one to model himself after his grandfather, resumed the practice in 2016 with the Seventh Party Congress. The Eighth Party Congress in January 2021 convened a little less than two weeks before the United States was about to inaugurate a new president. A few days into the Party Congress, Kim delivered an ambitious report outlining the many successes of the country's nuclear weapons development efforts under the five-year period that had just elapsed since the last party congress and, most importantly, outlined an ambitious set of quantitative growth and qualitative improvement objectives for the country's nuclear forces. Kim's report, which was paraphrased by state media and promptly translated into English, was among the most detailed documents on nuclear matters ever delivered by a North Korean leader – with no comparable analog in his by then nine years in power. Despite his detailed survey of military and nuclear modernization matters, Kim offered no indication of interest in diplomatic negotiations with the United States.

Kim outlined a long wish list of military and nuclear modernization goals, showcasing his seemingly limitless ambition to place North Korea among the ranks of the world's most capable nuclear powers. Kim called for better missiles, longer-range missiles, hypersonic missiles, new nuclear warheads, and military reconnaissance satellites. He also called for investments in naval nuclear propulsion technology and the development of new uncrewed aerial vehicles. Most importantly, perhaps, at the Eighth Party Congress, for the first time, Kim called for the development of "tactical nuclear weapons." For years, North Korea had euphemistically referenced its own nuclear weapons by the moniker "strategic weapon," conveying a sense that any nuclear use would have strategic effects. Kim now appeared to believe that his nuclear weapons needed to be "smaller and lighter for more tactical uses."[32]

From a strategic perspective, this was unsurprising and made good sense for a country with North Korea's predicament. North Korea isn't the first nuclear weapons possessor to have faced the problem of deterring a conventionally superior, territorially contiguous adversary. Like NATO during the 1960s facing overwhelming Soviet armor and conventional forces and, much later, Pakistan facing a conventionally dominant India, offsetting conventional weakness with nuclear weapons means the adoption of a diverse range of options, including lower-yield nuclear weapons for use against military targets at short ranges. Kim did not explain what he considered to be a "tactical" nuclear weapon – indeed, there is no universal definition of such a capability – but a range of evidence in the aftermath of his turn toward lower-yield weapons in 2021 indicated that North Korea viewed range, reduced explosive yield, and contingent delegative command and control arrangements as important.[33] Tactical nuclear weapons had a long history on the Korean Peninsula during the Cold War, albeit on the southern side of the Demilitarized Zone that separates the two Koreas. Between 1958 and 1991, the United States deployed a wide variety of such systems on South Korean soil. Indeed, the December 1991 departure of the last U.S. tactical nuclear weapon from South Korea,[34] in part, created the conditions for Seoul and Pyongyang to agree in January 1992 to a mutually endorsed goal of "denuclearization of the Korean Peninsula." Despite this change in practice, after December 1991 North Korea never acknowledged or accepted that U.S. nuclear weapons had left the Korean Peninsula and, to make the case for its own nuclear weapons, would often opportunistically allude to the possibility that such weapons remained deployed.

As the Biden administration entered office in January 2021, North Korea showed little interest in resuming negotiations with the United States and instead pressed forward with the implementation of the modernization plan Kim had called for. Over the course of the next few years, North Korea slowly but surely began to check off boxes from Kim's Eighth Party Congress wish list. To start with, Pyongyang began to emphasize its efforts to render its nuclear forces more survivable to potential disarming preemptive strikes by the United States and South Korea – a key strategic priority. As discussed earlier in this book, because stable deterrence depends on the ability of a state to assure its adversaries that it will be able to maintain some survivable retaliatory capability with which to inflict unacceptable damage, this becomes a logical priority, and especially so for a state with a smaller force like North Korea. Pyongyang, lacking the knowledge and resources to seek something like a continuously deployed nuclear-propelled, nuclear-armed submarine at sea at all times, instead has to seek survivability through other means. So Kim began showing off a range of capabilities that would complicate military planning for his adversaries. He launched nuclear-capable missiles from rail cars, from submerged pontoons in inland lakes, from fixed silos, from all-terrain road-mobile transporter-erector-launchers, and from diesel-propelled submarines. Cumulatively, these diverse basing modes would create a nightmare for any U.S. or South Korean military planners seeking to comprehensively disarm North Korea of its nuclear forces in a conflict. As a result, their leaders would have to contend with the possibility, in a war, that choosing to escalate would entail the certain acceptance of a high level of risk that a North Korean nuclear warhead would arrive on target in either U.S. or South Korean territory.

In May 2022, South Korea inaugurated a new conservative president, Yoon Suk Yeol, who had campaigned on taking a hard line against Pyongyang. Yoon sharply criticized his predecessor Moon Jae-in's interest in diplomacy and engagement with Pyongyang, and instead suggested that South Korea would pursue a strategy of "peace through strength," borrowing former U.S. President Reagan's turn of phrase.[35] In practice, this meant repeatedly emphasizing Seoul's growing capability to hunt North Korea's nuclear forces and its leadership. Under a previous conservative government, Seoul had started to develop a plan to kill North Korea's leadership in the course of a war – in retaliation for any nuclear use.[36] This "decapitation" approach has a long history in military strategy, but is particularly dangerous in a nuclear context. During the Cold War, for instance, U.S. and Soviet strategists quickly learned the value of at least *appearing* in a war to not threaten the other side's central nervous system, or leadership. Doing so – or being perceived as seeking to do so – may deprive the adversary of any incentive to practice restraint in the prosecution of a war. In other wars, leadership targeting is a very good way to have what might otherwise be a limited conventional skirmish turn into an unlimited nuclear war. North Korea takes this prospect particularly seriously; Kim's father, Kim Jong Il, watched in horror in 2003 as the United States tried – and failed – to kill Iraqi leader Saddam Hussein in a decapitation strike attempt at the outset of its invasion of Iraq that year.[37]

Even though South Korea's strategy of holding leadership at risk, as communicated, was one of *reprisal* (i.e., threatening North Korea's leadership with punishment in the event of nuclear weapons use in a crisis), Kim could hardly take this assurance at face value. Especially paired with Seoul's parallel ambitions to preempt his nuclear forces, Kim, on some level, had to take the possibility of *preemptive decapitation* seriously. As a result, North Korea turned again, as it did with tactical nuclear weapons, to a logical – if dangerous – solution. In 2022, its Supreme People's Assembly, the country's notional parliament, updated a 2013 law codifying various doctrinal measures on nuclear weapons matters. In this law, Pyongyang for the first time communicated that it had formally adopted what nuclear strategists term a fail-deadly command and control posture. The law said, in no uncertain terms, that should the country's nuclear command and control systems or leadership suffer attacks, it would respond by "automatically and immediately" launching nuclear attacks. As explained earlier in this book, nuclear deterrence rests on the conveyance of a real sense of risk: for Pyongyang, it made good sense to communicate to its adversaries that taking out the country's nuclear central nervous system would not be a "get-out-of-nuclear-war-free" card. It would be quite the opposite.

The year 2022 thus marked a serious spike in tensions between the two Koreas as the Yoon administration settled into office and increased the visibility of South Korea's own preparations to deal with Pyongyang. That year, North Korea launched more missiles in the course of exercises and tests than it had in any previous year by more than a factor of three. By the end of 2022, the old practice of journalists reflexively describing North Korean missile launches as "tests" was no longer suitable; instead, most launches in the country were exercises. North Korea, simply put, was ensuring that its military forces were nimble and operationally ready in case of a major war, including a nuclear war. As 2023 dawned, Kim identified an important modernization priority for the year ahead – one that he had alluded to at the WPK's Eighth Party Congress a little less than two years earlier. He called for the development of "another ICBM system, whose main mission is quick nuclear counterstrike."[38] Kim was alluding to a solid-propellant ICBM. This would confer substantial strategic advantages to North Korea compared to the liquid-propellant ICBMs he had already shown off in 2017. Unlike their liquid-propellant counterparts, which would likely need to be fueled and prepared immediately prior to launch, solid-propellant missiles have their fuel cast into the missile's airframe at the time of manufacture. In a crisis, this would mean that these ICBMs would be available for rapid use, depriving the U.S. and South Korean militaries of crucial time that could be used to preemptively destroy them. He also ordered an "exponential" expansion of the country's nuclear stockpile, an aspiration meant to be taken seriously, if not literally.

On April 13, 2023, two days before his grandfather Kim Il Sung's birthday, Kim Jong Un oversaw the first flight-test of the Hwasong-18, North Korea's first solid-fuel ICBM. Remarkably, despite North Korea never having tested or fielded a large-diameter, multistage solid-propellant missile before, the three-stage Hwasong-18 appeared to perform to spec, giving North Korea's strategic forces a substantial boon. Kim tested the missile twice again that year, in July and December. The third test, in December, was described by North Korean state media as a "launching drill," indicating that this missile had quickly moved from a developmental system to one that probably had reached something resembling an initial operational capability. This was the first indication from North Korea that *any* of its ICBM systems had been operationally deployed; an analogous indication was never offered for its older liquid-propellant systems, or the larger Hwasong-17 ICBM. Based on the observed characteristics of the Hwasong-18 across its three flight-tests in 2023, the missile appeared to be capable of ranging the entirety of the continental United States with a nuclear warhead. Kim expressed great satisfaction with the successful realization of this capability; his modernization plans were proceeding according to plan.

Against the backdrop of these developments following the collapse of the 2019 Hanoi Summit between Trump and Kim, Pyongyang had started to cultivate closer ties with China, its traditional partner, and with Russia. Though North Korea's relationship with China is often presented as a stalwart alliance, much mistrust exists between Beijing and Pyongyang. North Korea bristles at its unavoidable economic dependency on China. Beginning in 2022, Pyongyang appeared to perceive an immense strategic opportunity as Russia's invasion of Ukraine prompted a dramatic schism between Moscow and the West. Starting in late 2019, both Russia and China had grown supportive of an adjustment in international sanctions on North Korea, but Russia's invasion of Ukraine created the conditions to thrust Moscow and Pyongyang closer together than they had been since the Cold War. In July 2023, Vladimir Putin dispatched his defense minister, Sergei Shoigu, to North Korea to attend the country's commemoration of the seventi-eth anniversary of the Korean War Armistice.[39] Shoigu, along with Li Hongzhong, a member of the Politburo of the Chinese Communist Party, attended a military parade to commemo-rate the occasion.[40] The presence of these senior Russian and Chinese figures in North Korea was especially notable at this time, as the country had barely opened up after its self-imposed Covid lockdown. What was especially notable, however, was that on the day of the commemorative parade, Kim himself took Shoigu to a defense exposition featuring the full array of advanced missile and other military capabilities that North Korea had been developing. In a set of photos released by North Korean state media, Shoigu was seen closely observing the North Korean wares, with Kim by his side. Shoigu was also flanked by Alexei Krivoruchko, a Russian official involved in weapons acquisition. This was hardly a subtle signal: the Russians had come to Pyongyang to go shopping – and they did not care who knew.

Shoigu's visit was the herald of a real strategic shift in North Korea's relationship with Russia. In September 2023, Kim finally traveled overseas for the first time since the country had locked down in early 2020. He went to the Russian far east to meet Putin and gave the Russian president his full sup-port in what he called the "sacred fight" against the West.

Kim further extended his "support for all the measures taken by the Russian government" in the course of the war against Ukraine. Putin, for his part, indicated his willingness to assist North Korea with the construction of satellites. Kim was also taken to visit a factory involved in the production of fighters for the Russian Air Force, indicating his interest in potentially importing Russian hardware. The summit between the two leaders largely appeared to crystallize what was North Korea's greatest geopolitical opportunity in the post-Cold War era. Putin's full-scale embrace of Kim – what appeared to be, by all accounts, the launch of a strategic partnership – was as great of a boon for North Korea as the collapse of the Soviet Union had once been a tragedy. The North Korean leader stood to benefit tremendously from this cooperation, gaining the support of a powerful patron with a veto at the United Nations Security Council, a land border over which to conduct unrestricted trade, and a rich menu of sophisticated technologies and raw materials with important defense applications. Russia, too, benefited in the short term. By December 2023, North Korean artillery, mortars, and short-range ballistic missiles had started seeing use against Ukrainian cities and other targets. By February 2023, the U.S. Department of State assessed that more than 10,000 munitions containers had arrived in Russia from North Korea.[41] According to the Ukrainian government, around 1.5 million artillery pieces were in Russia by March 2024[42] and approximately fifty North Korean short-range ballistic missiles had been launched against Ukraine.[43] These marked the first-ever uses of North Korean ballistic missiles in war. By early 2024, North Korea's mass production capabilities for its new generation of solid-propellant, short-range ballistic missiles were almost exclusively devoted to meeting Russian orders for delivery.[44] During the 2024 springtime U.S.–South Korea military exercises – a time when North Korea would normally be expected to carry out missile launches of its own – Pyongyang remained relatively restrained and carried out demonstrations involving its conventional military forces, including tanks, artillery units, and special forces. Earlier in 2024, Kim oversaw a spate of cruise missile tests. The lack of ballistic missile testing during this period was likely a function of the depleted domestic inventory of missiles in North Korea due to the massive exports to Russia.

Through its history, North Korea has been a state that has endured periods of great geopolitical mayhem and flux, often seeking to gain advantage as the major powers jostle for influence in its region. The country was founded in the aftermath of the Second World War and the circumstances resulting on the Korean Peninsula after Japan's surrender; Kim Jong Un's grandfather was hand-picked by Josef Stalin and Lavrentiy Beria.[45] Later, North Korea would maneuver during the Sino-Soviet split to seek benefit from both Moscow and Beijing while maintaining a healthy degree of skepticism toward both major powers. The collapse of the Soviet Union, the third great period of geopolitical flux, appeared to motivate, in part, early research and development work in the country on nuclear weapons – likely to hedge against the loss of what had been a significant patron. At the dawn of the new nuclear age, amid what may be the fourth great period of geopolitical flux, North Korea has not only emerged as a capable nuclear power in its own right, but has found an opportunity that may have been unimaginable for Kim Jong Un as late as 2019. Moscow's broader schism with the West has also given Kim a powerful opportunity to lessen his dependence on Beijing, where the Russia–North Korea rapprochement likely has not been warmly received. During their first meeting in March 2018, Chinese President Xi Jinping impressed on Kim two important principles: that "high-level exchanges" would have to play a "guiding role" in their relationship, and that "strategic communication" should be a priority.[46] That Kim's first visit after his country's pandemic lockdown was to the Russian far east was unlikely to be reassuring for China, which has traditionally preferred to maintain its position as Pyongyang's preferred great power patron.

Despite this grim trajectory and rapid development of capability, the key states seeking to manage the nuclear threat from North Korea remain tethered to a moribund and intractable policy objective of "denuclearization." This continues to be the basis of U.S., South Korean, Japanese, and European policy toward the Korean Peninsula – even if few officials working on these issues would privately admit to believing that there is a real possibility over any reasonable time frame of Pyongyang relinquishing its nuclear capability. Fundamentally, North Korea has fully arrived as a nuclear-armed state; it is no longer treatable as the proliferation problem that it once was. This is a country armed with thermonuclear weapons and ICBMs, and a seemingly endless appetite for greater capabilities. The Korean Peninsula presents a particularly concerning flashpoint in the new nuclear age: North Korea's offensively oriented nuclear forces and its low threshold for resorting to the use of nuclear weapons present a significant risk for escalation in a range of possible future crises. The most meaningful way to begin addressing these risks would be for the states seeking to negotiate with Pyongyang to place the prevention of nuclear war as their first-order interest, with denuclearization a more distant goal.

The looming specter of an Iranian bomb

Nine states possess nuclear weapons at the dawn of this new nuclear age, but the prospect of a tenth may loom large. Since 2018, the prospect of an Iranian nuclear weapon capability has risen significantly. That year, the United States, under President Trump, announced that it would withdraw from the Joint Comprehensive Plan of Action (JCPOA), a meticulously negotiated multilateral agreement designed to constrain the possibility that Tehran could sprint to the bomb. The JCPOA, in form and function, was unprecedented in the history of nuclear nonproliferation. Over more than 150 pages, the document described a wide range of technical measures that, cumulatively, were designed to ensure that Tehran would remain at least one year away from amassing sufficient weapons-grade nuclear material for use in a bomb. These measures were to be verified with a range of intrusive means. Trump – and, by extension, many U.S. Republicans – had long lambasted the deal, which had been negotiated by his predecessor, Barack Obama. For President Obama, the JCPOA was a political firecracker; it took the expenditure of substantial political capital to bring a skeptical Congress – including more than a few Democrats – around to tolerating, if not embracing, the deal.

The JCPOA notably was not solely the result of negotiations between the United States and Iran, but was the outcome of years of talks between the so-called P5+1, which included the five permanent members of the United Nations Security Council (the United States, Russia, China, France, and the United Kingdom), and Germany.[47] In July 2015, the six countries, the European Union, and Iran announced that they had arrived at a mutually acceptable set of compromises in the form of the JCPOA. In broad strokes, the agreement worked by offering Iran relief from a range of unilateral and international economic sanctions in exchange for its compliance with the technical parameters outlined in the agreement. Tehran preserved important face-saving priorities in the course of the negotiations, including a continued ability to enrich uranium under monitoring for use in its peaceful nuclear energy ambitions.

As it was architected, the JCPOA included the following sets of concessions for Iran. Tehran agreed to reduce its stockpiles of uranium by 98 percent from pre-deal levels and agreed to hold no more than 300 kilograms of low-enriched uranium (LEU). The LEU it could hold would be verifiably enriched to levels no greater than 3.67 percent uranium-235, keeping Tehran away from the higher enrichment levels, including high-assay LEU, that could speed up a potential sprint to a bomb. While retaining a so-called "right to enrich" that was important to the Iranian government politically, Tehran further agreed to restrict the sophistication of its enrichment activities by agreeing only to use its comparatively less efficient first-generation IR-1 gas centrifuges. It further agreed to reduce the total count of centrifuges it operated across its enrichment facilities, and also, importantly, to cease all enrichment activity at the underground Fordow site where a little more than 1,000 centrifuges would remain for research purposes only. In addition, the agreement ensured that an Iranian heavy water reactor under construction at Arak would undergo a significant redesign to render it unsuitable for the production of plutonium, an alternative path to a potential nuclear weapon. The agreement also prohibited any work on heavy water reactors in Iran for fifteen years, and all spent fuel produced at the redesigned reactor was destined to be shipped out of the country, further limiting proliferation potential. Finally, all of these measures were underwritten by a set of unprecedently intrusive and bespoke verification and monitoring measures that were to be overseen by the International Atomic Energy Agency. IAEA inspectors were to continuously monitor all Iranian declared facilities, account for all nuclear materials in the country, and have access to address potential disputes with Iran as needed. In exchange for the above measures, Iran was assured that it would see a "comprehensive lifting" of all United Nations Security Council sanctions, multilateral and national sanctions "related to [its] nuclear programme" and on its "access in areas of trade, technology, finance, and energy." The intention behind these relief measures was to broadly normalize Tehran's access to the global economy.[48]

On May 8, 2018, Trump announced that the United States was withdrawing from the JCPOA, saying that "the heart of the Iran deal was a giant fiction: that a murderous regime desired only a peaceful nuclear energy program."[49] Trump also cited a trove of documents sourced from Iran, procured by Israeli intelligence, that showed evidence of Tehran's prior work on nuclear weapons. These documents, while new, were not revolutionary. The entire reason the JCPOA negotiations took place in the first place was precisely due to evidence and concerns, dating back to the early 2000s, that Tehran may seek to build a nuclear weapon. At the time of Trump's speech, neither the United States' intelligence community nor the IAEA had deemed Iran to be noncompliant with the terms of the deal. The Trump administration's alternative to the JCPOA was designed from the start to be unacceptable to the Iranians, demanding, effectively, Tehran's total capitulation. Mike Pompeo, then the U.S. secretary of state, spoke days later at the Heritage Foundation, a conservative think-tank in Washington, and outlined plans for a "coming pressure campaign on the Iranian regime."[50] This included a list of twelve demands – simply asserted against Tehran by the United States with no specific offer of benefits in particular. The list included everything from a complete confession from Tehran concerning its past work into nuclear weapons research and development, to a total end to its support for terrorist organizations in the Middle East, to the complete cessation of missile sales to and missile development efforts, and a willingness to cease all uranium enrichment. While many of these demands concerned real, malign Iranian activities that were detrimental to peace and security in the Middle East, the JCPOA negotiations had already demonstrated that compartmentalizing the nuclear file allowed for progress. Instead, the Trump administration's basic position toward Tehran was tantamount to saying that, in order to solve anything, Tehran must first give up everything. Many of the technical demands on the nonproliferation side too – such as the demand for a cessation to all enrichment activities in the country – had long been identified as nonstarters for the Iranians. Later that year, Pompeo reiterated this broad strategy of pressure.[51]

The Trump administration's decision to cast aside the JCPOA and turn toward coercion and pressure did not immediately implode the deal. The remaining members of the so-called P5+1 reiterated their support to see through its implementation, even if the economic benefits anticipated by Iran would be severely limited given the United States' withdrawal. After one year, cracks finally began to appear in what remained of the JCPOA. In May 2019, Iran began a slow but steady process of gradually – and deliberately – violating the negotiated technical limitations on its nuclear program that had been articulated in the JCPOA. After twelve months of giving the remaining P5+1 countries a chance to salvage the agreement, Tehran saw effectively no upside to complying with the deal's limitations. In the meantime, the United States had announced additional sanctions against Iran, seeking to intensify its coercive pressure. This sparked a pressure-for-pressure cycle, in effect, whereby Iranian violations of the technical limitations stipulated in the JCPOA – an agreement first abandoned by the United States – led to reciprocal coercive steps by the United States.

As tends to be the case with a build-up of pressure in any closed system, the cycle quickly intensified. Outside the nuclear file, Iran's Islamic Revolutionary Guard Corps (IRGC) began intensifying its support for its regional proxies – the so-called "axis of resistance." On December 27, 2019, an air base near the Iraqi city of Kirkuk that hosted both Iraqi and U.S. troops was struck by rockets launched by members of the Iran-aligned Kataib Hezbollah militia, killing one U.S. civilian contractor.[52] This was the proximal spark for a series of further escalations, including U.S. air strikes against Iran-aligned groups in Iraq and Syria, that culminated in a January 3, 2020, targeted killing of Major General Qasem Soleimani, commander of the IRGC's Quds Force. Soleimani, widely considered at the time to be

among the most influential men in Iran, was a near mytho-
logical figure within the IRGC, and particularly revered by
Iranian hardliners who already viewed the Trump administration as uncompromisingly hostile toward Tehran. Following
Soleimani's death, Iranian leaders vowed to retaliate. Within
less than a week, Iran had launched an unprecedentedly
intense set of ballistic missile strikes against two bases hosting
U.S. forces in Iraq, marking the first direct use of conventional
military force by Tehran against U.S. forces since the Cold
War. Though the missiles used were remarkably precise,[53]
miraculously, no U.S. forces were killed. The Pentagon, however, later noted that 110 U.S. troops had sustained traumatic
brain injuries during the attack.[54] Anticipating possible further
escalation in turn, Iran heightened its military readiness, in the
course of which, Iranian air defense operators mistakenly shot
down a departing Ukrainian civilian airliner leaving Tehran,
killing all 176 crew and passengers.[55] Despite the potential for
significantly greater escalation, the crisis petered out – though
hostility between the Trump administration and the Iranian
government would persist and intensify.

Iranian behavior did not improve as a result of increased
U.S. pressure. In fact, two days after Soleimani's assassination, Iran announced that it would "end its final limitations in
the nuclear deal," specifying that this meant "limitation in the
number of centrifuges." The statement, the result of a National
Security Council meeting in Tehran, further clarified that
"Iran's nuclear program will have no limitations in production
including enrichment capacity and percentage and number
of enriched uranium and research and expansion." By March
that year, the IAEA reported that Iran had tripled its stockpile
of low enriched uranium. This began to raise the urgency of
potential Iranian breakout; while this low enriched uranium
would not itself be suitable for use in a nuclear weapon, it
would begin to compress the time required for further enrichment that would indeed yield weapons-useable material. The

2015 deal had been designed to provide enough of a verifiable buffer against Iran breaking through the stipulated limits that even this tripling of the stockpile did not immediately represent an immediate crisis, but Tehran's "breakout" time was slowly becoming more compressed. Moreover, in contrast to some of the steps Iran had taken before the Soleimani assassination, but after its 2019 decision to deliberately begin violating the JCPOA, Iran was now taking more dangerous – and less easily reversible – steps. Tehran had started by exceeding the limits on stockpiling heavy water and enriched uranium, but after the Soleimani killing the country slowly also moved toward beginning to enrich using more advanced centrifuges that had been restricted under the JCPOA, as well as initiating enrichment at the underground Fordow facility. Despite these steps, Iran had not made a political decision to seek nuclear weapons, but insisted that these activities were limited to its civil nuclear program.

Through the remainder of Trump's first term in office, Iran continued to push toward the bomb. Israel, long hostile to the JCPOA and supportive of the Trump administration's pressure campaign against Tehran, took matters into its own hands to try and stymie a possible sprint to the bomb by Tehran. On November 27, 2020, Mohsen Fakhrizadeh, then the top technical figure on nuclear science in Iran, was killed in an ambush by what was later reported to have been a remotely operated autonomous gun.[56] Fakhrizadeh had played a continuing role of prominence in civil nuclear activities in Iran, but was also suspected to have overseen the country's prior work on nuclear weapons in the early 2000s under what was known as the AMAD program. A month after the assassination, the Iranian *Majlis*, the country's legislature, gave its imprimatur to a law that institutionalized a push toward greater nuclear capabilities, including work on uranium metallurgy that could further reduce the time necessary for the country to assemble a nuclear weapon.[57] This law probably was not a direct response to Fakhrizadeh's death, given the evidence of preparatory work dating back to the summer, but the killing broadly shaped Tehran's strategic communications around the law. Though parliamentary imprimatur is not a necessity for policy change in the Iranian system, the law was approved by the country's powerful Guardian Council. Like other Iranian steps since the United States' withdrawal from the JCPOA, the law predicated many of the steps on the contingency that the sanctions relief that had been promised under the 2015 agreement would not be forthcoming.

Critically, both Fakhrizadeh's killing and the passage of the law, took place at the time of the presidential transition in the United States. Then-president-elect Joe Biden had been clear on the campaign trail that he would support a return to the JCPOA, describing the move by Trump to withdraw from the agreement variously as a "dangerous failure." and a "self-inflicted disaster."[58] The new president, however, was in no rush to negotiate following his inauguration, inheriting a country still mired by the economic and human costs of the Covid-19 pandemic and the many sources of bureaucratic malaise left over within the executive branch by the Trump administration. The Iran file was part of a long list of broader foreign policy priorities, chief of which included a broader reassurance tour for allies and partners in Europe, Asia, and the Middle East. When the administration did begin to talk about the issue with Iran, the rest of the P5+1, and the world at large, the formula proposed was one of "compliance for compliance": the United States would itself return to compliance with the agreement, provided that Iran did the same. While this was broadly positive for a possible return to the agreement in early 2021, it introduced the problem of sequencing. The Iranians, for their part, appeared to insist – not unreasonably – that given that Washington had taken the step initially to leave the agreement in 2018, it should be the first side to demonstrate good faith by offering Tehran economic concessions. Javad Zarif, the

Iranian foreign minister who was central to the negotiations for the JCPOA under the Obama administration, outlined this position as late as April 2022 – when little progress had been made: the "U.S. unconditionally and effectively lift all sanctions imposed, re-imposed, or re-labelled by Trump. We will then immediately reverse all remedial activities."[59] What Biden did *not* do was take any unilateral action to bring the United States back into the JCPOA, which was not a treaty requiring the advice and consent of the U.S. Senate, but a political commitment that had been unilaterally abandoned. By contrast, the new administration did use the president's pen to restore U.S. participation in the 2015 Paris climate accord hours after his inauguration.[60]

Several factors appeared to influence the administration's broader approach toward Iran. First, by early 2021, there were not only concerns about the steps that Iran had taken to break the limitations placed on it under the JCPOA, but also about the suitability of returning to that agreement given the fast-approaching expirations on certain key capabilities. Many – but not all – of the restrictions on Iran's program negotiated back in 2015 had so-called sunset dates, with several key milestones: in October 2023, July 2024, January 2026, January 2031, and January 2036. The longest sunset concerned the IAEA's monitoring of Iran's uranium mining and milling activity and would have run through January 2041. Given the more proximal sunsets, many Democrats believed that a "compliance-for-compliance" return to the JCPOA may not be workable. While the JCPOA certainly had greater support among the Democratic Party, it was far from universally supported across the party. Domestic political concerns also shaped the early environment in which the Biden administration framed its Iran policy. These factors appeared to weigh strongly against any decisive or unilateral U.S. action; instead, after framing the broader compliance-for-compliance formula, the administration slowly began to work toward negotiations with Tehran. Complicating matters, Iran held a presidential election in June 2021, which brought Ebrahim Raisi to power. Raisi, unlike Rouhani, who had overseen the conclusion of the JCPOA negotiations and the implementation of the agreement, was generally more skeptical about it, and was seen as more sympathetic to the hardliners who opposed diplomacy with Washington.[61] Despite Raisi's skepticism, however, Supreme Leader Ayatollah Ali Khamenei, the ultimate political authority on these matters, broadly supported a return to negotiations on restoring the agreement.

After Raisi's takeover, precarious negotiations continued – as did Iranian measures to increase pressure on the United States and the rest of the P5+1. In July 2021, the IAEA confirmed that Iran had started to produce uranium metal enriched up to 20 percent. By August that year, the Iranians had started enriching some uranium to 60 percent levels – a major escalation. The amount of separative work – the process of enriching uranium and separating the highly fissile, weapons-useable uranium-235 isotope from the uranium-238 isotope – required to go from 60 percent to weapons-grade is marginal compared to the separative work required to go from the 3.67 percent-levels agreed in the JCPOA to 20 percent. No other non-nuclear weapon state enriched uranium to these levels. By late-2021, the IAEA's broader fidelity concerning Iran's nuclear activities had started to suffer as well – a result of the deal's fraying as Tehran continued its deliberate transgressions of the negotiated thresholds. Fundamentally, Western officials in Washington, Paris, and Berlin appeared to hold the view that Iran, though content to negotiate after Raisi's inauguration, was not fundamentally seeking a return to the JCPOA.[62] On the one hand, having witnessed the capriciousness with which political agreements with the United States can be swiftly demolished, Tehran could hardly count on negotiating with yet another Democratic administration only to have a potential Republican successor pull the rug out once more. This would not have been highly speculative for the Iranians, either: in March 2022, forty-nine Republican senators publicly told the Biden administration that any restored JCPOA would not see their support.[63] Other evidence for this view was the addition of what Robert Malley, the special envoy for Iran under the Biden administration, described as "extraneous" demands by the Iranians every time the P5+1 and Tehran came close to a deal.[64]

What lies ahead then for Iran? For years, the country's approach to its civil nuclear program has been seen as an archetypical case of what might be termed nuclear hedging.[65] This was acknowledged well before the JCPOA as well. In 2012, the U.S. Director of National Intelligence James Clapper observed that "Iran is keeping open the option to develop nuclear weapons, in part by developing various nuclear capabilities that better position it to produce such weapons, should it choose to do so."[66] As of 2024, Iran stands out for being the sole NPT non-nuclear weapons state to possess a significant stockpile of uranium enriched to 60 percent levels. According to U.S. intelligence assessments, by February 2023, Iran's effective breakout time had dropped to twelve days: it could, if a political decision were taken, amass sufficient weapons-grade fissile material for a single device in that amount of time.[67] Around the same time, the director-general of the IAEA, Rafael Mariano Grossi, told European lawmakers that the Iranians had "amassed enough nuclear material for several nuclear weapons, not one at this point."[68] Tehran's rapidly expanding nuclear program after May 2019 has been part of a diplomatic strategy of pressure, but may also be designed to credibly lay the groundwork for a form of non-weaponized deterrence of the sort that Indian and Pakistani leaders appeared to have pursued prior to their 1998 nuclear tests. In July 2024, U.S. intelligence assessments evolved, noting that Iran had started to undertake work that "could shrink the knowledge gap Tehran faces in mastering the ability to build a weapon."[69] Given that Iran's regional adversaries – and the United States – understand its broader proximity to the bomb, Tehran may see no particular urgency to transgress the politically irreversible threshold of actually proceeding with direct weaponization and nuclear testing.

The question of a possible Iranian bomb, thus, may not be resolved soon – even if Iran does remain the most likely "next proliferator" in this new nuclear age. Tehran may choose to persist in its contemporary limbo as a threshold nuclear state and a credible hedger. It may even derive certain nuclear deterrence effects from its practical latency. As in the South Asian case, despite neither India nor Pakistan having possessed actual nuclear weapons, a number of crises in the late 1980s and early 1990s appeared to demonstrate a certain degree of caution by both states – partially out of a recognition that significant escalation could lead to a demonstration of nuclear capability.[70] Given that Israel, Iran's chief regional adversary in the Middle East, maintains a policy of nuclear opacity and has long vowed "not to be the first to introduce nuclear weapons" to the region, Tehran may see this option to grant it the greatest possible latitude.[71] Announcing an overt decision to seek the bomb could beget preemptive strikes by Israel, potentially catalyzing a devastating regional war. Even without the prospect of preemptive war, successfully sprinting to the bomb and carrying out a nuclear test to announce its nuclear status would likely spark broader proliferation in the Middle East. Saudi Arabia, in particular, has long viewed the prospect of a nuclear-armed Iran as fundamentally unacceptable. Saudi Crown Prince Mohammed Bin Salman has repeatedly and openly alluded to the kingdom's intention to seek its own nuclear weapons should Iran acquire the bomb: "Saudi Arabia does not want to acquire any nuclear bomb, but without a doubt if Iran developed a nuclear bomb, we will follow suit as soon as possible," he told an American reporter in 2018.[72] Tehran would further need to consider the implications of weaponization on its relations with its nuclear-armed neighbor to the east, Pakistan. The two countries are no strangers to intermittent crises between them. In January 2024, Iran carried out ballistic missile strikes against Pakistani territory to target militant groups, drawing strong condemnations from Islamabad.[73]

Iran's decision will likely come down to a broader consideration of the costs and benefits of proceeding with overt weaponization. Under the second Trump administration or another Republican administration that appears to be uncompromisingly hostile, Tehran could begin to see certain benefits to weaponized nuclear deterrence. Unlike North Korea, which tested a nuclear device for the first time in 2006 and only demonstrated a capability to range the United States in 2017, Tehran could choose also to make additional progress on long-range missiles that could be suitable for nuclear delivery against the U.S. homeland. Iran does not have a formal ICBM program and has kept to a self-imposed missile range limitation of 2,000 kilometers for years now, but it has also maintained a separate civil space program that may allow for the cross-pollination of a nascent ICBM capability.[74] Iran and North Korea, too, have maintained close cooperation on missile development; Pyongyang employed an Iranian space launch vehicle's upper stage engine in an ICBM it tested in 2017.[75] Of course, in sprinting to the bomb, Iran would risk potentially transgressing certain technical thresholds that could precipitate a preventive war. The United States, Israel, Saudi Arabia, and other regional opponents to a nuclear-armed Iran have hardly clarified their red lines. Besides, as the skeletal remains of the JCPOA's verification and monitoring provisions rapidly have atrophied since 2019, the prospect of Iran putting in place the means to covertly "sneak out" toward a near-weaponized nuclear capability grow.

Looking ahead

Multipolar nuclear dynamics in the twenty-first century are shaping up to be intrinsically more complex than the two-way, bipolar competition of the Cold War. The United States' strategic competition with two opposing nuclear superpowers – China and Russia – is just part of the story. A stable equilibrium between these three players – two of which are aligned, but not allied – appears to be an elusive prospect. With the demise of strategic arms control between the United States and Russia, Washington may choose to increase the size of its nuclear force, potentially drawing Moscow and Beijing into subsequent expansions in their own force. A three-way arms race among these superpowers is far from a remote possibility. Moreover, the emergence of North Korea as a third nuclear adversary for Washington adds yet another player to the mix. Finally, the relationship between India and Pakistan, once the focal point of nuclear escalation concerns in the second nuclear age, is increasingly likely to feel the ripple effects of a growing Chinese nuclear arsenal in response to longstanding concerns in Beijing about the United States.

While focusing on the traditional strategic "dyads" – primarily, the U.S.–Russia, U.S.–China, India–Pakistan, India–China, and U.S.–North Korea dyads – remains useful, it is no longer sufficient in making sense of the increasingly interlinked nature of nuclear competition. The major powers, critical as they are to the global nuclear balance, coexist in a world of other, newer nuclear players, each with its own interests and idiosyncrasies. Nuclear risks and contagion are hardly confined. Beyond the flashpoints described in this chapter, this new nuclear age may seek the arrival of new, less foreseeable flashpoints, which may implicate existing nuclear-armed states in novel ways.

6

What to Do About the Bomb?

Throughout the previous chapters, I have made the case that much about contemporary nuclear dangers in the 2020s and going forward evinces meaningfully new dynamics at play. If, conceptually, it mattered to recognize after the Cold War that a second nuclear age had dawned, so too does it now matter to recognize the arrival of a new, third nuclear age. While the fundamental prescriptions of the nuclear revolution and the theory and practice of nuclear deterrence are unlikely to be upended, this new nuclear age marks the collision of old problems with a plethora of new variables: from intensifying three-way superpower rivalry between the United States, China, and Russia, rapid technological flux, and the fraying of global norms and institutions around nuclear weapons. Given these shifts, humanity is not prepared for what may well be a long future with the bomb (if we are fortunate). The novel complexities of this new nuclear age are set to collide with a world more primed for major interstate conflict than at any time since the end of the Cold War, between great powers and regional powers alike. As much as we may seek to simply wish it away, the bomb will continue to cast a long shadow over international affairs. The possibility of nuclear escalation, once again, will become central in interstate crises. Throughout this book, we have seen the myriad ways in which nuclear deterrence – the best solution that humanity has been able to muster out of an unsatisfying short list of alternatives – is growing increasingly frail and unstable. Peering into the looking glass, it may be tempting to reason teleologically about the bomb: to view nuclear weapons and the possibility of their use as humanity progresses as the narrative equivalent of Anton Chekhov introducing in the first act of a play a gun that must go off later. This would be a mistake of the highest order. The precarity necessitated by nuclear deterrence deliberately manifests risk, but fatalism about nuclear war and the ultimate failure of deterrence need not be our course.

If nuclear weapons and the possibility of major nuclear war were in the periphery of international politics in the post-Cold War period, they have now once again returned to the core. As a consequence, political leaders, decision-makers, their advisors, and military planners no longer have the luxury of relegating the consideration of nuclear war to the realm of the unthinkable. Decades of nuclear non-use have bred complacency, overconfidence, and a tendency among far too many thinkers to dismiss the possibility of nuclear catastrophe. Eight decades of nuclear non-use are the result of luck, fortune, and some degree of success in the practice of nuclear deterrence. But, perversely, this period – long when viewed from the perspective of an average human lifespan, but short in the grand scheme of human history – may allow future leaders to sleepwalk into a nuclear crisis.

Behavioral economists have shown that human beings are exceptionally poor at reasoning about extremely low-probability events. The availability heuristic, for instance, refers to the propensity of individuals to reason about the probability of a given event based on how many similar instances they might recall.[1] Because we have had zero interstate nuclear exchanges since 1945, even well-informed thinkers about the possibility of nuclear war may be tempted to treat the probability of such an event as essentially zero. Predicting *how* a nuclear war might begin requires imagination – or thinking *about* the unthinkable, as Herman Kahn famously put it. But, essentially, the problem is one of so-called Knightian uncertainty. Named for the economist Frank Knight, this refers to an event shrouded in the sort of uncertainty for which we have no usefully quantifiable past information. Even poring over the historical records of the many nuclear near-misses from during the Cold War and after might tell us little about how we might avert future nuclear wars that may emerge from entirely unforeseeable circumstances. Of course, should nuclear deterrence ever fail, another tempting cognitive bias – the hindsight bias – will likely kick in. We will have no shortage of thinkers, talkers, and shouters explaining that the risks were plainly visible all along.[2]

Given all this, what should we do about the bomb in this new nuclear age?

Testing patience

In the summer of 1996, a flurry of activity was under way by Chinese technicians to run cabling and other instrumentation into a tunnel in the desert of eastern Xinjiang. China was preparing at the time for what would be its final nuclear test before the announcement of a moratorium on nuclear testing. On July 29 that year, a 3-kiloton nuclear device was detonated within the tunnel. Two days later, on August 1, China announced that it had "start[ed] a moratorium on nuclear testing effective from 30 July 1996."[3] This was China's forty-fifth and final nuclear test. A little more than a month later, the United Nations General Assembly adopted the Comprehensive Nuclear Test-Ban Treaty (CTBT) after more than two years of multilateral negotiations. The CTBT was opened for signatures from September 24, 1996. The treaty was ambitious in scope: it sought to ban all nuclear testing for any purposes – civilian or military – in any mode. It represented the culmination of a slow-building norm against nuclear testing that had snowballed since the 1960s, beginning first with a ban on atmospheric testing, underwater testing, and space-based testing in 1963, and a later ban by the two superpowers on any nuclear tests with a yield over 150 kilotons. China's 1996 test remains the last by any of the five recognized NPT nuclear states, but seventeen additional nuclear test explosions have since taken place: five by India and six by Pakistan in May 1998, and six by North Korea between 2006 and 2017. Pyongyang, meanwhile, has indicated an interest in carrying out additional nuclear tests as needed.

More than twenty years after it opened for signature, the CTBT has yet to enter into force. During negotiations in the early 1990s, it was agreed that all states with active nuclear power programs, including research reactors, would be classified under a special annex. These so-called Annex 2 states – broadly, states with the potential to weaponize nuclear technology – would be required to sign and ratify the treaty for its entry into force. As of 2024, nine Annex 2 states had not yet ratified the treaty. Five – China, Egypt, Iran, Israel, and the United States – have signed, but not ratified, the treaty, while India, North Korea, and Pakistan have refused to sign it. Russia, in 2023, announced that it would withdraw its ratification of the treaty to achieve what it described as "strategic parity" with the United States.[4] However, in the post-1996 world, a strong norm against nuclear testing has emerged. While the CTBT has failed to enter into force – and likely will not do so in the coming decades given growing geopolitical friction among many of the Annex 2 states – it has succeeded in reinforcing this norm. It has further contributed to the exceptionalization of nuclear weapons as military capabilities that are set apart from all other weapons, which, with some exceptions, can be regularly tested.

But, as Russia's revocation of its prior ratification of the CTBT suggests, the nuclear testing norm may not be sacrosanct in the new nuclear age. North Korea remains the only state to have conducted nuclear tests in the twenty-first century; as a global pariah, it has hardly seen the norm against nuclear testing as an important constraint on its own behavior. Now, however, as other nuclear-armed states and potential proliferators like Iran look ahead to a more dangerous world, the temptation to test – to validate the reliability of existing weapons designs or for the development of new weapons altogether – is growing. Moreover, the three major nuclear superpowers – Russia, China, and the United States – have maintained their primary former nuclear test sites at an alarming degree of readiness despite their stated moratoria on nuclear testing.[5] As mistrust between these three states grows, there is concern that others may be the first to test – and, as a result, each needs to maintain its capability to rapidly constitute and carry out tests to various ends. Meanwhile, proponents of nuclear testing exist in all three countries and promote a return to testing on various grounds: to exhibit political resolve, to pursue new weapons designs, and to signal the continued effectiveness of their existing nuclear deterrents. In the United States, technical experts at the U.S. Department of Energy's National Nuclear Security Administration note that, at least for Washington, there is no technical need to test nuclear weapons to validate existing designs, or to maintain the stated U.S. objective of a "safe, secure, and effective" nuclear deterrent. Russian and Chinese experts have expressed concerns that as the United States manufactures the first new nuclear warhead since the end of the Cold War, it may seek to carry out nuclear tests. These concerns have manifested around the W93, a new warhead designed to meet requirements for the U.S. Navy's Trident D5 submarine-launched ballistic missiles. In 2021, Charlie Nakhleh, the associate laboratory director for Weapons Physics at Los Alamos National Laboratory in the United States, categorically ruled out the need for testing associated with the W93.[6] This view is shared widely among technical experts across the U.S. nuclear weapons complex.

For China, in particular, the temptation to test will likely be born out of perceived technical necessity. The United States and Russia have the advantage of data derived from hundreds of Cold War-era legacy nuclear tests: 1,054 for the United States and 715 for Russia, respectively. Between its first test in 1964 and its final test in 1996, China carried out 45 tests. While these tests have given Beijing sufficient confidence in its existing nuclear weapons designs, China may wish to revisit nuclear testing to meet new requirements as it carries out an unprecedented nuclear build-up. One particularly important reason to test may concern what is known as yield-to-mass optimization: holding yield constant for a nuclear warhead while reducing its physical mass and size. Because China's nuclear testing preceded its adoption of newer delivery systems, such as hypersonic glide vehicles, and focused largely on larger, high-yield nuclear warheads, Beijing's legacy testing data may provide a lower level of confidence with which more compact warheads can be built. China, however, has not publicly acknowledged whether any of its newer delivery systems, including the DF-17 hypersonic glide vehicle or any long-range cruise missiles, are intended for an eventual nuclear delivery role. Thus, while some in the United States see political value in nuclear testing,[7] the United States would have much to lose if other countries, including China, decided to resume testing in turn. The marginal value to the United States of additional nuclear tests would be substantially limited compared to that for China.

Unlike China, Russia does not face a need to conduct nuclear testing to produce new types of nuclear warheads, but the impulse to resume testing is likely born more out of political factors than technical ones. The Russian de-ratification of the CTBT in October 2023 was linked to broader malaise in Moscow's relations with the United States and the West.[8]

Beyond seeking "strategic parity" with the United States, which has never ratified the CTBT, senior figures in the Russian government, including President Vladimir Putin, may fear that the United States could resume nuclear testing. Russian experts commonly express concerns about such an eventuality in exchanges with American experts, and their concerns are not entirely unfounded given intermittent discussions of the value of nuclear testing in U.S. politics. Notably, in 2020, the Trump administration seriously deliberated the prospect of resuming nuclear testing.[9] Reiterating these longstanding concerns, when Putin announced the revocation of Russia's CTBT ratification, he also noted that "if the United States conducts tests, then we will," indicating that Moscow would not be the first to test – at least for the moment.[10]

In recent years, the United States has publicly stated its concern that Russia and China have started carrying out very small nuclear tests that do not meet the spirit or letter of the "zero-yield" standard set out by the CTBT.[11] In 2020, for example, the U.S. Department of State alleged that Russia "has conducted nuclear weapons experiments that have created nuclear yield and are not consistent with the U.S. 'zero-yield' standard."[12] That same year, the United States said that a "lack of transparency" at China's Lop Nur nuclear test site, along with observed infrastructure activity, raised "concerns regarding its adherence to the 'zero yield' standard." In 2019, Lieutenant General Robert Ashley, then director of the U.S. Defense Intelligence Agency, noted that "the United States believes that Russia probably is not adhering to its nuclear testing moratorium in a manner consistent with the 'zero-yield' standard."[13] Ashley added that DIA believed "Russia's testing activities would help it to improve its nuclear weapons capabilities."

The "zero-yield" controversy concerns the matter of whether explosive experiments to support nuclear weapons maintenance, research, and production produce a self-sustaining supercritical chain reaction. In the United States, experiments of these kind are exclusively subcritical and do not produce such a chain reaction. Technical experts, including those within the U.S. National Nuclear Security Administration, note that there may be reasons for Russia and China to carry out tests that fail to meet the U.S. zero-yield standard that have nothing to do with the potential intention to develop new nuclear weapons. For instance, these types of tests can be more economical and far easier to prepare than subcritical tests that would provide comparable insights. Short of obviously large-yield tests, which could be detected unambiguously by international monitoring efforts, including the CTBT's International Monitoring System, very-small-yield tests are not obviously likely to contribute to the design and manufacture of new nuclear weapons designs.[14] Proponents of a U.S. return to nuclear testing and of a U.S. nuclear build-up, however, now commonly assert that Russia and China are likely pursuing new nuclear warhead designs. The general lack of transparency around activities ongoing at the Russian and Chinese nuclear test sites does little to dispel these concerns.

New temptations to test might not be easily eliminated as tensions fester between the three major nuclear powers, but efforts at increasing transparency could mitigate perceived pressures. In the weeks leading up to Russia's de-ratification of the CTBT, the United States publicly broached the idea of allowing international observers – including Russian observers – to view U.S. nuclear weapons experiments to verify that they remained subcritical in nature and were unlikely to support a return to full-yield testing.[15] While this proposal met with typical skepticism from naysayers with any sort of good faith in efforts to build confidence with Russia and China,[16] it serves as a useful litmus test for whether testing temptations in Beijing and Moscow are truly born of a concern that the United States could be the first to test, or out of perceived technical needs to advance new weapons designs regardless of U.S. intentions. Transparency concerning nuclear testing is not unprecedented, and once even supported progress toward legally binding arms control between the United States and the Soviet Union – despite political concerns in both countries. In 1988, for instance, in a rare and remarkable late Cold War episode of U.S.–Soviet technical cooperation, scientists from both countries carried out a joint experiment to verify that the 1974 Threshold Test Ban Treaty, which sought to limit both sides to underground nuclear test explosions under 150 kilotons, could be effectively verified.[17] The experiment brought Soviet inspectors to the U.S. test site in Nevada and U.S. inspectors to the Semipalatinsk test site. The confidence in verification gained in the course of this experiment finally persuaded the U.S. Senate to offer its consent for the treaty's ratification, which occurred in 1990. This episode should hold lessons for leaders and policymakers in the new nuclear age.

The question of what transpires if the dam breaks on nuclear testing is fundamentally disconcerting. Perhaps there can be no surer starting pistol shot on a new arms race aside from a nuclear test by any country other than North Korea. Testing anywhere is likely to result in testing most places, if not everywhere. If any of the major powers were to test, India and Pakistan could return to testing as well in order to support a range of objectives. In India, there have been longstanding calls among hawks to fully validate the country's higher-yield thermonuclear weapon designs given credible reports that New Delhi's sole test of such a device fizzled in 1998.[18] As nuclear norms fray, if this nuclear age is to be contained in scope in at least one major way, it must be in the form of staying the hands that seek to resume the practice of explosive testing.

Rediscovering arms control

One of the most enduring lessons of the first nuclear age continues to be that nuclear deterrence, absent any supporting mechanisms built on negotiated restraint, is simply too dangerous. Arms control and confidence-building measures designed to reduce the risk of unwanted war are an essential component of ensuring that humanity might continue to uneasily coexist with the bomb, and that the bomb might remain unused in war, as it has since 1945. The new nuclear age began with a relative reset, practically speaking, on the arms control mechanisms that legally constrained the vast nuclear arsenals of the United States and Russia. Meanwhile, despite their precipitously declining relationship, the United States and China have yet to get the ball rolling on even general talks on strategic stability (including their respective definitions of the very concept). While India and Pakistan maintain a bevy of confidence-building measures and communication lines between them, the potential for severe crises – and attendant escalation – is still insufficiently managed by existing measures. Meanwhile, insecurity festers on the Korean Peninsula as North Korea pursues a full-bore nuclear modernization project and the United States, South Korea, and Japan hang on to the comfortable fiction that Pyongyang's denuclearization remains possible in the short-term. The potential arrival of new nuclear players, including Iran, threatens to add further precarity.

These geopolitical realities are not propitious for new forms of arms control, but restraint, in some form, will be necessary. Because the alternative is simply too risky. There is some good news, too: there is no shortage of good ideas concocted by technical experts when it comes to arms control, and, unlike during the Cold War, at least Washington and Moscow have decades of experience managing the delicate balance of terror through a range of tools. Some of the late Cold War arms control advances, like a 1988 agreement to offer notification of long-range land and sea-based ballistic missile tests[19] and a 1989 agreement to notify the other side of major strategic military exercises,[20] have remained intact despite the collapse of major agreements like New START. But all of this provides little salve in the near term as nuclear risks continue to rise. Ideas and experience with arms control do little good when geopolitics has sapped all political will to reinvigorate progress.

In the United States, as U.S.–Russia relations have declined substantially in the aftermath of Russia's invasion of Ukraine, the Biden administration has sought to expand the aperture on what arms control may look like in practice going forward. The term "framework," as opposed to "treaty," in particular, came to be favored by 2022. In a statement released at the outset of the tenth review conference for the NPT, Biden noted that the United States was "ready to expeditiously negotiate a new arms control framework to replace New START when it expires in 2026."[21] The choice of this term was deliberate and sought to communicate a degree of flexibility to Moscow on what the terms of a potential negotiation could entail. By the same token, there is much skepticism in Washington concerning whether any U.S. president could ever negotiate an arms control treaty with Russia again whose text is both acceptable to Moscow and able to win sufficient support in the U.S. Senate to win its advice and consent as required by the U.S. Constitution.[22] The U.S. Senate has not granted its advice and consent to any treaties pertaining to matters of national security since New START in 2010.[23] Two-thirds of U.S. senators must support a treaty – a threshold that appears elusive in the hyperpolarized environment of Washington in the 2020s and beyond.

Politics aside, the U.S. intelligence community, in its 2024 report on global threats, did not mince its words on the prognosis for arms control: "Arms control efforts through 2035 will change in scope and complexity as the number of strategic technologies and the countries that have them grow."[24] Rediscovering arms control in the new nuclear age will depend on several conditions. First, as during the Cold War, adversaries must be willing to acknowledge – to themselves and to each other – their shared interest in survival alongside the

dangers of unbounded nuclear competition. This most fundamental condition does not exist at the heart of any of the major
competitive nuclear relationships today, but it can perhaps be
created through the willingness of national leaders to take risks
and muster the political will to reduce nuclear risks. Arms
control has never been an act of altruism for one's adversary.
Rather, it is the pursuit of one's own interests – in lowering the
costs of an arms race, the consequences of deterrence failure,
and the risk of war in general – that should motivate this.
Secondary to this, and a central challenge specific to this new
nuclear age, will be the question of whether military establishments in nuclear-armed states will be able to find reasons to
embrace the stabilizing logic at the heart of the theory of the
nuclear revolution: that the possession of secure second-strike
capabilities, and vulnerability to an adversary's secure second-
strike capabilities, can help engender something resembling
stability. In a fast-changing technological context paired with
high political distrust, this will require costly reassurances.
Where verification of intent is difficult – or perhaps verges
on the impossible – states will need to talk and determine
whether political arrangements can be acceptable. Finally,
progress toward arms control in a dangerous and complex
new nuclear age can be slow and gradual – as long as it trends
toward restraint. Leaders must resist the impulse to treat everything that stands between the dangerous, unbounded status
quo before us and a more stable nuclear world as deserving of
a full-scale arms control treatment right off the bat. If nothing
can be solved before everything can be solved, there will be
little to do.

While it may be tempting to conclude that the problems
facing arms control in the twenty-first century will be primarily technological – after all, the intersecting cocktail of nuclear
weapons, space systems, AI, cyber operations, non-nuclear
missiles, and the rest can be dizzying – the core obstacle to
progress is political. The politics of arms control are difficult

both internally within states, where inviting one's adversary to an arrangement of mutual restraint is easily painted by opponents as a demonstration of weakness, and externally, where inviting an adversary to adopt forms of restraint is seen but as another tool of self-interested statecraft, designed to sow advantage. In Washington, it would not be too far-fetched to suggest that any arms control arrangement – legally or politically binding – that may be acceptable to Vladimir Putin, Xi Jinping, or Kim Jong Un would be politically a nonstarter. The mere idea of shared interests with adversaries, even with the risk of nuclear conflict looming, is controversial. In Beijing, Moscow, and Pyongyang, meanwhile, skepticism will abound about any proposals emerging from the United States. Their political concern is about the very survival of their regimes, after all, and the perception that Washington seeks absolute advantage and security at their expense. Some of this may even stand between these states and their willingness to sit down with the United States to talk about arms control matters at all. Their leaders may view the American approach to arms control processes as former U.S. President Richard Nixon once did: "Unless you know what the other guy wants, you just – you don't know how to screw 'em."[25]

One way out of the problems of domestic and international politics – and the problems of appearances – would be to embrace quieter, less public channels. This would be less viable as a form of arms control, which would require nuclear-armed states (especially democracies) to subject any agreement to the appropriate legal processes that would confer legitimacy on an arrangement. However, assurances designed to reduce the risks of nuclear war can be conveyed privately and even acted upon without public dissemination. After all, the *quid pro quo* that ended the Cuban Missile Crisis after thirteen days was not shouted from the rooftops, and only became known years later. Today's world is undoubtedly leakier and more prone to rapid, free-flowing information and disinformation dissemination, but leaders and decision-makers interested in a safer world have little to lose by exploring clandestine channels for communication with their adversaries. These mechanisms are best established and, where possible, regularized during times of relative peace precisely so that they may be used to manage the worst possible risks in a time of crisis. These mechanisms may have special value in the nuclear competitive relationships that have the least in the way of a legacy of other arms control or crisis communications, such as the U.S.–China and U.S.–North Korea relationships.

Rethinking verification

Throughout this book, I've underscored the many sources of unprecedented complexity – from multipolarity to new technologies – that permeate all aspects of this new nuclear age. Contemplating arms control, if it is to manifest in ways that might constrain some of the most concerning sources of risk, will require rethinking verification – both politically and technically. Verification – the process of determining whether parties to an arms control agreement are behaving in manners consistent with that agreement – has long been seen, particularly in the United States and the broader West, as an essential *sine qua non* of robust arms control. To be politically saleable to a skeptical Senate in Washington, arms control agreements with the Soviet Union and later Russia had to be seen as reasonably verifiable. The purpose of verification wasn't just to ensure that the other guy wouldn't cheat, but that the protocols agreed on concerning verification would deter cheating altogether because the risk of being caught cheating would be too high. Critics of arms control agreements as negotiated would often cite concerns about the sufficiency of verification protocols, of course – in many cases failing to accept that what they might consider sufficient would be outside the realm of what the counterparty in a negotiation would consider acceptable. The 154-page Joint Comprehensive Plan of Action with Iran, for instance, was historic and unprecedented in its intrusiveness and granularity on verification. Despite this, Republican critics of the agreement, which had been negotiated by a Democratic administration, regularly cited concerns over verification, using the matter largely as a cudgel to chip away at the viability of an agreement that they fundamentally viewed as unworthy of sustainment.

The politics of arms control verification are unlikely to get much easier in the new nuclear age. Even so, rethinking verification modalities and investing in the potential application of new technologies and methods could expand the scope of what future arms control negotiators might be able to rely on when the conditions for arms control manifest again, be it among the major powers or in regional contexts. The traditional Cold War model of treaty-based arms control verification, as practiced by the United States and Russia, was based on the ability of the two countries to feel confident that their technical experts and intelligence communities could rely on verification to detect activities that were inconsistent with agreements as negotiated – particularly those activities that would be militarily significant.

This explains, for instance, why the United States chose to make an issue out of a Soviet-built radar near Krasnoyarsk under the Reagan administration, citing the facility as a violation of the 1972 ABM Treaty's spirit and letter. The U.S. believed that this radar would violate the Treaty's mutually agreed probation against radars that could support missile defense intercepts of incoming reentry vehicles versus providing simple early warning of nuclear attacks.[26] The massive Soviet radars were originally detected by U.S. satellites, or what were euphemistically termed "National Technical Means" (NTM) in the treaty parlance on verification at the time. The Krasnoyarsk radar was a matter of compliance concern due both to technical and political factors at the time. Contrast with this episode the longstanding concerns within the United States and NATO about the Russian Iskander-M (9K720; NATO: SS-26) short-range ballistic missile. Though the 1987 INF Treaty banned Russia and the United States from possessing any ground-launched missiles with ranges between 500 and 5,500 kilometers, the Iskander-M, as an endoatmospheric missile capable of aerodynamic maneuvering, was scrutinized for years. If necessary, the Russians could have flown the missile to ranges in excess of 500 kilometers, but the United States chose not to raise this as a treaty compliance concern. When, in 2014, the United States did for the first time express concerns that Russia had violated the treaty, it did so over a completely different missile – one that demonstrated a violation of the letter and spirit of the treaty in clear technical terms.

The decades-long experience that Moscow and Washington have had with navigating questions of arms control verification have been deeply studied in both countries and around the world. They certainly bear lessons for the future of arms control, but the aperture of what future negotiators will need to consider in negotiations is set to grow increasingly more challenging.

One solution to this problem is to simply limit future arms control negotiations and agreements to the relatively simple issues where experience can prove useful. One way to do this in the context of U.S.–Russia negotiations would be to pick up on the precedents set by START and New START, to include data-sharing, on-site inspections, notifications, and other monitoring methods. This principle of respecting precedents has informed successive treaty negotiations between the two countries. In 2009, Barack Obama and his Russian counterpart at the time, Dmitry Medvedev, issued a joint statement outlining their vision for what would become New START, noting that the new treaty would "include effective verification measures drawn from the experience of the Parties in implementing the START Treaty."[27] With relations between the two countries at their worst since the end of the Cold War in the aftermath of Russia's 2022 invasion of Ukraine and the suspension of New START by Russia, getting back to a place where arms control matters can be negotiated – let alone verification measures – will not be easy. Still, the legacy of longstanding bilateral experience and understanding, paired with NTM capabilities, for instance, contributed to the ability of the U.S. Department of State's Bureau of Arms Control, Deterrence, and Stability (ADS) to assess, in January 2024, that Russia "likely did not exceed the New START Treaty's deployed warhead limit in 2023."[28] Nevertheless, the ADS report further noted that "due to the uncertainty generated by Russia's failure to fulfill its obligations with respect to the Treaty's verification regime, the United States was unable to verify that the Russian Federation remained in compliance throughout 2023 with its obligation to limit its deployed warheads on delivery vehicles subject to the New START Treaty to 1,550." An assessment of the state of play, in this case, did not amount to a verification of continued Russian compliance with its politically stated intent to adhere to the Treaty's central limits despite Putin's suspension decision.

Outside the unique U.S.–Russia context, arms control verification may look quite a bit different. China and North Korea, for instance, do not appear politically disposed to permit intrusive verification of the sort that Russia has been able to stomach with the United States. China does participate in limited conventional arms control verification activities with its neighbors to the West, but this verification activity is seen as an expression of trust and something to be done in a context of good diplomatic relations.[29]

In the new nuclear age, technical and policy experts will need to consider the value that untested but conceptually rich verification approaches might yield in future negotiations. Probabilistic verification approaches, for instance, seem intuitively appealing in an era of increasing mistrust and complexity.[30] Instead of striving for the stringent and ideally intrusive verification means that may be necessary to offer high confidence in a state's compliance with an agreement, a probabilistic approach could instead involve the monitoring of a wider number of activities relating to a country's nuclear forces. Even if the probability of detecting noncompliance might vary wildly across activities – for instance, it may be much easier to verify the fact of proscribed missile tests from space than uranium enrichment activity at a centrifuge plant – the aggregate probability of detecting *some* noncompliance across all monitored activities would increase as more activities are monitored. Such an approach may be promising with a state like North Korea where traditional monitoring is unlikely to be accepted by the government.

In favor of organizational change

It will be important for those policymakers seeking to make progress on the reduction of nuclear risks to not lose all hope despite the grim prognosis for arms control. After all, what if the risks of nuclear war – or of conventional wars escalating uncontrollably – could be managed without having to necessarily cooperate or speak with one's adversary? This basic idea should be appealing given the practical geopolitical realities now prevalent: given the difficulties of negotiating restraint with Russia, China, and North Korea, can the United States and its allies find other ways to address the risk of nuclear war? The basic approach here concerns what might be known as organizational change, introspection, and adaptation. Well-meaning military procurement programs, operational plans, and doctrines can contribute to a heightened risk of nuclear escalation – particularly unintentional nuclear escalation. One way to mitigate these risks would simply be for states to look inward, identify the practices within their own organizations and systems that contribute to these risks, and enact policy and planning changes as needed to lower the risk of nuclear conflict. This would not fall under the traditional rubric of what might be called "arms control," but it would certainly qualify as nuclear risk reduction.

Consider, for instance, the U.S. policy of pursuing a comprehensive missile "defeat" strategy against an adversary like North Korea. Missile defeat, in contrast to just missile defense, consists of seeking to disable or destroy missile threats both before and after their launch; missile defense traditionally focuses on post-launch threats. In 2017, a leaked U.S. Department of Defense document suggested that the U.S. harbored the goal of destroying North Korea's ability to launch nuclear-armed missiles through "non-kinetic" means, strongly implying a potentially highly classified and exquisite cyberweapon. For Kim Jong Un, in the course of a crisis, the mere possibility that such a weapon might exist and could sever him from his nuclear weapons at any time and without warning would be a huge source of escalatory incentive. Kim would have to use whatever nuclear weapons he could to seek advantage lest he lose his ability to do so entirely. The Biden administration was less explicit about these ambitions as it rolled out its *Missile Defense Review* in 2022 on the "left of launch" component of targeting North Korean missile forces, but one senior administration official noted at a public event that it maintained the goal of comprehensive missile defeat, which would entail planning "to take actions on the left and the right of launch."[31] If the United States seeks to deprive Kim Jong Un of incentives to use nuclear weapons – as it should – then a change to this policy could be one way of reducing the risk of nuclear war without necessarily sitting down for a chat with Kim himself. Washington could even promulgate a broader effort for other states to offer political commitments that they would not interfere in the nuclear command and control systems of other countries with cyber-weapons.

Another particularly feasible and attractive option for all nuclear-armed states would be to borrow from the United States' decision, in 2022, to carry out a "failsafe review." The U.S. Congress, in its 2022 National Defense Authorization Act for the 2022 fiscal year, mandated that the U.S. government establish an independent advisory committee to study the security and reliability of U.S. nuclear forces, top to bottom, and to simultaneously study the factors that could precipitate unauthorized, inadvertent, or accidental nuclear use. We know from the United States' own post-1945 history that several accidents involving nuclear weapons have occurred, mostly during the heyday of the Cold War when Washington endorsed dangerous ideas in the pursuit of deterrence like persistently flying bombers with live nuclear weapons on board. While other nuclear-armed states are less transparent about their own histories and mistakes with the bomb, there are no doubt countless other cases – from Russia to China to India to North Korea. To reduce the risk of nuclear war, in general, states should seek to carry out such reviews. While the autocratic nuclear states may be resistant to carrying out such an introspective review, which could expose politically sensitive organizational shortfalls, democratic nuclear possessors should be able to undertake such studies more proactively.

Finally, it should be incumbent also on non-nuclear states that fear potential conflicts with nuclear-armed states to similarly introspect about their doctrines, policies, and military plans. As described earlier in this book, technological change in the new nuclear age has all but ensured that many sophisticated non-nuclear states will possess the military means to raise anxieties in their nuclear-armed adversary in ways that could beget inadvertent escalation. For instance, non-nuclear NATO allies could carry out long-range strikes implicating Russian nuclear weapons storage facilities, or related units, in the course of a conventional war. South Korea and Japan, meanwhile, have explicit ambitions to target North Korean nuclear forces. Across these states, the risks of potential conventional military operations against nuclear forces need to be more deeply studied and understood.[32] Such a review need not compromise the deterrence that these states seek against their nuclear-armed rivals. They should instead undertake such a review out of their own interest in averting unwanted nuclear escalation while seeking to achieve their deterrence and military goals.

Prudence at the core

In the hours before his inauguration on January 20, 2017, Donald Trump arrived at Blair House in Washington, DC, to receive a briefing on the United States' nuclear capabilities and, critically, what he would have to do in order to issue an order for the use of the country's nuclear weapons. Four years later, Joe Biden would undergo the same briefing. As commanders-in-chief, both men – and their predecessors dating back to Harry Truman – exercised the exclusive and sole authority over the country's nuclear forces. No other official at the highest ranks of the U.S. government or military – not the secretary of defense, and not the chairman of the Joint Chiefs of Staff – is formally involved in the nuclear chain-of-command. Trump, Biden, or any other U.S. president would be able to issue an order that would be faithfully carried out by the country's National Military Command Center (NMCC), provided it were valid and legal. For an order to be valid, the president must authenticate his or her identity by citing a code, generated in a cryptographically secure manner by the U.S. National Security Agency daily, printed on a laminated card known as the Sealed Authenticator System – colloquially known as the nuclear "biscuit." The legality of an order – as measured against the laws of war – cannot in all cases be guaranteed, but in most plausible launch scenarios, the president would be able to select a strike "package" encased within a large, leather satchel carried at all times by a military aide in his or her proximity. This satchel, known colloquially as the "nuclear football," also contains a means of secure communication with the NMCC.[33] Once the criteria of validity and legality are met, hundreds of billions of dollars of assets involved in the complex, redundant, and reliable U.S. nuclear command and control system are designed to ensure that launches are carried out promptly. In this way, a nuclear war involving potentially the use of hundreds of weapons can be started by just one person.

When I talk about the above-described procedures for a nuclear launch in the United States at public events or with non-specialists, I am often met with incredulity: *Surely that can't be it? Surely the secretary of defense or the chairman of the Joint Chiefs of Staff must advise the president, or be involved? Congress, which has the constitutional power to declare war, must be involved, no?* These questions are a natural response, and entirely reasonable, but the answers are yes, no, and no. Even U.S. lawmakers bear misunderstandings about the nuclear chain of command. In 2024, after it became known that the U.S. secretary of defense had been hospitalized without notifying the White House, congressional outcry focused – incorrectly – on the compromising effect this could have had on the United States' ability to carry out a nuclear launch, if necessary. "The secretary of defense is the key link in the chain of command between the president and the uniformed military, including the nuclear chain of command, when the weightiest of decisions must be made in minutes," Tom Cotton, a Republican senator from Arkansas, said in a statement.[34] Don Bacon, a congressman from Nebraska, told the press: "Nuclear command and control is priority number one, and the SECDEF is a key authority in this chain of command . . . The confusion here undermines deterrence."[35] These expressions of concern about the secretary of defense's role in nuclear matters were incorrect. The authority for the U.S. president as commander-in-chief to use nuclear weapons is absolute, requires no second opinion, and, once issued, an order likely cannot be remanded in sufficient time. The reasons for this are partly political and partly born of Cold War strategic anxieties. The origins of sole authority in the United States rest with Harry Truman, who ultimately saw nuclear weapons as not just another rung in the tools of conventional warfare, but as supreme political weapons after their initial uses in the final weeks of the Second World War. The sources of customary presidential authority in the United States, thus, date to August 1945, but the legal codification of the practice arrived with the passage of the Atomic Energy Act in 1946. Truman's interests in codifying presidential authority were also partly concerned by the prospects for escalation should the U.S. military perceive nuclear weapons as simply another class of useable weaponry.

A little less than two decades later, at the height of the Cold War, the strategic anxieties that have since informed the operationalization of U.S. nuclear command and control began to take on increased salience. In the United States – and the Soviet Union for that matter – there was an acute fear that no matter how robust nuclear forces grew in practice, command and control systems and personnel – specifically, the president – were a significant vulnerability. If an adversary perceived an advantage in striking first to "decapitate" the president or otherwise sever the central nervous system of the national nuclear force, U.S. forces could be thrown into disarray, undermining the threat of certain, robust retaliation that was seen as central to maintaining effective nuclear deterrence. In the case of a decapitation attack seeking to take out the president, authority would devolve – to the vice president, the speaker of the house, and so on – but maintaining deterrence of a broader war was still a key priority. Under the Eisenhower administration, the United States partly solved these problems by moving toward the delegation of nuclear use authority to field officers in Europe in a crisis, ensuring that nuclear weapons could be used at least in Europe without the president's direct involvement.[36] This practice would later be abandoned, given the obvious dangers of unwanted nuclear use by anxious military officers. The introduction of ICBMs introduced new dilemmas, however. U.S. leaders had to now contend with the possible obliteration of large swathes of the country's nuclear forces and possibly their own lives in a strike that could take on the order of thirty minutes. To partly dissuade such a strike and to ensure the certainty of their ability to retaliate before their own missiles were destroyed, the United States adopted the option of launching its nuclear forces "under attack." In other words, if sufficient warning were available of inbound Soviet ICBM reentry vehicles from space- *and* land-based sensors simultaneously, the president would be notified and, on the order of minutes, have the option of issuing a launch order. Because of the necessary time urgency involved in such a decision, the president's sole authority, which had by this time become a customary and legal component of U.S. nuclear employment plans, was a boon – not a liability. By contrast, the introduction of additional decision-making agents into this process would add undesirable friction.

Though the strategic circumstances of the Cold War that drew out this preference largely receded after the Soviet Union's collapse, the United States has maintained the option to launch its nuclear forces under attack. There have been some attempts to deemphasize this option. The Obama administration, in its 2013 employment guidance for U.S. nuclear weapons, directed the Department of Defense to "examine and reduce the role of launch under attack," and that, while the United States would retain this capability, it would "focus planning on the more likely 21st century contingencies."[37] The Trump administration's 2020 employment strategy dropped the language on deemphasizing this option, but noted that while "U.S. nuclear forces do not *rely* on launch-under-attack to ensure a credible response," (emphasis added) they are "postured to withstand an initial attack and provide maximum decision-making time for a President to gather information and respond in a time, place and manner of our choosing."[38] While this stated aspiration was laudable, the option of launching U.S. nuclear forces under attack remained available to the president.

The U.S. option to launch its nuclear forces under attack and the president's sole authority may appear to be complementary puzzle pieces, but digging deeper exposes the significant risks associated with this. In a scenario in which Russia decides to launch ICBMs at the United States, the president would have in the order of roughly fifteen minutes after such a launch is detected, verified, and communicated to issue an order to launch.[39] Because such an attack would likely target U.S. ICBM silos, whose locations are fixed and known, a decision to wait for additional information could result in the loss of these missiles, depriving the United States of a significant portion of its nuclear retaliatory capability. The psychological stressors on any president in such a scenario would be massive – not least because the president himself might also have been targeted by sea-based Russian missiles that could arrive sooner than the ICBMs. Faced with the prospect of having to make a humanity-altering decision, even the most prudent and sober leader would balk. In those fifteen minutes, the president may likely choose to elicit the advice of close advisors, including possibly the secretary of defense and other senior cabinet officials; but again, there is no requirement that he or she do so prior to issuing a launch order for U.S. nuclear weapons. Even the choice of choosing *not to launch* and to ride out the attack – or to see if the warning of an attack may have come in error – would be stressful. Inherent in the principle of sole authority is the requirement that these nigh-incomprehensible burdens be placed on one person whose background will almost certainly not be in nuclear strategy, but in politics. Emulating these stressors is challenging, but one attempt to recreate these burdens in a virtual reality setting showed that people with a variety of backgrounds, dispositions, and values will tend to choose to launch.[40] As unlikely as a bolt-out-of-the-blue first strike against the United States might be, the inability to rule out such a scenario has largely kept sole authority in the picture.

I began this section with an intimate description of the U.S. launch process because that is what is most known in the public domain about these procedures, but a broader and more fundamental problem facing humanity at the dawn of this new nuclear age is that the capability to resort to nuclear use in many cases rests in the hands of individual leaders, shielded from political or democratic accountability, in all too many cases. In Russia today, it is strongly suspected that Vladimir Putin could authorize nuclear use unilaterally, despite some available evidence that there is a formal resort to a multi-actor authorization process, with the involvement of as many as three analogs to the U.S. "football."[41] Russia's 2014 military doctrine notes that "the decision to use nuclear weapons shall be taken by the President of the Russian Federation."[42] This was reiterated in a separate statement on the foundations guiding nuclear deterrence in Russia.[43] In China, similarly, Xi Jinping, in his capacity as the head of the Central Military Commission of the Communist Party of China – one of his many roles – could authorize the use of nuclear weapons *in extremis* without consulting with other senior political figures, including members of China's traditionally powerful Politburo Standing Committee.[44] Similarly, Kim Jong Un in North Korea, in his capacity as the chairman of the State Affairs Commission, enjoys "monolithic command" over the country's nuclear forces, per a law adopted by the country's rubber-stamp parliament in 2022.[45] That same law, however, does note that "state nuclear forces command organization composed of members appointed by the president of the State Affairs of the DPRK shall assist the president of the State Affairs of the DPRK in the whole course from decision concerning nuclear weapons to execution," somewhat formalizing, if not mandating, a consultative arrangement for Kim with senior military leaders. As in the United States and other cases, a resort to consultative deliberations and collective decision-making could be just a luxury born of time that may not be available in a fast-moving nuclear crisis. Notably, India and Pakistan, each with a collective National Command Authority overseeing nuclear weapons use decisions, do not adopt a monolithic command model.

Between the leaders of the United States, Russia, China, and North Korea alone, there is plenty of room for psychologically born, catastrophic shortfalls in judgment manifesting in nuclear war. In the United States, the matter of sole authority hardly seemed to feature in post-Cold War debates on nuclear matters, but came roaring to the forefront of national security debates in Washington following the election of Donald Trump in 2016. Trump, like no other U.S. president before him, behaved overtly in ways that created concerns about his propensity to look at the nuclear option prematurely in crises, or to simply seek the use of nuclear weapons preemptively. The concerns festered repeated threats toward North Korea in 2017, including a pledge to bring "fire and fury" to the country if Kim continued developing his missile capabilities.[46] In November 2017, amid this crisis, the U.S. Senate Foreign Relations Committee held, for the first time since the Cold War, a hearing on the president's nuclear weapons launch authority. The hearing was born of bipartisan concerns.[47] Trump, despite his many public demonstrations of flawed judgment, served as the ultimate case study in the dangers of nuclear sole authority. For proponents of the status quo, he provided arguably one of the most difficult cases against which to reconcile their beliefs: if you were alright with Trump having the sole finger on the proverbial U.S. nuclear button, then perhaps you were alright with the principle in general. Few were. Despite this, there was no successful effort to reform sole authority, and the Biden administration did not take measures to limit the president's power in this regard. All this despite nearly two-thirds of the American public, in 2023 polling, expressing discomfort with the centralization of nuclear use authority in one person.[48]

It should go without saying that nuclear war is simply too significant and devastating an event to be left up to the vagaries of individuals. While the United States' democratic system suggests that its approach to sole authority may be the most plausibly modified, it is far from clear that the entrenched strategic anxieties about a possible launch-under-attack scenario that have germinated now for decades will allow for such a change. In a different sense, there will be a need for American voters, politicians, and advisors to center on the importance of prudence in leadership. This need not be prudence as formally defined by Plato in his *Republic*, and later expanded upon by Aristotle, but a more general sense of the term as something analogous to cautiousness. In the broadest sense, prudent leaders will be those who, through experience, temperament, courage, and, where relevant, expert advice, are able to avoid taking their nations – and humanity – into the abyss.

Arguably, this sort of prudence manifested, in perhaps a weak sense, between Kennedy and Khrushchev during those fateful thirteen days in October 1962. Kennedy, despite his initial shock and anger at Khrushchev's decision to deploy missiles to Cuba, was able to find himself in a position by the end of the crisis – against the best advice of much of his gathered Executive Committee advisors – to agree the secret deal to remove U.S. missiles from Turkey. With the exception of George Ball, the under-secretary of state, opposition to the proposal was unanimous among Kennedy's key advisors – as it was with the Turks and NATO.[49] Transcripts from the crisis show, mechanistically, how Kennedy appeared to cognitively experience prudence, explaining to his advisors who opposed the deal that failing to take this off-ramp would lead to worse choices still. If "we wouldn't take the missiles out of Turkey, then maybe we'll have to invade or make a massive strike on Cuba, which may lose Berlin. That's what concerns me," Kennedy said. "We all know how quickly everybody's courage goes when the blood starts to flow, and that's what's going to happen in NATO ... When we start these things, and [the Soviets] grab Berlin ... everybody's going to say, 'Well, that [Jupiter deal] was a pretty good proposition.'" He went on to say: "Today it sounds great to reject it, but it's not going to, after we do something." In the end, Kennedy was vindicated, the crisis ended, taking the Soviet Union and the United States away from the brink.[50] Kennedy's expert advisors, including McGeorge Bundy, his national security advisor, suggested that the U.S. missiles in Turkey and the Soviet missiles in Cuba were two entirely separate issues, with only one of them at the center of the crisis. Bundy was also especially concerned about what message the deal would send to U.S. allies about Washington's credibility. While this might have had *intellectual* appeal for many of Bundy's ExComm colleagues, charged with defending U.S. and allied interests, it failed to solve the crisis at hand.[51] Indeed, until the late-1980s, the mythology of how the Cuban Missile Crisis had come to an end emphasized steely, masculine, all-American resolve, causing the Soviets to blink – until the truth about the wise decision to take the secret deal emerged.[52]

Kennedy's willingness to push against his advisors, ultimately, allowed for a way out. And this wasn't a sudden *eureka* moment for the U.S. president toward the end of the crisis, but the apotheosis of a line of prudent thinking that he first articulated just four days after the first images of the Soviet missiles in Cuba were acquired. "The question really is," President Kennedy said, "what action we take which lessens the chances of a nuclear exchange, which obviously is the final failure." This line of thinking, as long as it can remain at the forefront of the minds of contemporary leaders in crises, may have value. Two other factors in the Cuban Missile Crisis case appear to have been operative, too. The first includes the ability of Kennedy – and Khrushchev – to empathize with the predicament the other finds himself in. This "strategic empathy" bent the arc of what otherwise could have been a devastating game of rational brinkmanship toward concession and compromise. The second – perhaps less difficult to demonstrate – may have to do with the experience that both leaders personally had with the horrors of large-scale conventional war. Though neither had personally experienced nuclear Armageddon, both possessed sufficient imagination to see a series of events that could possibly lead to nuclear war as unacceptable – the "final failure," as Kennedy put it.[53]

It is possible to overlearn these lessons from the Cuban Missile Crisis, of course. Only decades later did the world learn just how much of a role dumb luck had played, given the experience of the Soviet *B-59* submarine crew. But prudence appears to be a principle that has continued to bear relevance. In October 2022 – coincidentally, the month of the sixtieth anniversary of the Cuban Missile Crisis – officials in the Biden administration feared that Russia may have been in the process of taking steps that could have seen the use of tactical nuclear weapons in Ukraine. At the time, one U.S. intelligence estimate put the odds of a nuclear strike on Ukraine at a coin flip's odds – far too high to be tolerable.[54] This sparked an intense spate of effort to deter such use and, fearing the worst, a response, if needed. It built on a real sense of nuclear escalation risk that had informed the administration's efforts starting a few days into the war. Above all, from the highest levels of the U.S. government, efforts were imbued with a genuine feeling of peril about the prospects of nuclear use; in other words, the fear of a significant, intolerable escalation prompted this effort to think through all eventualities from the get-go. October 2022 passed without any escalation, in the end, and U.S. officials would later note that, in addition to their messaging, which had included a threat of a massive conventional attack on Russian forces, interventions at the highest levels of the Chinese and Indian governments toward Putin on the unacceptability of any nuclear use may also have played a role. The impulse in those two states to convey their concerns to Russia, similarly, is yet another example of prudent leadership at work.

Perhaps most important for a return to restraint, outside the specifics of any given crisis, will be the courage of leaders to seek a way out of an unbounded arms race. While much of the story of how the United States and Russia lurched slowly toward a world devoid of strategic arms control begins in 2002, with the U.S. decision to leave the ABM Treaty, the final blows to New START were dealt largely by a Russian president who appeared determined to subjugate arms control to proximal concerns on the battlefield of Ukraine. From private exchanges with Russian experts and scholars – including some close to the Kremlin – it is clear that there are still many in that country who understand the value of arms control for their national interests, but until Putin – or his successor – decides to once again seek proactive arms control diplomacy, little progress may be possible. Just as leaders can create opportunities, they can also shut doors. North Korean leader Kim Jong Un, too, appears determined, after the collapse of the bout of unprecedented diplomacy between the United States and his country in 2018 and 2019, to shut the door on engagement, instead turning toward Putin and a strategic arms build-up of his own.

While the U.S.–China case does not appear propitious for restraint at the dawn of this new nuclear age, Washington, under the Biden administration, did coalesce around a belief that the only way to move the needle is for the U.S. president to personally appeal to his Chinese counterpart. In November 2021, for the first time, Joe Biden raised the United States' interest in exploratory talks on arms control; according to officials with knowledge of what transpired in that virtual meeting, Xi simply nodded and smiled in return, making no clear commitments.[55] However, almost two years later, Beijing and Washington were able to convene a director-general-level dialogue on arms control.[56] While this was largely an exchange of talking points, it demonstrated, for the first time since the Obama administration, a willingness to probe issues in this area. High-level exchange has moved China on nuclear matters in the past. During the negotiations in the 1990s, for what became the CTBT, then-President Clinton and his secretary of defense, Bill Perry, were critical interlocutors with Beijing.

As it was during the Cold War, it may take a crisis so compelling as to make the nuclear shadow that looms over the United States, China, and other nuclear states so obvious as to be central in their relationship. It is not uncommon to hear the recommendation made that a "modern Cuban Missile Crisis" could inject a healthy dose of nuclear prudence into today's leaders – be it a crisis in the Taiwan Strait, a near-miss in Europe, or even in South Asia. While there may be truth to this, it ignores the attendant risks. Inviting crisis can hardly be risk-free, and the U.S. and Russian officials who lived those thirteen fateful days in October 1962 would later recount their real sense of fear that nuclear war was more likely than not. A fundamental task facing anyone working within the defense bureaucratic systems of the major nuclear powers – and especially those in proximity to national leaders – is to ensure that nuclear dangers remain high on their minds. For prudence to manifest in times of crisis – and to ensure that the fingers that may push the proverbial button are stayed by rational fear of the "final failure" – leaders will have to imagine the consequences of nuclear war. They must similarly hope to never find themselves asking what they might have done differently should nuclear weapons be employed.

Survival in the new nuclear age

Peering into the challenges that loom ahead, the fundamental question that political leaders, their advisors, military planners, and the rest of us need to keep at the front of our minds is: *how much longer can we keep going as we have*? This book has surveyed the tremendous complexities underpinning global nuclear dynamics – complexities born of multipolarity, of growing geopolitical rivalry, and of technological changes. The enterprise of nuclear deterrence that remains central to how, if not humanity, then the nuclear-armed states, manage their affairs remains central. Despite its detractors, we continue to have evidence that nuclear deterrence *works* – even if what it accomplishes can be entirely unsatisfying. In 2022, Russia and NATO were mutually deterred by each other's nuclear capabilities from transgressing key thresholds in the early days of the former's invasion of Ukraine, even if the consequence of this deterrence hardly allowed either side to pursue their objectives without limits. For years, even as North Korea continues to amass weapons-useable fissile material and missiles, preventive war has largely been an unserious policy option in Seoul and Washington – owing in no small part to the benefits that Pyongyang avails from its nuclear capabilities. Underpinning China's nuclear build-up that began in the early 2020s, too, may be the notion that a more robust nuclear force – and the attendant deterrence benefits it might bring along – will cause the United States and its allies to act with caution in future crises.

Deterrence exists, however, as a function of the terror inherent in nuclear weapons – in the abhorrent effects that nuclear detonations might one day cause to human flesh, bone, and civilization alike. For the states that choose to depend on nuclear deterrence for their security – those with nuclear weapons and those allied with those with nuclear weapons – this is rarely said openly. Nuclear deterrence is, after all, most comfortably discussed in the antiseptic language of defense intellectual jargon. But the terror *is* the central feature; it is not a bug or a deficiency. Nuclear deterrence cannot be neat and antiseptic because it is precisely the possibility of Armageddon – of plunging into the unknown, but assuredly and intolerably painful – that keeps the world humming along. Ultimately, nuclear deterrence is practiced – and worshipped by the establishments that profess its benefits – at the risk of calamity. It, by definition, *cannot* be rendered perfectly safe, after all. Without the risk of plunging over the brink, nuclear deterrence cannot function.

And, so, we must ask again: *how much longer can we keep going as we have*? Is nuclear deterrence, ultimately, sustainable for the long haul? Optimists look at seventy-five-plus years – and going – of no nuclear weapons detonated in anger in a time of war or crisis and think that it may well be possible. Pessimists, on the other hand, look to the propensity inherent in human beings for fallible, imperfect decision-making, to the tendency of large organizations to make errors, and to the inability of technology to impose sufficient guardrails and answer "no." A puzzle, however, continues to be the plentiful evidence of imprudent, impulsive leaders with access to nuclear weapons and a long list of nuclear "near misses" from during and after the Cold War, and still no mushroom clouds over cities exploded in anger in a war. There is a real sense that luck has saved humanity more than a few times: from ensuring that the crew on the Soviet *B-59* submarine during the Cuban Missile Crisis in 1962 did not release their nuclear-armed torpedoes, to allowing for de-escalation in 2019 between India and Pakistan after an Indian pilot was shot down, but lived, allowing for a prisoner exchange and off-ramp away from broader war. For the optimists, the tales of near misses are never fully persuasive. After all, for nuclear deterrence to be practicable, its failure must paradoxically be both imaginable and possible; what matters to the optimists, then, is not that the near misses did not happen, but that deterrence ultimately held despite what may have been a realistically imaginable pathway into the abyss. The pessimists may lack the empirics to persuade, but they might pose a different question: *what is the frequency of nuclear wars in the long run of human history?*

A core concern brought about by the many trends described in this book, underpinning this new nuclear age, is that humanity is about to begin to observe the effects of nuclear deterrence in an unprecedented environment. Not all that defines this new, third nuclear age is actually new, but the precise mix of dynamics at play represents complexity beyond that which we have observed in the past. Over the relatively short, seventy-five-plus-years of history since *Trinity*, nuclear weapons – and the threats they posed to mankind – were largely only observed under conditions of intense, bipolar superpower competition, and under a more unipolar world (where regional nuclear states nevertheless experienced crises). This new nuclear age, in a real sense, may represent the final opening of Pandora's box when it comes to nuclear weapons and nuclear deterrence. The long-term stability of deterrence in a more multipolar, entangled world, with anxieties about the ability of new technologies to nullify secure second-strike capabilities, of three-way great power arms races amid atrophied arms control, and a fraying nonproliferation order, is fundamentally more questionable. Given the many plausible pathways to initial nuclear use in a range of imaginable interstate crises, from the Korean Peninsula to South Asia to the Baltic region in Europe and the Taiwan Strait, a larger nuclear exchange is all too imaginable. Even if humanity stays the bomb's destructive potential for eighty years after Nagasaki while accepting nuclear deterrence, can that record be sustained indefinitely?

This should lead to a fundamental rethink of how we – humans in states with nuclear weapons, states dependent on other's nuclear weapons, and states without nuclear weapons – reflect on nuclear deterrence and the problem of war more generally. This must begin with the centering of the notion that nuclear deterrence cannot be a permanent solution to the problem of large-scale war between powerful countries. Instead, it should be conceived as an effective, if fallible, temporary salve – giving the states that possess these weapons, and humanity as a whole, sufficient time to seek a better world, less primed for interstate conflict. Under the shadow of nuclear deterrence, world leaders must be able to move to resolve their grievances and differences. The problem of war, the most fundamental problem in international politics, cannot be fully eliminated, but an environment in which states are able to seek cooperation and address their political differences through diplomacy rather than resorts to force or threats will be safer, ultimately, for nuclear deterrence. This was, in many ways, the world that existed briefly in the interlude between the Cold War and the dawn of this new nuclear age – explaining perhaps why nuclear weapons receded as they did into the relative background of international politics. Our task ahead will be to ensure then that the Cold War and this new nuclear age are not humanity's steady-state when it comes to nuclear weapons, but the aberration.

There is a separate, but related, problem that will be especially acute in this new nuclear age. Earlier in this book, I described the growing allure of limited nuclear use, born of a belief that crises, and even wars, could be successfully terminated after initial nuclear attacks because of the inherent fear in escalation to an unlimited nuclear exchange. This world has not yet manifested, but it represents perhaps the ultimate in the deterrence optimist's hubris: that nuclear weapons can be "tailored," or serve the role of a "scalpel."[57] As long as nuclear weapons remain political tools for coercion – and as long as leaders and military planners fail to account for the possibility of escalation spiraling unpredictably and in unwanted ways – this temptation will loom. But even if a nuclear weapon can be used short of sparking an all-out nuclear *war*, we will have crossed a dangerous Rubicon. The third use of nuclear weapons since August 1945 may not be the last, and humanity might find itself sliding into a world where nuclear deterrence is wholly insufficient for our longer-term survival.

Even if a single nuclear weapon detonating in a war does not mark an existential event for humanity, inviting – or tolerating – this possible future will have far-reaching and devastating consequences. The most obvious of these is that nuclear use, despite the best efforts of military establishments in nuclear-armed states, leads to general Armageddon after escalation fundamentally proves uncontrollable. Millions perish and, among those who survive, famine, protracted climatic effects, and civilizational breakdown follow. If escalation can be managed – through luck, or through adept communication and reason – we will have a more paranoid, desperate, and dangerous world. Far from intolerable weapons that must be kept forever sheathed, nuclear weapons would take on even greater salience, imploding the nonproliferation order in the process. In a misguided search for safety in such a world, leaders may easily reach for increasingly risky solutions, such as automated nuclear retaliatory systems.

As unsatisfactory a solution as nuclear deterrence may be to the perils of humanity's coexistence with the bomb, its fundamental prescription is to *fear* the bomb. This fear need not paralyze action, but merely temper the instinct to march forward, proudly, toward the brink. Nuclear weapons have returned to the fore of international politics, and will be here to stay. Averting catastrophe will require that we take the prospect of nuclear escalation seriously.

Notes

Introduction

1 Dylan Spaulding, "The Anthropocene as a Nuclear Age," *The Equation* (November 2, 2023).

2 "Presidential Review Memorandum/NSC-10," National Security Archive (February 18, 1977); https://nsarchive.gwu.edu/media /28643/ocr.

3 M. Taylor Fravel, "China's 'World-Class Military' Ambitions: Origins and Implications," *The Washington Quarterly* 43, no. 1 (January 2, 2020): 85–99.

4 Robert Zoellick, "Whither China: From Membership to Responsibility?" Bureau of Public Affairs, U.S. Department of State (September 21, 2005); https://2001-2009.state.gov /s/d/former/zoellick/rem/53682.htm. Amitai Etzioni, "Is China a Responsible Stakeholder?" *International Affairs* (Royal Institute of International Affairs 1944–) 87, no. 3 (May 2011): 539–53.

5 Andrew Desiderio, "Milley: Beijing's Fears of U.S. Attack Prompted Call to Chinese General," *POLITICO* (September 28, 2021).

6 Author's interview with a U.S. military intelligence official in 2023.

7 "Statement by Peking on Nuclear Test," *New York Times* (October 17, 1964), sec. Archives.

8 Rosemary J. Foot, "Nuclear Coercion and the Ending of the Korean Conflict," *International Security* 13, no. 3 (1988): 92–112.

9 Thomas C. Reed, "The Chinese Nuclear Tests, 1964–1996," *Physics Today* 61, no. 9 (September 1, 2008): 47–53.

10 For a deeper exploration of these trends, see *Missile Technology: Accelerating Challenges* (IISS, December 2022), Ch. 5; https://www.iiss.org/en/publications/strategic-dossiers/mdi-missile-technology-accelerating-challenges/.

11 *Military and Security Developments Involving the People's Republic of China, 2021,* Annual Report to Congress, Office of the Secretary of Defense, p. 92; https://media.defense.gov/2021/Nov/03/2002885874/-1/-1/0/2021-cmpr-final.pdf.

12 See, for instance, Hans M. Kristensen and Robert S. Norris (2018) "Chinese Nuclear Forces," *Bulletin of the Atomic Scientists* 74, no. 4 (June 28, 2018): 289–95, and Hans M. Kristensen and Matt Korda, "Nuclear Notebook: Chinese Nuclear Forces, 2020," *Bulletin of the Atomic Scientists* 76, no. 6 (2020): 443–57.

13 Dmitry Stefanovich, "Russia to Help China Develop an Early Warning System," *The Diplomat* (October 25, 2019).

14 President of Russia, "Joint Statement of the Russian Federation and the People's Republic of China on the International Relations Entering a New Era and the Global Sustainable Development" (February 4, 2022); http://www.en.kremlin.ru/supplement/5770.

15 Patricia M. Kim, "The Limits of the No-Limits Partnership," *Foreign Affairs* (February 28, 2023).

16 Max Seddon and Chris Cook, "How Russia War-Gamed a Chinese Invasion," *Financial Times* (February 29, 2024), sec. FT Investigations.

Chapter 1: Slouching Toward a New Nuclear Age

1 For a detailed history of the Manhattan Project, see Richard Rhodes, *The Making of the Atomic Bomb*, repr. ed. (New York: Simon & Schuster, 2012 [1986]).

2 Casualty estimates for the Hiroshima and Nagasaki bombings remain debated. For a historically informed exploration, see Alex Wellerstein, "Counting the Dead at Hiroshima and Nagasaki," *Bulletin of the Atomic Scientists* (blog), (August 4, 2020).

3 One megaton refers to an explosive force equivalent to one million tons of Trinitrotoluene, or TNT, a chemical explosive material.

4 "Foreign Relations of the United States, 1961–1963, Volume XIV, Berlin Crisis, 1961–1962," Office of the Historian, U.S. Department of State (May 31, 1961); https://history.state.gov/his toricaldocuments/frus1961-63v14/d30.

5 Andreas Lutsch, "West Germany and NATO's Nuclear Force Posture in the Early 1960s (Part 1)," *Journal of Cold War Studies* 24, no. 4 (December 16, 2022): 4–58.

6 William Alberque, "The NPT and the Origins of NATO's Nuclear Sharing Arrangements," *Proliferation Papers* 57, Ifri (February 2017), p. 19; https://www.ifri.org/sites/default/files/atoms/files /alberque_npt_origins_nato_nuclear_2017.pdf.

7 Hans M. Kristensen and Robert S. Norris, "A History of US Nuclear Weapons in South Korea," *Bulletin of the Atomic Scientists* 73, no. 6 (November 2, 2017): 349–57.

8 William Burr, "The United States and South Korea's Nuclear Weapons Program, 1974–1976," Wilson Center (March 14, 2017); https://www.wilsoncenter.org/article/the-united-states-and -south-koreas-nuclear-weapons-program-1974-1976.

9 Vipin Narang, *Seeking the Bomb: Strategies of Nuclear Proliferation* (Princeton, NJ: Princeton University Press, 2022), p. 43.

10 "60th Anniversary of Irish Resolution: A Forerunner of the NPT," National Security Archive (October 29, 2018); https://nsarchive .gwu.edu/briefing-book/nuclear-vault/2018-10-29/60th-anniver sary-irish-resolution-forerunner-npt.

11 Richard A. Paulsen, *The Role of US Nuclear Weapons in the Post-Cold War Era* (Maxwell Air Force Base, AL: Air University Press, 1994).

12 Michael Krepon, "The Golden Age of Nuclear Arms Control," Arms Control Wonk (April 22, 2019); https://www.armscon trolwonk.com/archive/1207168/the-golden-age-of-nuclear-arms-control/.

13 Paul Bracken, *The Second Nuclear Age: Strategy, Danger, and the New Power Politics* (New York: St. Martin's Griffin, 2013), p. 1.

14 "Resolution 984 (1995): S/RES/984 (1995)," United Nations Security Council (April 11, 1995); http://unscr.com/files/1995 /00984.pdf.

15 Peter Liberman, "The Rise and Fall of the South African Bomb," *International Security* 26, no. 2 (2001): 45–86.

16 Bob Woodward, "Pakistan Reported Near Atom Arms Production," *Washington Post* (November 4, 1986).

17 Terence Neilan, "Bush Pulls Out of ABM Treaty; Putin Calls Move a Mistake," *New York Times* (December 13, 2001), sec. World.

18 Austin Long, "Red Glare: The Origin and Implications of Russia's 'New' Nuclear Weapons," RAND Corporation (March 26, 2018); https://www.rand.org/pubs/commentary/2018/03/red-glare-the -origin-and-implications-of-russias-new.html.

19 See, for example, Li Bin, Zhou Baogen, and Liu Zhiwei, "Missile Defense: China Will Have to Respond," *Bulletin of the Atomic Scientists* 57, no. 6 (November 1, 2001): 25–28.

20 Rebecca Davis Gibbons and Matthew Kroenig, "Reconceptual-izing Nuclear Risks: Bringing Deliberate Nuclear Use Back In," *Comparative Strategy* 35, no. 5 (October 19, 2016): 407.

21 Former U.S. official in a conversation with the author, 2023.

22 Robert G. Gard, Jr., "JFK's Nuclear Proliferation Warnings: Up to 25 Countries With Nuclear Weapons," *Council for a Livable World* (blog), (May 11, 2012).

23 "Remarks by President Barack Obama in Prague as Delivered," Office of the Press Secretary, The White House (April 5, 2009); https://obamawhitehouse.archives.gov/the-press-office/remarks -president-barack-obama-prague-delivered.

24 Joby Warrick, "China Is Building More Than 100 New Missile Silos in its Western Desert, Analysts Say," *Washington Post* (June 30, 2021).

25 Matt Korda and Hans M. Kristensen, "China is Building a Second Nuclear Missile Silo Field," *Federation Of American Scientists* (blog), (July 26, 2021).

26 Roderick Lee, "PLA Likely Begins Construction of an Intercontinental Ballistic Missile Silo Site near Hanggin Banner," U.S. Air Force, China Aerospace Studies Institute (August 12, 2021); https://www.airuniversity.af.edu/CASI/Display/Article/27297 81/pla-likely-begins-construction-of-an-intercontinental-ballis tic-missile-silo-si/.

27 *Military and Security Developments Involving the People's Republic of China*, Annual Report to Congress, Office of the Secretary of Defense (2021), p. 8; https://media.defense.gov/ 2021/Nov/03/2002885874/-1/-1/0/2021-CMPR-FINAL.PDF.

28 Rosemary J. Foot, "Nuclear Coercion and the Ending of the Korean Conflict," *International Security* 13, no. 3 (1988): 92–112.

29 Isaac Stanley-Becker, "Top General Was So Fearful Trump Might Spark War that He Made Secret Calls to his Chinese Counterpart, New Book Says," *Washington Post* (September 14, 2021).

30 Vladimir Isachenkov, "Putin Signs Bill to Suspend Last Nuclear Arms Pact with US," AP News (February 28, 2023).

31 Michael R. Pompeo, "U.S. Withdrawal from the INF Treaty on August 2, 2019," U.S. Department of State (August 2, 2019); https://2017-2021.state.gov/u-s-withdrawal-from-the-inf-treaty-on-august-2-2019/. Ryan Browne, "US Formally Withdraws from Open Skies Treaty That Bolstered European Security," CNN (November 22, 2020). "DOD Statement on Open Skies Treaty Withdrawal," U.S. Department of Defense (May 21, 2020); https://www.defense.gov/News/Releases/Release/Article /2195239/dod-statement-on-open-skies-treaty-withdrawal/.

32 Ankit Panda, *Kim Jong Un and the Bomb: Survival and Deterrence in North Korea* (Oxford: Oxford University Press, 2020).

33 Alastair Gale, "U.S. Confronts the Reality of North Korea's Nuclear Program," *Wall Street Journal* (July 20, 2022), sec. World.

34 Warren P. Strobel and Matthew Luxmoore, "Russia Has Lost Almost 90% of Its Prewar Army, U.S. Intelligence Says," *Wall Street Journal* (December 12, 2023).

35 Ankit Panda, "Missiles, Preemption, and the Risk of Nuclear War on the Korean Peninsula," Arms Control Association (March 2024); https://www.armscontrol.org/act/2024-03/features/mis siles-preemption-risk-nuclear-war-korean-peninsula.

36 Karen DeYoung and Missy Ryan, "U.S. in No Hurry to Provide Ukraine with Long-Range Missiles," *Washington Post* (July 24, 2023).

37 "Blinken Says U.S. Neither Encourages nor Enables Ukraine to Strike inside Russia," Reuters (December 6, 2022), sec. Europe.

38 The Soviet Union once detonated a 30-kiloton nuclear device to extinguish a burning gas well in Uzbekistan, for example.

39 Thomas C. Schelling, "An Astonishing Sixty Years: The Legacy of Hiroshima," The Nobel Prize (2005); https://www.nobelprize.org /prizes/economic-sciences/2005/schelling/lecture/.

40 Nina Tannenwald, "The Nuclear Taboo: The United States and the Normative Basis of Nuclear Non-Use," *International Organization* 53, no. 3 (1999): 433–68.

41 Heather Williams et al., "Deter and Divide: Russia's Nuclear Rhetoric and Escalation Risks in Ukraine," Center for Strategic and International Studies (2024); https://features.csis.org/deter -and-divide-russia-nuclear-rhetoric.

42 Hanna Notte, "The West Cannot Cure Russia's Nuclear Fever," *War on the Rocks* (July 18, 2023).

43 Peter Baker and Choe Sang-Hun, "Trump Threatens 'Fire and Fury' against North Korea if it Endangers U.S.," *New York Times* (August 8, 2017), sec. World.

44 "Have We Kept Our Nuclear Bomb for Diwali, Asks Narendra Modi," *The Hindu* (April 21, 2019), sec. Lok Sabha 2019.

45 Daryl G. Press, Scott D. Sagan, and Benjamin A. Valentino, "Atomic Aversion: Experimental Evidence on Taboos, Traditions,

and the Non-Use of Nuclear Weapons," *The American Political Science Review* 107, no. 1 (2013): 188–206.

46 "Joint Statement of the Leaders of the Five Nuclear-Weapon States on Preventing Nuclear War and Avoiding Arms Races," The White House (January 3, 2022); https://www.whitehouse.gov/briefing-room/statements-releases/2022/01/03/p5-statement-on-preventing-nuclear-war-and-avoiding-arms-races/.

Chapter 2: From Terror, Peace

1 Dexter Masters, *One World or None: A Report to the Public on the Full Meaning of the Atomic Bomb* (New York: The New Press, 2007), p. xiii.

2 "Russell-Einstein Manifesto," Atomic Heritage Foundation; https://ahf.nuclearmuseum.org/ahf/key-documents/russell-einstein-manifesto/.

3 "The Baruch Plan (Presented to the United Nations Atomic Energy Commission, June 14, 1946)," Atomic Archive; https://www.atomicarchive.com/resources/documents/deterrence/baruch-plan.html.

4 Henry Lewis Stimson, "The Decision to Use the Atomic Bomb," *Harper's Magazine* (February 1947).

5 Gar Alperovitz, *The Decision to Use the Atomic Bomb* (New York: Vintage, 2010).

6 Rosemary J. Foot, "Nuclear Coercion and the Ending of the Korean Conflict," *International Security* 13, no. 3 (1988): 92–112.

7 "President Says Atom Bomb Would Be Used Like 'Bullet'; Eisenhower Talks of Atom 'Bullet,'" *New York Times* (March 17, 1955), sec. Archives.

8 John Foster Dulles, "Challenge and Response in United States Policy," *Foreign Affairs* 36, no. 1 (1957): 31.

9 William Burr, ed., "U.S. Presidents and the Nuclear Taboo," National Security Archive (November 30, 2017); https://nsarchive.gwu.edu/briefing-book/nuclear-vault/2017-11-30/us-presidents-nuclear-taboo.

10 Bernard Brodie, *The Absolute Weapon: Atomic Power and World Order* (Freeport, NY: Ayer Co. Publishers, 1946).

11 Jacob Viner, "The Implications of the Atomic Bomb for International Relations," *Proceedings of the American Philosophical Society* 90, no. 1. (January 1946): 55.

12 Robert Jervis, *The Meaning of the Nuclear Revolution: Statecraft and the Prospect of Armageddon* (Ithaca, NY: Cornell University Press, 1990).

13 Robert Jervis, "The Nuclear Revolution and the Common Defense," *Political Science Quarterly* 101, no. 5 (1986): 689–703.

14 See Paul C. Avey, "Just Like Yesterday? New Critiques of the Nuclear Revolution," *Texas National Security Review* (April 20, 2023). Brendan Rittenhouse Green, *The Revolution that Failed: Nuclear Competition, Arms Control, and the Cold War* (New York: Cambridge University Press, 2020). Mark S. Bell, *Nuclear Reactions: How Nuclear-Armed States Behave* (Ithaca, NY: Cornell University Press, 2021).

15 Eisenhower may not have believed this himself. See "Memorandum of Discussion at the 364th Meeting of the National Security Council," Office of the Historian, U.S. Department of State (May 1, 1958); https://history.state.gov/historicaldocuments/frus1958 -60v03/d23.

16 IPPNW, "Ukraine War Shows Nuclear Deterrence Doesn't Work; We Need Disarmament," IPPNW Peace and Health Blog (March 27, 2022). "What about 'Nuclear Deterrence' Theory? Do Nuclear Weapons Help Keep the Peace?," ICAN; https://www. icanw.org/what_about_nuclear_deterrence_theory.

17 "Remarks of President Joe Biden – State of the Union Address As Prepared for Delivery," The White House (March 1, 2022); https://www.whitehouse.gov/briefing-room/speeches-re marks/2022/03/01/remarks-of-president-joe-biden-state-of-the -union-address-as-delivered/.

18 Sacha Pfeiffer, Lauren Hodges, and Christopher Intagliata, "Former NATO Commander Says a No-Fly Zone over Ukraine Must Be on the Table," *NPR* (March 3, 2022), sec. Europe.

19 Adam Kinzinger (Slava Ukraini), "(1) The fate of #Ukraine is being decided tonight, but also the fate of the west. Declare a #NoFlyZone over Ukraine at the invitation of their sovereign govt. Disrupt Russia's air ops to give the heroic Ukrainians a fair fight. It's now, or later," Twitter (February 26, 2022).

20 Jonathan Swan, Zachary Basu, and Sophia Cai, "Scoop: Zelensky Pushes Biden on No-Fly Zone," Axios (February 28, 2022).

21 Richard D. Hooker Jr., "A No-Fly Zone over Ukraine? The Case for NATO Doing It," Atlantic Council (blog), (March 18, 2022).

22 Susan Milligan, "Biden Stands Firm Against No-Fly Zone as Zelenskyy Prepares to Address Congress," *U.S. News and World Report* (March 15, 2022).

23 Aaron Blake, "Analysis | Why Biden and the White House Keep Talking about World War III," *Washington Post* (March 18, 2022).

24 McGeorge Bundy, *Danger and Survival: Choices About the Bomb in the First Fifty Years* (New York: Random House, 1988), p. 127.

25 Bakhti Nishanov [@b_nishanov], "General Breedlove at @ HelsinkiComm hearing on containing Russia: 'We are constantly reacting to Putin. We should be the ones dictating the substance and tempo of this engagement. We are almost fully deterred, while Putin is almost fully undeterred,'" Twitter (March 23, 2022).

26 Susan B. Glasser, "Jake Sullivan's Trial by Combat," *The New Yorker* (October 9, 2023).

27 Jill Lawless, "The BBC Says a Russian Pilot Tried to Shoot down a British Plane over the Black Sea Last Year," AP News (September 14, 2023).

28 AnneClaire Stapleton et al., "Deadly Russian Missile Struck Close to Zelensky and Greek Leader's Convoy," CNN (March 7, 2024).

29 "A Senior U.S. Intelligence Official Says Russian Missiles Crossed into NATO Member Poland, Killing Two People," AP News (November 15, 2022).

30 Two such statements appeared on social media. Artis Pabriks [@Pabriks], "My condolences to our Polish brothers in arms. Criminal Russian regime fired missiles which target not only

Ukrainian civilians but also landed on NATO territory in Poland. Latvia fully stands with Polish friends and condemns this crime," Twitter (November 15, 2022). Jaro Nad [@JaroNad], "Very concerned by Russian missiles dropping in Poland. Russia must explain what happened. Senseless attacks on infrastructure must stop immediately. Russia's recklessness is getting out of hand. Will be in close contact w/@mblaszczak and allies to coordinate response @Slovakia_NATO," Twitter (November 15, 2022).

31 Herman Kahn, *Thinking About The Unthinkable* (New York: Avon Books, 1962).

32 Anne Applebaum, "The War Won't End Until Putin Loses," *The Atlantic* (May 23, 2022).

33 Thomas C. Schelling, "The Threat That Leaves Something to Chance," RAND Corporation (August 10, 1959); https://www.rand.org/pubs/historical_documents/HDA1631-1.html.

34 This view was expressed by multiple U.S. officials and European officials in London and Berlin in the course of interviews conducted in the summer and autumn of 2023.

35 Thomas C. Schelling, *The Strategy of Conflict: With a New Preface by the Author*, repr. ed. (Cambridge, MA: Harvard University Press, 1981). I am indebted to Schelling for the contours of the analogy set out in this paragraph.

36 Theresa Hitchens, "The Nuclear 3 Body Problem: STRATCOM 'Furiously' Rewriting Deterrence Theory in Tripolar World," *Breaking Defense* (blog), (August 11, 2022).

37 Scott D. Sagan and Allen S. Weiner, "The Rule of Law and the Role of Strategy in U.S. Nuclear Doctrine." *International Security* 45, no. 4 (2021): 139. Guy Pollard, the United Kingdom's deputy permanent representative to the Conference on Disarmament in 2015, stated that the United Kingdom "would not use any of our [nuclear] weapons contrary to international law": Statement by Mr. Guy Pollard, "2015 Review Conference of the Treaty on Non-Proliferation of Nuclear Weapons: New York, 27 April – 22 May 2015"; https://www.reachingcriticalwill.org/images/documents/Disarmament-fora/npt/revcon2015/statements/1May_UK.pdf.

38 Albert Wohlstetter, "The Delicate Balance of Terror," RAND Corporation (1958); https://www.rand.org/pubs/papers/P1472 .html.

39 Paul H. Nitze, "Assuring Strategic Stability in an Era of Détente," *Foreign Affairs* 54, no. 2 (1976): 207–32. Ted Greenwood and Michael L. Nacht, "The New Nuclear Debate: Sense or Nonsense?" *Foreign Affairs* 52, no. 4 (1974): 761–80.

40 Robert McNamara, "Recommended FY 1966–1970 Programs for Strategic Offensive Forces, Continental Air and Missile Defense Forces, and Civil Defense," U.S. Department of Defense (December 3, 1964); https://nsarchive.gwu.edu/document/252 24-document-23-intolerable-punishment-any-industrialized -nation-memorandum-secretary.

41 Charles L. Glaser, James M. Acton, and Steve Fetter, "The U.S. Nuclear Arsenal Can Deter Both China and Russia," *Foreign Affairs* (October 5, 2023).

42 Fred Kaplan, *The Wizards of Armageddon* (Stanford, CA: Stanford University Press, 1991), pp. 264–70.

43 Final Decision on MC 14/2 (Revised): "A Report by the Military Committee on Overall Strategic Concept for the Defense of the North Atlantic Treaty Organization Area," NATO Strategy Documents 1949–69 (May 23, 1957); https://www.nato.int/docu /stratdoc/eng/a570523a.pdf.

44 "The first objective would be to counter the aggression without escalation and preserve or restore the integrity and security of the North Atlantic area. However, NATO must be manifestly prepared at all times to escalate the conflict, using nuclear weapons if necessary. It is emphasised that NATO's capabilities to resist conventional aggression without resorting to nuclear warfare will depend on the enemy's actions, on the actions taken by NATO nations as a result of available warning, on the effectiveness of the military forces-in-being and reinforcements, and their conventional capability to defend forward. These factors will dictate the level of aggression at which NATO will have to commit itself to initiate the use of nuclear weapons," NATO

observed in MC 14/3. See Final Decision on MC 14/3: "A Report by the Military Committee on Overall Strategic Concept for the Defense of the North Atlantic Treaty Organization Area," NATO Strategy Documents 1949–69 (January 16, 1968); https://www.nato.int/docu/stratdoc/eng/a680116a.pdf.

45 United Nations Office for Disarmament Affairs, *Nuclear Weapons: A Comprehensive Study Stock for Standing Orders Only* (United Nations, 1992), p. 45.

46 Vasiliĭ Danilovich Sokolovskiĭ, *Military Strategy* (Stanford, CA: Stanford Research Institute, 1972), p. 236.

47 Fiona S. Cunningham and M. Taylor Fravel, "Dangerous Confidence? Chinese Views on Nuclear Escalation," *International Security* 44, no. 2 (October 1, 2019): 61–109.

48 One news report noted that the three Western nuclear powers "delivered a joint message to Russia vowing to retaliate with conventional weapons if Putin decided to use nuclear weapons in Ukraine, according to the former US and Russian officials." See Christopher Miller, Max Seddon, and Felicia Schwartz, "How Putin Blundered into Ukraine – Then Doubled Down," *Financial Times* (February 23, 2023), sec. The Big Read.

49 Author's interview with a U.S. official in October 2023.

50 This is reported in detail in Fred Kaplan, *The Bomb: Presidents, Generals, and the Secret History of Nuclear War* (New York: Simon & Schuster, 2020), 256–58.

51 Nina Tannenwald, "Stigmatizing the Bomb: Origins of the Nuclear Taboo," *International Security* 29, no. 4 (2005): 5–49.

Chapter 3: Technology and Escalation

1 "China's 2021 Orbital-Weapon Tests," IISS (March 2022); https://www.iiss.org/publications/strategic-comments/2022/chinas-2021-orbital-weapon-tests.

2 David E. Sanger and William J. Broad, "China's Weapon Tests Close to a 'Sputnik Moment,' U.S. General Says," *New York Times* (October 27, 2021), sec. U.S.

3 Matt Korda, "ICBM Advocates Say US Missile Subs Are Vulnerable. It Isn't True," Defense One (December 10, 2020); https://www.defenseone.com/ideas/2020/12/icbm-advocates-say-us-missile-subs-are-vulnerable-it-isnt-true/170677/.

4 Office of the Secretary of Defense, *Nuclear Posture Review* (February 2018), p. 45.

5 William Rosenau, "Coalition Scud-Hunting in Iraq, 1991," in *Special Operations Forces and Elusive Enemy Ground Targets: Lessons from Vietnam and the Persian Gulf War* (RAND Corporation, 2001), pp. 29–44; http://www.jstor.org/stable/10.7249/mr1408af.9.

6 James M. Acton, *Silver Bullet? Asking the Right Questions About Conventional Prompt Global Strike* (Washington, DC: Carnegie Endowment for International Peace, 2013).

7 President of Russia, "Presidential Address to the Federal Assembly" (March 1, 2018); http://en.kremlin.ru/events/president/news/56957.

8 "Statement of General Terrence J. O'Shaughnessy, United States Air Force, Commander, United States Northern Command and North American Aerospace Defense Command," United States Senate (February 13, 2020); https://www.armed-services.senate.gov/imo/media/doc/OShaughnessy_02-13-20.pdf.

9 Albert Wohlstetter, "The Delicate Balance of Terror," *Foreign Affairs* 37, no. 2 (1959): 211–12.

10 Morton H. Halperin, "The Decision to Deploy the ABM: Bureaucratic and Domestic Politics in the Johnson Administration," *World Politics* 25, no. 1 (1972): 87.

11 Steven C. Haas, "Reassessing Lessons from the ABM Treaty," *International Affairs (Royal Institute of International Affairs 1944–)* 64, no. 2 (1988): 233–40.

12 "Ballistic Missile Defense Intercept Flight Test Record," Missile Defense Agency (December 2018); https://www.defense.gov/Portals/1/Interactive/2018/11-2019-Missile-Defense-Review/ballistic-missile-defense-intercept-flight-test-record-UPDATED.pdf.

13 "Missile Defense Becomes Part of Great Power Competition," U.S. Department of Defense (July 28, 2020); https://www.defense.gov/News/News-Stories/Article/Article/2291331/missile-defense-becomes-part-of-great-power-competition/.

14 Fred Kaplan, "The Illogic of Nuclear Escalation," *Asterisk* (November 2022).

15 Christopher Clary and Vipin Narang, "India's Counterforce Temptations: Strategic Dilemmas, Doctrine, and Capabilities," *International Security* 43, no. 3 (February 1, 2019): 7–52.

16 Hunter Stoll, John Hoehn, and William Courtney, "Air Defense Shapes Warfighting in Ukraine," RAND Corporation (February 22, 2024); https://www.rand.org/pubs/commentary/2024/02/air-defense-shapes-warfighting-in-ukraine.html.

17 "Russia Deploys Avangard Hypersonic Missile System," BBC News (December 27, 2019).

18 Vann H. Van Diepen, "Six Takeaways from North Korea's 'Hypersonic Missile' Announcement," *38 North* (October 13, 2021).

19 Courtney Albon, "Missile Defense Agency Satellites Track First Hypersonic Launch," *Defense News* (June 14, 2024).

20 Cameron L. Tracy and David Wright, "Modelling the Performance of Hypersonic Boost-Glide Missiles," *Science & Global Security* 28, no. 3 (2020): 135–70.

21 Andrew Futter and Benjamin Zala, "Strategic Non-Nuclear Weapons and the Onset of a Third Nuclear Age," *European Journal of International Security* 6, no. 3 (August 2021): 257–77.

22 Ankit Panda, *Indo-Pacific Missile Arsenals: Avoiding Spirals and Mitigating Escalation Risks*, Carnegie Endowment for International Peace (October 31, 2023); https://carnegieendowment.org/2023/10/31/indo-pacific-missile-arsenals-avoiding-spirals-and-mitigating-escalation-risks-pub-90772.

23 The White House, "Remarks by National Security Advisor Jake Sullivan for the Arms Control Association (ACA) Annual Forum," The White House (June 2, 2023); https://www.whitehouse.gov/briefing-room/speeches-remarks/2023/06/02/remarks

-by-national-security-advisor-jake-sullivan-for-the-arms-con
trol-association-aca-annual-forum/.

24 Taylor Coe, "Where Does the Word Cyber Come From?,"
    OUPblog (March 28, 2015).

25 James P. Farwell and Rafal Rohozinski, "Stuxnet and the Future
    of Cyber War," *Survival* 53, no. 1 (February 1, 2011): 23–40.

26 Karen DeYoung, Ellen Nakashima, and Emily Rauhala, "Trump
    Signed Presidential Directive Ordering Actions to Pressure
    North Korea," *Washington Post* (September 30, 2017), sec.
    National Security.

27 Patrick Howell O'Neill, "Russia Hacked an American Satellite
    Company One Hour before the Ukraine Invasion," *MIT
    Technology Review* (May 10, 2022).

28 See, for instance, the U.S. National Security Agency's esti-
    mate from 2006, which suggested that cyberattacks would be
    "exceedingly hard to trace." "A Strategy for Surveillance Powers"
    (November 23, 2013); https://www.nytimes.com/interactive/
    2013/11/23/us/politics/23nsa-sigint-strategy-document.html.

29 Ellen Nakashima, "Russian Spies Hacked the Olympics and Tried
    to Make It Look like North Korea Did It, U.S. Officials Say,"
    Washington Post (February 26, 2018).

30 Thomas Rid and Ben Buchanan, "Attributing Cyber Attacks,"
    Journal of Strategic Studies 38, no. 1–2 (January 2, 2015):
    4–37.

31 William J. Broad and David E. Sanger, "U.S. Strategy to Hobble
    North Korea Was Hidden in Plain Sight," *New York Times*
    (March 4, 2017), sec. World.

32 Spencer Ackerman, "Revealed: Pentagon Push to Hack Nuke
    Missiles Before They Launch," *Daily Beast* (May 22, 2018), sec.
    Politics.

33 For a more detailed discussion, see Ankit Panda, "The Right Way
    to Manage a Nuclear North Korea," *Foreign Affairs* (November
    19, 2018).

34 Krystal Hu, "ChatGPT Sets Record for Fastest-Growing User Base
    – Analyst Note," Reuters (February 2, 2023), sec. Technology.

35 Nilay Patel, "Exclusive: Google's Sundar Pichai Talks Search, AI, and Dancing with Microsoft," *The Verge* (May 12, 2023).

36 Herbert A. Simon and Allen Newell, "Heuristic Problem Solving: The Next Advance in Operations Research," *Operations Research* 6, no. 1 (1958): 3.

37 Claude E. Shannon, "Programming a Computer for Playing Chess," *Philosophical Magazine* 41, no. 7 (1950): 256–75.

38 David Hoffman, "'I Had A Funny Feeling in My Gut,'" *Washington Post* (February 10, 1999).

39 Herman Kahn, *On Thermonuclear War* (Princeton, NJ: Princeton University Press, 1960), 145–55.

40 Terry Mikesell, "Dark Satire on Nuclear War Was Right on Target in '64," *The Columbus Dispatch* (August 2, 2012).

41 Emily M. Bender et al., "On the Dangers of Stochastic Parrots: Can Language Models Be Too Big?" in *Proceedings of the 2021 ACM Conference on Fairness, Accountability, and Transparency* (March 2021), pp. 610–23.

42 Saurabh Bagchi, "Why We Need to See Inside AI's Black Box," *Scientific American* (May 26, 2023).

43 See "2020 Review Conference of the Parties to the Treaty on the Non-Proliferation of Nuclear Weapons," Working paper submitted by France, the United Kingdom of Great Britain and Northern Ireland and the United States of America (July 20, 2022); https://reachingcriticalwill.org/images/documents/Disarmament-fora/npt/revcon2022/documents/WP70.pdf.

44 Emilia David, "China Mandates that AI Must Follow 'Core Values of Socialism,'" *The Verge* (July 14, 2023).

45 David Hoffman, *The Dead Hand: The Untold Story of the Cold War Arms Race and Its Dangerous Legacy* (New York: Anchor, 2010).

46 "DPRK's Law on Policy of Nuclear Forces Promulgated," KCNA Watch (September 9, 2022).

47 Adam Lowther and Curtis McGiffin, "America Needs a 'Dead Hand,'" *War on the Rocks* (August 16, 2019).

48 Alan J. Vick et al., "Aerospace Operations Against Elusive Ground Targets," RAND Corporation (January 1, 2001); https://www.rand.org/pubs/monograph_reports/MR1398.html.

49 See Christopher Clary, "Survivability in the New Era of Counterforce," in Vipin Narang and Scott D. Sagan, *The Fragile Balance of Terror: Deterrence in the New Nuclear Age* (Ithaca, NY: Cornell University Press, 2023), pp. 171–4.

50 Edward Geist, *Deterrence under Uncertainty: Artificial Intelligence and Nuclear Warfare* (New York: Oxford University Press, 2023), pp. 170–88.

51 General James Dickinson, statement before the Senate Armed Services Committee (April 21, 2021); https://www.armed-ser vices.senate.gov/imo/media/doc/Dickinson04.20.2021.pdf.

52 James M. Acton, "Escalation through Entanglement: How the Vulnerability of Command-and-Control Systems Raises the Risks of an Inadvertent Nuclear War," *International Security* 43, no. 1 (August 1, 2018): 56–99.

53 Office of the Secretary of Defense, *Nuclear Posture Review* (February 2018), p. 21; https://media.defense.gov/2018/Feb/02/2001872886/-1/-1/1/2018-nuclear-posture-review-final-report.pdf.

54 Author's interview in 2022.

55 "Global Counterspace Capabilities: An Open Source Assessment," Secure World Foundation (April 2023), pp. 03–09; https://swfound.org/media/207567/swf_global_counterspace_capa bilities_2023_v2.pdf.

56 Alexey Arbatov, Vladimir Dvorkin, and Petr Topychkanov, "Entanglement as a New Security Threat: A Russian Perspective – Entanglement: Chinese and Russian Perspectives on Non-Nuclear Weapons and Nuclear Risks," Carnegie Endowment for International Peace (November 8, 2017), p. 38; https://carnegie moscow.org/2017/11/08/entanglement-as-new-security-threat -russian-perspective-pub-73163.

57 Marcia Smith, "U.N. Approves Resolution Not to Conduct Destructive ASAT Tests," Space Policy Online (December 7,

2022); https://spacepolicyonline.com/news/u-n-approves-resolu
tion-not-to-conduct-destructive-asat-tests/.

58 Ankit Panda and Vipin Narang, "Deadly Overconfidence: Trump
Thinks Missile Defenses Work Against North Korea, and That
Should Scare You," *War on the Rocks* (October 16, 2017).

59 "Aerospace and AI are Future of Defense Industry, Says Yoon,"
Korea JoongAng Daily (October 17, 2023).

Chapter 4: The New Nuclear Disorder

1 Sheldon M. Stern, *The Week the World Stood Still: Inside the
Secret Cuban Missile Crisis* (Stanford, CA: Stanford University
Press, 2005), 157.

2 "Recollections of Vadim Orlov (USSR Submarine B-59),"
National Security Archive; https://nsarchive2.gwu.edu/nsa/cuba_
mis_cri/020000%20Recollections%20of%20Vadim%20Orlov.pdf.

3 Marion Lloyd, "Soviets Close to Using A-Bomb in 1962 Crisis,
Forum is Told," *The Boston Globe* (October 13, 2002).

4 Mark Leonard and Rob Blackhurst, "'I Don't Think Anybody
Thought Much about Whether Agent Orange Was against the
Rules of War,'" *Guardian* (May 19, 2002), sec. World news.

5 William Burr and Leopoldo Nuti, "The Jupiter Missiles and the
Endgame of the Cuban Missile Crisis: Sealing the Deal with
Italy and Turkey," Wilson Center (April 20, 2023); https://www.
wilsoncenter.org/blog-post/jupiter-missiles-and-endgame-
cuban-missile-crisis-sealing-deal-italy-and-turkey.

6 Steven E. Miller, "Nuclear Hotlines: Origins, Evolution,
Applications," *Journal for Peace and Nuclear Disarmament* 4,
suppl.1 (March 5, 2021): 117.

7 "Memorandum From the President's Press Secretary (Salinger)
to President Kennedy," Office of the Historian, U.S. Department
of State (February 14, 1962); https://history.state.gov/historical
documents/frus1961-63v05/d154?_s=34jwqcfexqkxghsupwuv.

8 Richard Smoke, 1984. *National Security and the Nuclear
Dilemma: An Introduction to the American Experience* (New
York: Random House, 1984), p. 138.

9   Hal Brands, "Progress Unseen: U.S. Arms Control Policy and the Origins of Détente, 1963–1968," *Diplomatic History* 30, no. 2 (2006): 253–85.

10 "Russian Noncompliance with and Invalid Suspension of the New START Treaty," U.S. Department of State (blog), (June 1, 2023); https://www.state.gov/russian-noncompliance-with-and -invalid-suspension-of-the-new-start-treaty/.

11 Shannon Bugos, "Russia Suspends New START," Arms Control Association (March 2023); https://www.armscontrol.org/act/ 2023-03/news/russia-suspends-new-start.

12 "U.S. Countermeasures in Response to Russia's Violations of the New START Treaty," U.S. Department of State (blog), (June 1, 2023), https://www.state.gov/u-s-countermeasures-in-response -to-russias-violations-of-the-new-start-treaty/.

13 Robert G. Gard, Jr., "JFK's Nuclear Proliferation Warnings: Up to 25 Countries With Nuclear Weapons," Council for a Livable World (May 11, 2012); https://livableworld.org/jfks-nuclear-pro liferation-warnings-up-to-25-countries-with-nuclear-weapons/.

14 "The Treaty on the Non-Proliferation of Nuclear Weapons (NPT)," Department for Disarmament Affairs, United Nations (May 2005); https://www.un.org/en/conf/npt/2005/npttreaty .html.

15 For an overview of nuclear force reductions over time, see "Status of World Nuclear Forces," *Federation of American Scientists* (blog), (March 31, 2023).

16 "Nuclear Non-Proliferation Treaty (NPT): Accomplishments and Challenges," Bureau of Public Affairs, U.S. Department of State (October 19, 2001); https://2001-2009.state.gov/t/isn/rls/ fs/2001/5485.htm.

17 Harald Müller and Carmen Wunderlich, "Nuclear Disarmament without the Nuclear-Weapon States: The Nuclear Weapon Ban Treaty," *Daedalus* 149, no. 2 (2020): 171–89.

18 Martha Finnemore and Kathryn Sikkink, "International Norm Dynamics and Political Change," *International Organization* 52, no. 4 (1998): 887–917.

19 Toby Dalton et al., "Dimming Prospects for U.S.–Russia Nonproliferation Cooperation," Carnegie Endowment for International Peace (March 14, 2024); https://carnegieendow ment.org/2024/03/14/dimming-prospects-for-u.s.-russia-non proliferation-cooperation-pub-91958.

20 "'Objects Resembling Explosives' Planted at Zaporizhzhia Nuclear Plant, Says Kyiv," *Guardian* (July 5, 2023), sec. World news.

21 Gaukhar Mukhatzhanova, "10th NPT Review Conference: Why It Was Doomed and How It Almost Succeeded," Arms Control Today (October 2022); https://www.armscontrol.org/act/2022 -10/features/10th-npt-review-conference-why-doomed-almost -succeeded.

22 "Joint Leaders Statement on AUKUS," The White House (September 15, 2021); https://www.whitehouse.gov/briefing- room/statements-releases/2021/0915/joint-leaders-statement -on-aukus/. "AUKUS Leaders' Level Statement," The White House(April 5, 2022); https://www.whitehouse.gov/briefing-room/ statements-releases/2022/04/05/aukus-leaders-level-statement/.

23 "Inaugural Address by President Joseph R. Biden, Jr.," The White House (January 20, 2021); https://www.whitehouse.gov/briefing -room/speeches-remarks/2021/01/20/inaugural-address-by- president-joseph-r-biden-jr/.

24 "Joint Statement Following Discussions With Chancellor Erhard," The American Presidency Project (December 21, 1965); https://www.presidency.ucsb.edu/documents/joint-statement -following-discussions-with-chancellor-erhard-1.

25 William Burr, "The United States and South Korea's Nuclear Weapons Program, 1974–1976," Wilson Center (March 14, 2017); https://www.wilsoncenter.org/article/the-united-states -and-south-koreas-nuclear-weapons-program-1974-1976.

26 David Albright and Andrea Stricker, *Taiwan's Former Nuclear Weapons Program: Nuclear Weapons On-Demand* (Washington, DC: Institute for Science and International Security, 2018).

27 "Address to the Nation on the War in Vietnam," The American

Presidency Project (November 3, 1969); https://www.presidency
.ucsb.edu/documents/address-the-nation-the-war-vietnam.

28 Leon Whyte, "Evolution of the U.S.–ROK Alliance: Abandonment
     Fears," *The Diplomat* (June 22, 2015).

29 "Memorandum of Conversation: Foreign Relations of the United
     States, 1961–1963, Volume XIV, Berlin Crisis, 1961–1962,"
     Office of the Historian, U.S. Department of State (May 31, 1961);
     https://history.state.gov/historicaldocuments/frus1961-63v14
     /d30.

30 Ankit Panda, "Seoul's Nuclear Temptations and the U.S.-South
     Korean Alliance," *War on the Rocks* (February 3, 2023).

31 Toby Dalton, Karl Friedhoff, and Lami Kim, "Thinking Nuclear:
     South Korean Attitudes on Nuclear Weapons," Chicago
     Council on Global Affairs (February 21, 2022); https://global
     affairs.org/research/public-opinion-survey/thinking-nuclear-
     south-korean-attitudes-nuclear-weapons.

32 Jeongmin Kim, "Full Text: Yoon Suk Yeol's Remarks on
     South Korea Acquiring Nuclear Arms," NK PRO (January 13,
     2023).

33 Scott D. Sagan, "Why Do States Build Nuclear Weapons?: Three
     Models in Search of a Bomb," *International Security* 21, no. 3
     (1996): 54–86.

34 Ankit Panda, "The Washington Declaration Is a Software Upgrade
     for the U.S.–South Korea Alliance," Carnegie Endowment for
     International Peace (May 1, 2023); https://carnegieendowment
     .org/2023/05/01/washington-declaration-is-software-upgrade
     -for-u.s.-south-korea-alliance-pub-89648.

35 "South Korean President Reiterates that Seoul Will Not Seek its
     Own Nuclear Deterrent," AP News (February 7, 2024).

36 Newell Highsmith, "Would the U.S. Sanction Allies Seeking the
     Bomb?" Carnegie Endowment for International Peace (April 20,
     2023); https://carnegieendowment.org/2023/04/20/would-u.s.-
     sanction-allies-seeking-bomb-pub-89587.

37 For a detailed exploration of the Cold War era West German
     and Japanese cases, see Tristan A. Volpe, *Leveraging Latency:*

How the Weak Compel the Strong with Nuclear Technology (New York: Oxford University Press, 2023).

38 Translated from the original German. See Fabian Reinbold, Georg Löwisch, and Jacobia Dahm, "Joschka Fischer: 'Ich schäme mich für unser Land,'" *Die Zeit* (December 3, 2023).

39 "Open Letter in Support of the Treaty on the Prohibition of Nuclear Weapons" (September 21, 2020); https://d3n8a8pro7v hmx.cloudfront.net/ican/pages/1712/attachments/original/ 1600645499/TPNW_Open_Letter_-_English.pdf.

40 Peter Baker, "Favoring Foes Over Friends, Trump Threatens to Upend International Order," *New York Times* (February 11, 2024).

41 "Wales Summit Declaration Issued by NATO Heads of State and Government (2014)," NATO (September 5, 2014); https://www .nato.int/cps/en/natohq/official_texts_112964.htm.

42 "Record 23 Countries Hit 2 Percent Defense Spending Target, NATO Says," *POLITICO* (June 17, 2024). "Defence Expenditure of NATO Countries (2014–2024)," NATO Press Release (2024); https://www.nato.int/nato_static_fl2014/assets/pdf/2024/6/pdf /240617-def-exp-2024-en.pdf.

43 See "A Conversation with Minister of Foreign Affairs of Poland Radosław Sikorski," Atlantic Council (February 26, 2024); https:// www.youtube.com/watch?v=SFOYe92FHxE.

44 Iain Rogers, "Germany Says Its Defense Spending Could Increase to 3.5% of GDP," Bloomberg (February 17, 2024).

45 Ulrich Kühn, "Germany Debates Nuclear Weapons, Again. But Now It's Different," *Bulletin of the Atomic Scientists* (blog), (March 15, 2024).

46 Dan Sabbagh, "Nato Chief Rebukes Donald Trump and Announces Record Defence Spending," *Guardian* (February 14, 2024), sec. World news.

47 Bruno Tertrais, "Will Europe Get Its Own Bomb?," *The Washington Quarterly* 42, no. 2 (April 3, 2019): 47–66.

48 Tertrais, "Will Europe Get Its Own Bomb?"

Chapter 5: Nuclear Flashpoints

1 Matthew Luxmoore, "Putin Puts Nuclear Forces in a 'Special Mode of Combat Duty,'" *Wall Street Journal* (February 27, 2022).

2 David Brunnstrom and Trevor Hunnicutt, "Biden Says U.S. Forces Would Defend Taiwan in the Event of a Chinese Invasion," Reuters (September 19, 2022), sec. World.

3 The Editorial Board, "Opinion: Who Would Win a War Over Taiwan?," *Wall Street Journal* (January 19, 2023), sec. Opinion. Mark F. Cancian, Matthew Cancian, and Eric Heginbotham, "The First Battle of the Next War: Wargaming a Chinese Invasion of Taiwan," Center for Strategic and International Studies (January 9, 2023); https://www.csis.org/analysis/first-battle-next-war-war gaming-chinese-invasion-taiwan.

4 Gregory Weaver, "The Role of Nuclear Weapons in a Taiwan Crisis," Atlantic Council (blog), (November 22, 2023).

5 Barton Gellman, "U.S. and China Nearly Came to Blows in '96," *Washington Post* (June 20, 1998).

6 Mallory Shelbourne, "Davidson: China Could Try to Take Control of Taiwan In 'Next Six Years,'" USNI News (blog), (March 9, 2021).

7 "China's Xi Says 'reunification' with Taiwan Is Inevitable," Reuters (January 1, 2024), sec. Asia Pacific.

8 "CIA Chief: China Has Doubt on Ability to Invade Taiwan," Voice of America (February 26, 2023).

9 Elliot Ji, "Rocket-Powered Corruption: Why the Missile Industry Became the Target of Xi's Purge," *War on the Rocks* (January 23, 2024).

10 For a broader assessment of the costs of "victory" for China, see Jude Blanchette and Gerard DiPippo, "'Reunification' with Taiwan through Force Would Be a Pyrrhic Victory for China," Center for Strategic and International Studies (November 22, 2022); https://www.csis.org/analysis/reunification-taiwan-through-force-would-be-pyrrhic-victory-china.

11 Caitlin Talmadge, "Would China Go Nuclear? Assessing the Risk of Chinese Nuclear Escalation in a Conventional War with the

United States," *International Security* 41, no. 4 (April 1, 2017): 50–92.

12 Weaver, "The Role of Nuclear Weapons in a Taiwan Crisis."

13 M. C. Rajan, "'New India' Will Pay Back Terrorists with Interest, says PM Modi," *Hindustan Times* (April 20, 2020).

14 "Indian Aircraft Violate LoC, Scramble Back after PAF's Timely Response: ISPR," DAWN e-paper (February 26, 2019).

15 Ansar Abbasi, "Hope India Knows What NCA Means?," *The News* (February 27, 2019).

16 Iain Marlow, "India Deployed Nuclear Subs, Carrier Group Amid Pakistan Tension," Bloomberg (March 18, 2019).

17 https://www.youtube.com/watch?v=hxZGbwCcCd0.

18 "Have We Kept Our Nuclear Bomb for Diwali, asks Narendra Modi," *The Hindu* (April 22, 2019).

19 For background on this period, see Jeffrey Lewis and Ankit Panda, "How Much Is Enough? Revisiting Nuclear Reliability, Deterrence, and Preventive War," in Vipin Narang and Scott D. Sagan, eds., *The Fragile Balance of Terror: Deterrence in the New Nuclear Age* (Ithaca, NY: Cornell University Press, 2023), pp. 123–53.

20 Christopher Clary and Ankit Panda, "Safer at Sea? Pakistan's Sea-Based Deterrent and Nuclear Weapons Security," *The Washington Quarterly* 40, no. 3 (July 3, 2017): 149–68.

21 See Rakesh Sood, "Managing the China, India and Pakistan Nuclear Trilemma: Ensuring Nuclear Stability in the New Nuclear Age," *Journal for Peace and Nuclear Disarmament* 5, no. 2 (July 3, 2022): 262–80. Jingdong Yuan, "External and Domestic Drivers of Nuclear Trilemma in Southern Asia: China, India, and Pakistan," *Journal for Peace and Nuclear Disarmament* 5, no. 2 (July 3, 2022): 296–314. Chunhao Lou, "Geopolitical 'Entanglements' and the China-India-Pakistan Nuclear Trilemma," *Journal for Peace and Nuclear Disarmament* 5, no. 2 (July 3, 2022): 281–95.

22 Rahul Singh and Deeksha Bhardwaj, "'Armed, but Followed Protocol': Govt," *Hindustan Times* (June 19, 2020).

23 "Indian Army Strengthens Mountain Strike Corps Looking after China Border," *Economic Times* (April 9, 2021).

24 "'India to Explain What Happened in Mian Channu,' says DG ISPR after Indian Projectile Falls in Pakistan," DAWN e-paper (March 10, 2022).

25 Mujib Mashal and Salman Masood, "India Accidentally Fires a Missile at Pakistan. Calm Ensues," *New York Times* (March 12, 2022), sec. World.

26 Privately, one senior Pakistani military officer also expressed this assessment of the March 2022 BrahMos misfire incident.

27 Françoise Mouly and Mina Kaneko, "Cover Story: Kim Jong-Un's Big Announcement," *The New Yorker* (January 8, 2016).

28 Nicholas L. Miller and Vipin Narang, "How North Korea Shocked the Nuclear Experts," *POLITICO Magazine* (August 26, 2017).

29 Ankit Panda and Vipin Narang, "The Hanoi Summit Was Doomed from the Start," *Foreign Affairs* (March 5, 2019).

30 Christy Lee, "North Korean Leader Kim Jong Un Signals He's Ready for 'New Way,' Experts Say," Voice of America (October 19, 2019).

31 Oliver Hotham, "Coronavirus Prevention a Matter of 'National Survival,' North Korean Media Says," *NK News* (January 29, 2020).

32 "Great Programme for Struggle Leading Korean-Style Socialist Construction to Fresh Victory On Report Made by Supreme Leader Kim Jong Un at Eighth Congress of WPK," KCNA Watch (January 9, 2021).

33 Ankit Panda, "A Call to Arms: Kim Jong Un and the Tactical Bomb," *The Washington Quarterly* 44, no. 3 (July 3, 2021): 7–24.

34 "S. Korea Now Free of Nuclear Arms, Roh Says," *Los Angeles Times*, December 19, 1991.

35 Ji Da-gyum, "Yoon Suk Yeol Pursues 'Peace through Strength' on the Korean Peninsula," *Korea Herald* (February 27, 2022).

36 Ankit Panda, "South Korea's 'Decapitation' Strategy Against North Korea Has More Risks Than Benefits," Carnegie Endowment for International Peace (August 15, 2022); https://carnegieendow ment.org/2022/08/15/south-korea-s-decapitation-strategy-against-north-korea-has-more-risks-than-benefits-pub-87672.

37 Bob Woodward, "Attack Was 48 Hours Old When It 'Began,'" *Washington Post* (January 25, 2024).

38 "Report on 6th Enlarged Plenary Meeting of 8th WPK Central Committee," KCNA (January 1, 2023); https://kcnawatch.org/newstream/.

39 Tong-hyung Kim, "North Korean Leader Kim Jong Un Meets with Russian Defense Minister to Discuss Military Cooperation," AP News (July 27, 2023).

40 "North Korea's Kim Vows to Boost Cooperation with China to 'New High,'" Reuters (July 29, 2023), sec. Asia Pacific.

41 "N. Korea Has Sent More than 10,000 Containers of Munitions, Materials to Russia since Sept.: State Dept.," *Korea Times* (February 24, 2024).

42 "Zelensky: DPRK Sent 1.5 Million Artillery Shells to Russia," Ukrinform (February 25, 2024).

43 "Ukraine: Russia Increasing Use of N. Korean-Made Ballistic Missiles," KBS World (March 15, 2024).

44 Kim Eun-jung, "Defense Chief Says N.K. Munitions Factories Operating at Full Capacity to Supply Russia," Yonhap News Agency (February 27, 2024).

45 "Soviet Officer Reveals Secrets of Mangyongdae," *DailyNK* (blog), (January 2, 2014).

46 "Xi Jinping, Kim Jong Un Hold Talks in Beijing," Xinhua (March 28, 2018).

47 The Europeans preferred to call this grouping the E3+3.

48 "Joint Comprehensive Plan of Action," U.S. Department of State (July 14, 2015); https://2009-2017.state.gov/documents/organization/245317.pdf.

49 "Remarks by President Trump on the Joint Comprehensive Plan of Action," The White House (May 8, 2018); https://trumpwhitehouse.archives.gov/briefings-statements/remarks-president-trump-joint-comprehensive-plan-action/.

50 "After the Deal: A New Iran Strategy," The Heritage Foundation (May 21, 2018); https://www.heritage.org/defense/event/after-the-deal-new-iran-strategy.

51 Michael R. Pompeo, "Confronting Iran," *Foreign Affairs* (October 15, 2018).

52 "US Civilian Contractor Killed, Several Troops Injured in Rocket Attack on Iraqi Military Base," ABC News (December 27, 2019).

53 "Iran's Attack on Iraq Shows How Precise Missiles Have Become," *The Economist* (January 16, 2020).

54 "U.S. Military Raises Injury Toll In Iran Missile Attack In Iraq," Radio Free Europe/Radio Liberty (February 22, 2020).

55 Farnaz Fassihi, "Iran Says It Unintentionally Shot Down Ukrainian Airliner," *New York Times* (January 11, 2020), sec. World.

56 Ronen Bergman and Farnaz Fassihi, "The Scientist and the A.I.-Assisted, Remote-Control Killing Machine," *New York Times* (September 18, 2021), sec. World.

57 Henry Rome, "Iran's Misunderstood Nuclear Law," The Washington Institute for Near East Policy (September 7, 2023); https://www.washingtoninstitute.org/policy-analysis/irans-misunderstood-nuclear-law.

58 Quint Forgey, "Biden Slams Trump's Iran Strategy as a 'Self-Inflicted Disaster,'" *POLITICO* (June 20, 2019).

59 Zarif quoted in Steven E. Miller, "The Struggle to Save the JCPOA: Negotiations to Nowhere?," in Paolo Cotta-Ramusino et al., eds., *Nuclear Risks and Arms Control: Problems and Progresses in the Time of Pandemics and War* (New York: Springer International Publishing, 2023), p. 128.

60 "Paris Climate Agreement," The White House (January 20, 2021); https://www.whitehouse.gov/briefing-room/statements-releases/2021/01/20/paris-climate-agreement/.

61 Henry Rome, "Iran Elected a Hard-Liner President. What Does That Mean for the Nuclear Deal?," *Washington Post* (June 21, 2021).

62 This was conveyed in the course of multiple interviews with officials in 2022 and 2023.

63 "49 Senate Republicans Tell President Biden: An Iran Agreement Without Broad Congressional Support Will Not Survive," United States Senate Committee on Foreign Relations (March 14, 2022);

https://www.foreign.senate.gov/press/rep/release/49-senate-republicans-tell-president-biden-an-iran-agreement-without-broad-congressional-support-will-not-survive.

64 Steve Inskeep, "A U.S. Special Envoy Responds to Iran on Nuclear Talks, Protests over a Woman's Death," *NPR* (October 7, 2022), sec. Asia.

65 Wyn Bowen and Matthew Moran, "Iran's Nuclear Programme: A Case Study in Hedging?," *Contemporary Security Policy* 35, no. 1 (January 2, 2014): 26–52.

66 James R. Clapper, "Unclassified Statement for the Record on the Worldwide Threat Assessment of the US Intelligence Community for the Senate Select Committee on Intelligence," U.S. Intelligence Community (February 16, 2012).

67 "Iran Can Make Fissile Material for a Bomb 'in about 12 Days' – U.S. Official," Reuters (February 28, 2023), sec. Middle East.

68 "Iran Has Enough Enriched Uraniam to Build 'several' Nuclear Weapons, UN Says," PBS News (January 26, 2023).

69 Laurence Norman and Michael R. Gordon, "Iran Is Better Positioned to Launch Nuclear-Weapons Program, New U.S. Intelligence Assessment Says," *Wall Street Journal* (August 9, 2024).

70 Lewis and Panda, "How Much Is Enough?"

71 Avner Cohen, *Israel and the Bomb* (New York: Columbia University Press, 1999), p. 338.

72 "Saudi Crown Prince Says Will Develop Nuclear Bomb If Iran Does: CBS TV," Reuters (March 15, 2018), sec. World. "Saudi Crown Prince: If Iran Develops Nuclear Bomb, So Will We," CBS News (March 15, 2018).

73 Jonny Hallam and Helen Regan, "Iran Missile Attack: Pakistan Condemns Deadly Strike on Its Territory as Tensions Spike across Region," CNN (January 17, 2024).

74 Defense Intelligence Ballistic Missile Analysis Committee, "Ballistic and Cruise Missile Threat," National Air and Space Intelligence Center (June 2017, 2020); https://irp.fas.org/threat/missile/bm-2020.pdf.

75 Ankit Panda, *Kim Jong Un and the Bomb: Survival and Deterrence in North Korea* (Oxford: Oxford University Press, 2020), pp. 155, 179.

Chapter 6: What to Do About the Bomb?

1 Amos Tversky and Daniel Kahneman, "Availability: A Heuristic for Judging Frequency and Probability," *Cognitive Psychology* 5, no. 2 (September 1, 1973): 207–32.

2 Neal J. Roese and Kathleen D. Vohs, "Hindsight Bias," *Perspectives on Psychological Science* 7, no. 5 (September 2012): 411–26.

3 Information Circular, IAEA (September 16, 1996); https://www.iaea.org/sites/default/files/publications/documents/infcircs/1996/inf522.shtml.

4 Maxim Starchak, "Russia's Withdrawal From the Nuclear Test Ban Treaty Is an Own Goal," Carnegie Endowment for International Peace (October 24, 2023); https://carnegieendowment.org/politika/90831.

5 "Nuclear Test Sites Are Too Damn Busy," Arms Control Wonk (September 23, 2023); https://www.armscontrolwonk.com/archive/1218750/nuclear-test-sites-are-too-damn-busy/.

6 Los Alamos National Laboratory, "Envisioning the W93" (July 26, 2021); https://discover.lanl.gov/publications/national-security-science/2021-summer/w93/.

7 Robert C. O'Brien, "The Return of Peace Through Strength," *Foreign Affairs* (June 18, 2024).

8 Ann M. Simmons, Michael R. Gordon, and Laurence Norman, "Russia Says It Will Step Back From Nuclear-Test Treaty," *Wall Street Journal* (October 6, 2023).

9 John Hudson and Paul Sonne, "Trump Administration Discussed Conducting First U.S. Nuclear Test in Decades," *Washington Post* (May 23, 2020).

10 Guy Faulconbridge, "Russia's Putin Issues New Nuclear Warnings to West over Ukraine," Reuters (February 22, 2023), sec. World.

11 Rebecca Hersman, "Decoding the Latest U.S. Report on Arms Control: Are Russia and China Really Cheating?," Centre for Strategic and International Studies (April 17, 2020).

12 "2020 Adherence to and Compliance with Arms Control, Nonproliferation, and Disarmament Agreements and Commitments," U.S. Department of State (June 2020); https:// www.state.gov/wp-content/uploads/2020/06/2020-Adherence -to-and-Compliance-with-Arms-Control-Nonproliferation-and -Disarmament-Agreements-and-Commitments-Compliance -Report-1.pdf.

13 Robert P. Ashley Jr., "Russian and Chinese Nuclear Modernization Trends," Defense Intelligence Agency (May 29, 2019); https:// www.dia.mil/News/Speeches-and-Testimonies/Article-View /Article/1859890/russian-and-chinese-nuclear-modernization -trends/.

14 This is according to a senior U.S. official involved with Defense Programs at the U.S. National Nuclear Security Administration.

15 Jonathan Tirone, "US Offers Nuclear-Test Inspections to Ease Russia, China Tension," Bloomberg (September 28, 2023).

16 Anthony Ruggiero and Richard Goldberg, "Biden's Plan to Expose Nuclear Secrets to Moscow and Beijing," Text, *The Hill* (blog), (October 19, 2023).

17 Sandra Blakeslee, "In Remotest Nevada, a Joint U.S. and Soviet Test," *New York Times* (August 18, 1988, sec. World).

18 Nataraja Sarma, "Nuclear 'fizzle' Chronicled Long Ago," *Nature India* (August 27, 2009).

19 "Agreement Between The United States of America and The Union of Soviet Socialist Republics on Notifications of Launches of Intercontinental Ballistic Missiles and Submarine-Launched Ballistic Missiles (Ballistic Missile Launch Notification Agreement)," U.S. Department of State (May 31, 1988); https:// 2009-2017.state.gov/t/avc/trty/187150.htm.

20 "Union of Soviet Socialist Republics-United States: Agreement on Reciprocal Advance Notification of Major Strategic

Exercises," *International Legal Materials* 28, no. 6 (November 1989): 1436–37.

21 "President Biden Statement Ahead of the 10th Review Conference of the Treaty on the Non-Proliferation of Nuclear Weapons," The White House (August 1, 2022); https://www.whitehouse .gov/briefing-room/statements-releases/2022/08/01/president -biden-statement-ahead-of-the-10th-review-conference-of-the -treaty-on-the-non-proliferation-of-nuclear-weapons/.

22 "About the Senate & the U.S. Constitution. Advice and Consent: Treaties," U.S. Senate; https://www.senate.gov/about/ origins-foundations/senate-and-constitution/advice-and-con sent-treaties.htm.

23 Since New START received the Senate's advice and consent, two free trade treaties and the Kigali Amendment to the Montreal Protocol regulating hydrofluorocarbons are the sole treaties to have cleared ratification with the Senate's support.

24 "Annual Threat Assessment of the U.S. Intelligence Community," Office of the Director of National Intelligence (February 5, 2024); https://www.dni.gov/files/ODNI/documents/assessments/ATA -2024-Unclassified-Report.pdf.

25 Douglas Brinkley and Luke Nichter, *The Nixon Tapes, 1971–1972* (Boston, MA: Houghton Mifflin Harcourt, 2014), p. 414.

26 Jack Ruina, "Threats to the ABM Treaty," *Security Dialogue* 26, no. 3 (1995): 265–75. Colin Norman, "A Dispute over Soviet ABM Plans," *Science* 235, no. 4788 (1987): 524–6.

27 Office of the Press Secretary, The White House (April 1, 2009); https://obamawhitehouse.archives.gov/the-press-office/joint- statement-dmitriy-a-medvedev-president-russian-federation- and-barack-obama-pr.

28 "2023 Report to Congress on Implementation of the New START Treaty," U.S. Department of State (blog), (January 31, 2024); https://www.state.gov/2023-report-to-congress-on-imple mentation-of-the-new-start-treaty/.

29 See, for instance, "China and Neighbor Countries Kick off Annual Border Disarmament Compliance Inspection," Ministry

of National Defense of the People's Republic of China (June 26, 2019); http://eng.mod.gov.cn/xb/News_213114/TopStories/4844446.html.

30 Mareena Robinson Snowden, "Probabilistic Verification: A New Concept for Verifying the Denuclearization of North Korea," Arms Control Association (September 2019); https://www.arms control.org/act/2019-09/features/probabilistic-verification-new -concept-verifying-denuclearization-north-korea.

31 Radio Free Asia (November 4, 2022); https://www.rfa.org/korean/in_focus/nk_nuclear_talks-11042022165933.html.

32 For background, see Ankit Panda, "Indo-Pacific Missile Arsenals: Avoiding Spirals and Mitigating Escalation Risks," Carnegie Endowment for International Peace (October 31, 2023); https://carnegieendowment.org/2023/10/31/indo-pacific-missile-arsenals-avoiding-spirals-and-mitigating-escalation-risks-pub -90772.

33 For additional details on the launch authentication process, see Georgina DiNardo, "How the 'Nuclear Football' Remains a Potent Symbol of the Unthinkable," C4ISRNet (September 11, 2023).

34 "Cotton: Austin Must Address Troubling Hospitalization Report," U.S. Senator Cotton for Arkansas (January 6, 2024); https://www.cotton.senate.gov/news/press-releases/cotton-austin-must-address-troubling-hospitalization-report.

35 Andrew Solender, "Republicans Erupt over Secrecy around Defense Secretary Lloyd Austin's Hospitalization," Axios (January 7, 2024).

36 See William Burr, "Predelegation of Nuclear Weapons Use, 1959-1960," National Security Archive (May 18, 2001); https://nsarchive2.gwu.edu/NSAEBB/NSAEBB45/printindex.html. Peter J. Roman, "Ike's Hair-trigger: U.S. Nuclear Predelegation, 1953–60," *Security Studies* 7, no. 4 (June 1, 1998): 121–64.

37 "FACT SHEET: Nuclear Weapons Employment Strategy of the United States," The White House (June 19, 2013); https://obama

whitehouse.archives.gov/the-press-office/2013/06/19/fact-sheet-nuclear-weapons-employment-strategy-united-states.

38 "Report on the Nuclear Employment Strategy of the United States – 2020," U.S. Department of Defense, p. 6; https://www.esd.whs.mil/Portals/54/Documents/FOID/Reading%20Room/NCB/21-F-0591_2020_Report_of_the_Nuclear_Employement_Strategy_of_the_United_States.pdf.

39 For a detailed timeline of such a scenario, see Jeffrey Lewis, "Is Launch Under Attack Feasible?," The Nuclear Threat Initiative (blog), (August 24, 2017).

40 Susan D'Agostino, "A VR Journey into the Nuclear Bunker Offers Chilling Lessons on US Nuclear Policy," *Bulletin of the Atomic Scientists* (blog), (February 14, 2022).

41 David E. Hoffman, "The Russian Nuclear Button," *Foreign Policy* (blog), (March 14, 2024).

42 President of the Russian Federation, "Military Doctrine of the Russian Federation" (2014); https://web.archive.org/web/201805 01051233id_/https://www.offiziere.ch/wp-content/uploads-001 /2015/08/Russia-s-2014-Military-Doctrine.pdf.

43 "Foundations of State Policy of the Russian Federation in the Area of Nuclear Deterrence," CAN (June 2020); https://www.cna.org/reports/2020/06/state-policy-of-russia-toward-nuclear-deterrence.

44 Jeffrey G. Lewis and Bruno Tertrais, "OP #45: The Finger on the Button," Middlebury Institute of International Studies at Monterey, James Martin Center for Nonproliferation Studies (February 18, 2019), pp. 19–21; https://www.nonproliferation.org/op-45-the-finger-on-the-button/.

45 "DPRK's Law on Policy of Nuclear Forces Promulgated," KCNA Watch (September 9, 2022).

46 Peter Baker and Choe Sang-Hun, "Trump Threatens 'Fire and Fury' against North Korea if it Endangers U.S.," *New York Times* (August 8, 2017), sec. World.

47 Patricia Zengerle, "Senate Committee Questions Trump's Nuclear Authority," Reuters (November 14, 2017), sec. United States.

48 Lama El Baz, "Most Americans Are Uncomfortable with the Policy of Nuclear Sole Authority" (blog), The Chicago Council on Global Affairs (August 16, 2023).

49 Walter Pincus, "Transcript Confirms Kennedy Linked Removal of Missiles in Cuba, Turkey," *Washington Post* (December 30, 2023).

50 Quoted at length in Pincus, "Transcript Confirms Kennedy Linked Removal of Missiles in Cuba, Turkey."

51 "Black Saturday: Transcript," JFK Library, Atomic Gambit (October 25, 2022); https://www.jfklibrary.org/about-us/social -media-podcasts-and-apps/atomic-gambit/episode-4-black- saturday/transcript.

52 On this, see Leslie H. Gelb, "The Myth that Screwed up 50 Years of U.S. Foreign Policy," *Foreign Policy* (blog), (March 14, 2024).

53 While Kennedy's role in resolving the crisis is undeniably a case of prudent leadership at work, it should be noted that his decision-making in the lead-up to the crisis was far from prudent (including a lack of humility after the failed 1961 Bay of Pigs invasion attempt of Cuba).

54 See W. J. Hennigan, "The Brink," *New York Times* (March 4, 2024), sec. Opinion.

55 Author's interview with U.S. official in 2023. David Brunnstrom, Michael Martina, and Tom Daly, "Biden and Xi Agree to Look at Possible Arms Control Talks – Biden adviser," Reuters (November 17, 2021), sec. Media & Telecom.

56 Alan Wong, "US, China Held Nuclear Arms Talks Before Xi-Biden Meeting," Bloomberg (November 8, 2023).

57 These terms are often used in the strategic literature to describe limited nuclear use.

Index